The history of the
Royal Manchester College of Music
1893 –1972

Dedicated to
all staff and students,
past and present,
of the R.M.C.M.

Only those who are earnest enough to
sit with patience at the feet of the great
masters, and endeavour with infinite labour
to wrest from them their secrets, can ever
hope to be imbued with the true spirit of
music and become artists themselves.

Sir Charles Hallé

Dr Adolph Brodsky, Principal 1895–1929

Michael Kennedy

The history of the
Royal Manchester College of Music
1893–1972

Manchester University Press

Published by
Manchester University Press
316-324 Oxford Road
Manchester M13 9NR

ISBN 0 7190 0435 7

Made and printed in Great Britain
by William Clowes and Sons, Limited
London, Beccles and Colchester

Contents

List of plates

Grateful acknowledgement is due to Miss Laura Birchall, Miss
Dora Gilson, Mr Clifton Helliwell and the *Daily Telegraph* for
their help in obtaining the above illustrations.

Preface

This is not the first history of the Royal Manchester College of Music. In September, 1918, at the request of the Council, Stanley Withers, the Registrar from 1893 until 1927, wrote a short booklet to mark the 25th anniversary. In 1966 my colleagues on the Council honoured me by asking me to write this present book in view of the impending amalgamation of the College and the Northern School of Music into the new Northern College of Music, Manchester.

While Withers's task was therefore celebratory, mine could be—but I hope will not be—regarded as in some sense valedictory. For it is a case of 'The College is dead. Long live the College': the traditions, skills, loyalties and generosities recorded in the subsequent pages do not die because a marriage is arranged, a name is changed and a new home is entered. Or if they do, the ghosts of the past, with Charles Hallé and Gustav Behrens at their head, will surely rise up to rebuke us.

My thanks are principally due to the Principal, Mr Frederic R. Cox, and the members of the Council for placing at my disposal all College minutes, records, accounts, letters and other historical documents. Miss Laura Birchall, the Librarian, has helped me and has patiently dealt with my borrowings from the archives in her care. Many former students have given me reminiscences of the College and I am especially indebted to Mr Frank Merrick, Mr Clifford Knowles (whose assessments of Brodsky and Forbes were invaluable guides to me), Mr T. B. Pitfield, Miss Elsie Thurston and Miss Dora Gilson, Sir Leonard Behrens, Mr Alexander Goehr and others have also answered my questions. I wish to acknowledge permission to reprint extracts from *The Guardian* and *The Daily Telegraph* and I thank their respective editors.

I have designed this book as a companion volume to my *The Hallé Tradition*. As I did there, I have devoted several chapters to detailed surveys of the music performed at the College. These chapters are self-contained and can be 'skipped' by those not interested without any effect on the general narrative. But I know that many people are as interested as I

am by the development of musical tastes, and I have found
it fascinating to discover which works were played in the
formative years of artists who later achieved much. From such
a mass of material the selection has been arbitrarily personal;
my guide lines have been either the intrinsic interest of the
work performed or the fact that the student's name became
more widely known.

Some may think that not enough is said in the following
pages in detailed criticism of the teaching at colleges of music,
particularly as the methods are being challenged by a rising
generation of musicians. Frankly I do not feel qualified to
venture into such tricky academic waters. I am an historian,
and I present here nearly 80 years of achievements that, whatever the methods used, have been very considerable. Many
distinguished names occur in the following pages: they are
testimony to the effectiveness of the College's policy, from
1893 onwards, and to the skill and devotion of the professorial
staff. No doubt there have been failures; no doubt some talents
which might have flowered did not receive enough sunshine
at the right moment—these are unavoidable mishaps under
any human system. But the general result, it seems to me, has
been success on a large scale.

M.K.
Manchester, 1970

1
Foundation

In 1890 only two full-scale conservatoires of music existed in England, both in London: the Royal Academy of Music, founded in 1823, and the Royal College of Music, which opened its doors in May, 1883. English musical students attended one or other of these foundations or went abroad, usually to Leipzig. But since 1858 there had existed in Manchester a professional symphony orchestra playing year after year under the same conductor, its founder Charles Hallé. He had come to England from Paris after the Revolution of 1848 and had then settled in Manchester as conductor of the Gentlemen's Concerts Orchestra which had given regular concerts since the last quarter of the 18th century. Friend of Berlioz, Chopin, Mendelssohn and Wagner, and one of the finest pianists of his time, Hallé had first wanted to establish a conservatoire in Manchester in 1854. Over the years, especially after he had launched his own series of orchestral concerts, he had continued to press the need for a local training-ground for musicians. He knew how often he had had to obtain new players for his orchestra from Paris, Berlin or Leipzig, and he also knew how much native talent was wasted through lack of opportunity for training. 'Even among audiences composed chiefly of artisans and miners I had again and again been struck with the keen discernment of good and bad,' he wrote, 'and the unquestionable musical talent commonly revealed.'[1]

After his 70th birthday, in 1889, Hallé became anxiously concerned about the future of his concerts and the need for a conservatoire. At a meeting in the Town Hall on 3 December, 1891, he put forward a scheme for erection of a new concert-hall in Manchester which would also contain accommodation for a college—an early vision of an arts centre. If the hall was managed by a society, Hallé said, he would hand over to it his concerts, which were his private property and a profitable concern. A provisional committee was formed to consider this

[1] This and subsequent quotations from Hallé's views are taken from his article 'The Royal Manchester College of Music', published in the *Strand Musical Magazine* in 1895.

and 'the expediency' of founding a college. The familiar story of national economic crisis led Hallé's friends to the conclusion that an appeal to the public for funds to build the hall would inevitably fail. But they recommended, at another Town Hall meeting on 2 May, 1892, that steps should be taken towards a foundation of a college of music 'on the basis of the most successful musical institutions in this country and on the Continent'. The committee also decided to engage teaching staff 'of the highest order'. To do this would require 'ample revenue' so it was resolved to raise a guarantee fund, to be spread over five years, and to appeal for subscriptions from a wide area because it was hoped that 'the advantages of the Manchester Conservatorium of Music would be utilised by pupils residing in any part of the North of England, as well as in Manchester and its more immediate neighbourhood'. It was also stated with great pleasure that the committee 'had the promise of the cordial co-operation of Sir Charles Hallé in any efforts that might be made' to establish the college. At this meeting a large and representative general committee was appointed with power to frame a constitution and to collect subscriptions. Nine days later this committee met, named the proposed institution 'The College of Music, Manchester' and appointed an executive committee of a Chairman (Dr A. W. Ward, Principal of Owens College), a treasurer (Charles E. Lees) and an honorary secretary (Gustav Behrens).

The leading spirit in these early days was Gustav Behrens, who at this time was 46 years of age. He wrote to as many influential citizens as he thought likely to help, asking them to join the general committee. Letters were sent to the Dukes of Westminster and Devonshire, Earl Spencer, the Earl of Crawford and Balcarres, the Earls of Derby, Sefton and Ellesmere, the Marquess of Ripon, Lord Egerton of Tatton, Lord de Tabley, the Bishop of Manchester (Dr J. Moorhouse), the Dean of Manchester (the Very Rev. E. Craig Maclure), C. P. Scott, Editor of the *Manchester Guardian*, and several Members of Parliament including A. J. Balfour, J. W. Sidebotham and William Mather, and the mayors of about thirty Northern boroughs. Such was the enthusiasm for the scheme that on the day of the 11 May committee meeting Behrens was able to write to a prospective subscriber that 'there is every probability of our being able to commence operations . . . by October next, provided our appeal . . . meets with a sufficiently liberal re-

sponse'. This estimate proved to be correct. Already approaches
had been made to famous musicians to fill some of the professorial posts. Willy Hess, a Joachim pupil who had been leader
of Hallé's orchestra since 1888, was assured of the violin
professorship. It was hoped that Charles Santley, the most
celebrated singer of the day, would head the singing department, but he was not prepared to settle in Manchester and
suggested Anna Williams. It was tacitly assumed that Hallé
would be the Principal, but Behrens himself had some misgivings about this, probably because he knew that although
Hallé was in Manchester from October to March for his concerts he then went abroad on tour, often in partnership with
his second wife, the violinist Wilma Norman-Neruda. They
had toured Australia together, for instance, in 1890 and 1891.
Behrens, who probably would have preferred a younger man,
expressed his doubts in a letter to Hallé written on 24 May,
1892:

> Broadfield [E. J. Broadfield] was good enough to show me a
> letter which you wrote to him before your departure for Germany,
> and I have been giving a good deal of thought, as you may imagine,
> to your very interesting suggestions. Frankly speaking, however, my
> opinion is that it will be impossible for anyone to take the actual
> Principalship (I mean as far as executive work is concerned) for
> our College of Music unless combined with permanent and daily
> attendance in Manchester. So many questions are sure to arise in
> the daily conduct of so important an institution that, to my mind,
> it will be absolutely essential that the ruling spirit, whoever that
> may be, should be constantly on the spot. I consider that the posi-
> tion which you would occupy with most satisfaction to yourself and
> advantage to the College would be that of 'Chairman of the Execu-
> tive', unconnected with any teaching duties; my feeling being that
> the authority exercised by you in such a position will be infinitely
> greater as regards the teaching-staff and also as regards the lay
> committee than when combined with professorial duties. Of course
> I am expressing my own views, and I do not know whether Broad-
> field or any other member of the Committee is in harmony with
> me on this point. Anyhow, you will excuse my remarks, which are
> only dictated by my sincere desire to see our scheme thoroughly
> successful.

Behrens was perhaps not entirely alone in his views. A meeting of the executive on 14 June was 'unanimous in desiring
your co-operation as Principal', Behrens wrote to him, 'but at
the same time they feel that in case you are unable to be in
daily attendance it will be necessary to have a vice or deputy

Principal who being in thorough harmony with the Principal will be able to take charge of the management during his absence'. In a further letter to Broadfield, Hallé asked for advice on a 'fair' salary because 'my position will be changed so entirely through the new office (for I do not want to be merely an ornamental Principal), I shall have to give up so many things that I am afraid I shall have to open my mouth pretty wide'. No more was heard about a Deputy Principal.

Advertisements for applications for the permanent official post of organising secretary to the executive committee brought 800 replies. These were sifted to 40, and again to seven who were interviewed by the committee. None of the seven was appointed, the post going to Stanley Withers, of Brooklands, on a basis of a trial six months at a salary of £100 for the half-year period. When the College opened he became Secretary and Registrar, with a salary of £250 a year.

The rest of 1892 was taken up with campaigning to raise funds. Manchester was always accepted as the proper home for the College because of the existence of Hallé's orchestra from which teaching staff could be drawn, but it was emphasised that not only Mancunians would benefit, and public meetings were held in Oldham, Bolton, Kendal and other boroughs to enlist supporters for the scheme. Local committees were formed in some of the towns, and by the beginning of 1893 an aggregate of £11,000 had been promised in the form of a guarantee fund of nearly £2,000 a year for five years, in addition to £1,600 subscribed for initial outlay, particularly rental of premises suitable for the College. The erection of a specially designed building does not seem to have been considered. A building in what was then known as Ducie Street, off Oxford Road, was available: 'the most appropriate and commodious that could be obtained for the purpose'. It had been built for use as a club, but had never been used. Charles Lees, the treasurer, undertook to buy these premises and present them to the College as his personal gift. At first sight it seemed to offer all the advantages of what today would be called, alas, a 'purpose-built' college of music: a large central hall, suitable for concerts, seating over 400, with rooms leading from the hall on three of the four sides.

In the Town Hall on 27 February, 1892, with the Mayor of Manchester, Sir Anthony Marshall, in the chair, the General Committee and subscribers met and approved a draft constitu-

tion which the executive committee had drawn up. Its main
features were that the college should be governed by:

(a) the General Committee, comprising life members (donors
    of £100 or more), subscribing members (£1 per annum),
    representative members (three Northern M.P.s, a repre-
    sentative from Manchester City Council, Lancashire
    County Council and Salford Council, three nominees of
    other County Councils, the Principal, two professors, at
    least two and not more than five College diploma holders
    chosen by students, a representative from Owens College,
    one from the Victoria University, and not more than five
    from other selected Northern public bodies);
(b) the Council (not fewer than 12 and not more than 30 mem-
    bers, exclusive of the Principal who would be a member
    ex-officio). There would also be a President, to hold office
    for five years, and a Chairman of the Council to be elected
    annually.

The members of the first Council, elected as this meeting, were:
The Mayor, Gustav Behrens, Oliver Behrens, E. J. Broadfield,
Gustav Dehn, Charles Dunderdale, William Eller, T. W. Gilli-
brand, Dr Charles J. Hall, Sir Charles Hallé, Charles J. Heywood, Edward J. Heywood, Charles F. Lees, George R. Murray,
S. R. Platt and Dr A. W. Ward. At its first meeting, on
1 March, Dr Ward was elected chairman, C. J. Heywood vice-
chairman, Charles Lees honorary treasurer and Gustav
Behrens honorary secretary. It was agreed to offer the Principalship to Hallé, to engage teaching staff, to assess what
alterations to the building were needed, and to take steps towards incorporation. In a letter to Hallé, dated 9 March, Ward
set forth the terms of his engagement:

1. That you undertake the joint duties of Principal of the College
and Chief Professor of the Pianoforte in consideration of a remuneration at the rate of £1,000 per annum to be paid quarterly. . . .

2. That for the purposes of instruction you agree to attend
during the session two days weekly, viz. Wednesdays and Saturdays four to five hours each day.

3. That for the purpose of the duties connected with the Principalship you agree to attend personally at the College as often as
may be requisite; in any case, however, not less often than for such
times as may be necessary on three days weekly, viz. on Wednesdays, Thursdays and Saturdays.

Hallé replied three days later from St Andrews:

I am at this moment on professional tour through Scotland
which leaves me no time to consider your very kind letter of the

9th and to answer it at length; but I may say shortly that I accept the proposals of the Council and the terms, leaving minor details for future consideration. In great haste. Yours most sincerely.

Over the next months the Council, meeting fortnightly, tackled several issues. An architect's estimate of alterations to the building was requested; a petition to the Privy Council for a Royal Charter was prepared; it was decided to ask the Prince of Wales (later Edward VII) or, failing him, the Duke of York (later George V) to be the first president. In July Queen Victoria 'was graciously pleased to command' that the College be known as the Royal College of Music, Manchester. It is astonishing that the Council should have thought they could get away with this, and, sure enough, within a day or two they received a protest from Sir George Grove, Director of the Royal College of Music, who very reasonably pointed out that not only would this cause confusion but that, in the case of bequests, it might lead to serious consequences. The Council therefore decided to alter the title to The Royal Manchester College of Music, and this it became on 25 July, 1893.

But most important of all were preparation of the prospectus for students and appointment of the professorial staff. The academic year was divided into three terms; fees were £30 a year; and it was decided to award a performer's diploma on annual examination after candidates had completed three full years. The diploma entitled the holder to the designation Associate of the R.M.C.M. The main study courses were Singing, Pianoforte, Strings and Wind Instruments, Organ and Composition. Harmony and the piano were compulsory for all. Also all students had to attend the lectures on the history of music, the classes in sight reading and musical dictation and to join the choir. A weekly orchestra class was formed to which, on Hallé's insistence, non-students were admitted provided they were proficient enough and paid three guineas a year. As long as the Principal approved, students (on whom there was to be no age limit) were allowed to take a second study, supplementary to their main course, at no extra fee. From the first there was close co-operation with Owens College, the constituent college of the university, whereby College of Music students could proceed to the university degrees in music. Owens's harmony classes were held in the College of Music and the R.M.C.M. students were made eligible to attend the Owens class in acoustics.

Hallé wrote:

In no case was a student admitted for lessons on a single instrument alone. From the beginning the one vital aim of the College was by thoroughness in its teaching, if possible, to make artists of its students. And so, instead of unduly forcing students on in any one branch of music alone, we determined to make their education comprehensive and sound, if somewhat slow. . . . The more musical aptitude a pupil shows the greater is his need of thoroughly drastic training. Facility is the veritable pitfall of many would-be musicians. They learn easily and are satisfied with mediocrity. Only those who are earnest enough to sit with patience at the feet of the great masters, and endeavour with infinite labour to wrest from them their secrets, can ever hope to be imbued with the true spirit of music and become artists themselves.

The first teaching staff was:

Singing: Mrs Lemmens-Sherrington (£300 a year guaranteed); Anna Williams, Miss Lemmens-Sherrington, Andrew Black, Frederick H. Dale, John Acton.

Pianoforte: Sir Charles Hallé (£400 p.a.); Frederick Dawson, George Gunton, Lilias Shaw, Jeanne Brotey, Olga Neruda (£300 p.a. guaranteed).

Violin: Willy Hess (£500 p.a. guaranteed); C. Rawdon Briggs, £50 p.a. guaranteed); Simon Speelman (viola).

Violoncello: J. J. E. Vieuxtemps, Carl Fuchs.

Organ: Dr Kendrick Pyne.

Harp: J. H. Cockerill.

Flute: Edward de Jong, Firman Brossa.

Double bass: John Hoffman.

Horn: Franz Paersch.

Trumpet: Thomas Reynolds.

Oboe: Charles Reynolds.

Clarinet: G. A. Hoffman.

Bassoon: Desiré Lalande, Mr Knight.

Trombone: John Branston.

Harmony and Counterpoint: Dr Henry Hiles (£120 p.a.), Walter Carroll.

Choirmaster: Dr Henry Watson, R. H. Wilson.

For most of the staff the rate of payment was 7s. 6d. an hour, excepting Paersch and Pyne who were paid 10s. 6d., and Wilson and Carroll 5s. It was a distinguished assembly of musicians. The instrumental teachers were all members of Hallé's orchestra; Dr Hiles, who was 66, had been lecturer in harmony and composition at the Victoria University since

1879, having held the same post at Owens College from 1876. In addition to being an organist and conductor he had written several compositions, among them two oratorios, *David* and *The Patriarchs*. Frederick Dawson, who was under 30, had been a pupil of Hallé and Rubinstein; Olga Neruda was Hallé's sister-in-law and a pupil of Clara Schumann; Hellen Lemmens-Sherrington (1834–1906) had been a leading British soprano in opera and oratorio; Anna Williams (1845–1924) also had a high reputation in oratorio; Andrew Black (1859–1920) was making his name as the leading British baritone of his day; Kendrick Pyne was Manchester city organist. The names of Wilson and Carroll were additions to the original list submitted by the teaching staff sub-committee. Walter Carroll was among the youngest of the staff, being 24 when the College opened. He had left Longsight High School at the age of 14 to earn a living as an office boy but continued to study music at evening classes at Owens College. From 1889–93 he had studied privately with Hiles. He was an organist and choir-master and became Mus.B., Durham, in 1891 and Mus.B., Manchester, 1896. In 1900 he became the first Doctor of Music of the Victoria University.

All was set, then, for the College to open its doors to its first students on Monday, 2 October. At its meeting on 12 September the Council decided to have an opening ceremony in the form of a conversazione or reception, with light refreshments. But at their final meeting before the opening, two setbacks awaited the Council. They were informed by the Prince of Wales that he could not accept the Presidency of the College 'first, as he was the originator and president of a similar college [the R.C.M.] into competition with which the Manchester College should more or less enter, and secondly because the Manchester College was local rather than national in its aims'. It was decided therefore not to invite the Duke of York to be President and to leave the post open for the time being. More serious was the treasurer's report that there was a deficiency of £172 after the College had been made ready for actual tuition and that the first year's subscription would have to be called upon immediately. Thereupon the Council resolved that the Conversazione on 7 October should be restricted to subscribing members of the General Committee and that 'the resolution to provide light refreshments be rescinded'. Instead, the guests were treated to a programme of music performed by the Principal and professors.

2
Hallé's two years

According to Hallé's article and to the first annual report, 76
students registered their names 'before the actual work of
tuition began'; a minute of a Council meeting on 6 October
records that the number of students in the first week was 74.
Singing students were in the majority, with piano next, then
violin and organ. Almost at once certain snags about the building became apparent and the House Committee, a sub-committee of the Council, was instructed to inquire immediately
'into the question of deadening the sound'.

The acoustics of the building were tested by Professor
Arthur Schuster (later Sir Arthur Schuster) and as a result
ventilating tubes were cased with wood packed with cotton
waste, four baize doors were put in, curtains fitted in all rooms
and door curtains in the classrooms, carpets and mats were
laid, india-rubber feet fitted to a piano, canvas was stitched
to the ceiling of one classroom, partitions between two rooms
were packed with sawdust to a thickness of five inches and
a large curtain erected across the large hall.

From the first the College was the object of generosity from
private citizens and public organisations who had the good of
musical education at heart. It owed its premises to Lees; Mrs
Edward Hecht, widow of Hallé's first chorus-master at his
concerts, gave music from her husband's library and £50 to
form the nucleus of a free scholarship fund for poor students;
Miss Alice Curtis gave an annual gold medal for the best
singing student; John Broadwood & Sons were extremely
generous in providing pianofortes; Forsyth Bros. supplied
music for students at cut rates; the Gentlemen's Concerts
admitted students to the gallery free of charge; and Hallé
allowed them to attend rehearsals of his concerts and gave
concessions in the admission price. Besides the suitability of
the building the Council were specially concerned about two
matters: provision of an organ and provision of scholarships.
Several private benefactors had paid the fees of deserving
but poor students and had started a sustentation fund for this
purpose in April of 1893. But it was wisely realised that this

was not enough and it was gratifying when, at the Council's prompting, Lancashire County Council gave a lead by founding two musical scholarships and Cheshire County Council one. However, the eligibility for these awards was governed by the councils' administrative areas. No citizen of Manchester and Salford was able to compete, nor were the residents of Liverpool, Oldham, Blackburn, Burnley and Bolton. Only one borough, Ashton-under-Lyne, did its duty in this respect (and then only through the generosity of an individual) by founding a musical scholarship, tenable at the College, for its technical school students. The Council's hope that other towns would follow Ashton's example was supported by the wide area from which the first students were drawn, extending all over Lancashire, Cheshire and Derbyshire to Yorkshire, Lincolnshire and more distant parts such as Cheltenham, Kirkcaldy and Cowes.

The first weeks of the College's existence were not without their frictions. A meeting of the House Committee, of which George Murray was chairman, empowered Hallé to engage two cellists and two double basses for the Orchestra Class. Three weeks later, on 30 October, at its next meeting the Committee tetchily noted that this authority had not yet been acted upon and expressed the 'strong opinion that no delay should take place in the formation of the said class; and directs that a copy of this resolution be sent to the Principal tonight'. It further resolved to send a telegram to Hallé strongly urging him to be at the Council meeting on 1 November. Hallé did not attend the meeting which was adjourned to 8 November when matters were settled. But this impression that Hallé, as some of them had feared, was not giving the College a full share of his time, evidently caused further comment at a meeting on 20 December when reference was made to 'the expediency of the Principal being here at stated hours at least once a week for administrative purposes'. Hallé said that in future he would so attend. The House Committee had a further skirmish early in 1894 when it discussed sessional fees and sent a copy of its resolution on the subject to Hallé 'coupled with an expression of regret that he was not able to be present at the meeting . . . during the discussion of this and other important matters'. The rebukes had their effect, for Hallé's reports to the Council then became more detailed and numerous. He took part in the discussions on provision of an organ. Sir William Houldsworth, who in November was elected first

President of the College, offered to lend his private instrument, but Pyne reported that it was not suitable. In the meantime Charles Lees offered to buy the organ belonging to Sir Edward Burne-Jones, the painter, and to contribute most of the cost of its being removed from London and installed in the College on an enlarged platform. At the same time a bequest from a benefactor enabled purchase of a smaller practice organ from the Manchester firm of Kirtland.

If Hallé, who was now 75, found that the administrative and committee work involved in establishment of the College was tiresome, he certainly did not neglect his primary interests: music and musicians. He was instrumental in obtaining College training for its first prodigy. Arthur Catterall was born in Preston in 1883. His grandfather had been a professional musician and his father was an amateur violinist who bought Arthur a violin when he was four and began to teach him. Two years later the boy was giving recitals in his home town and by the time he was eight he had played Mendelssohn's concerto at Manchester Palace of Varieties. His father refused to capitalise on his boy's talents, despite an offer from a Chicago international exhibition, and insisted on his concentrating on general education. But he took Arthur to play to Lady Hallé and she, impressed, insisted that Sir Charles should hear him. Hallé took him to Willy Hess and admitted him to the College with a dispensation excusing him from any class except the violin class. The 10-year-old boy was taken to the College twice a week by a priest for his lessons with Hess. On 14 March, 1895, when Joachim attended open practices at the College, Catterall, accompanied by Hallé, played a Handel sonata. Joachim's and the Hallés' faith in the child was, of course, justified by his eventual career. After studying further under Brodsky, Catterall, at Hans Richter's request in 1902, played in the Bayreuth Festival Orchestra. While there he played at Cosima Wagner's receptions at Wahnfried and the following winter appeared as soloist in the Tchaikovsky concerto at a Hallé Concert. From 1905 to 1914 he was leader of Sir Henry Wood's Queen's Hall Orchestra, forming his own quartet in 1911. In 1913 he returned to Manchester as violin professor at the College and leader of the Hallé, a post he held until 1925 when he resigned partly because of a quarrel with Sir Hamilton Harty and also to undertake an increasing amount of solo work. Later he became leader of the B.B.C.

Symphony Orchestra; and throughout the 1920s and 1930s he shared with Albert Sammons the distinction of being England's best native-born violinist.

The Manchester businessmen who founded the College knew only too well that when a commercial rival appeared on the scene he was eyed with suspicion, not to say hostility. So they can hardly have been surprised when they learned that their petition to the Privy Council for a Royal charter, supported by the University, 50 Members of Parliament and many Lancastrian public bodies, was to be opposed by the joint board of the Royal College of Music and the Royal Academy of Music on the grounds that the new College's relatively small endowments did not amount to a guarantee of permanence. Counsel were briefed and the case was argued on 25 June, 1894. The College's petition was rejected. The cost of this fruitless application had amounted to over £400. This was not the only blow to befall the College during this summer. On 11 August its greatest single benefactor, Charles Lees, died, a 'severe calamity', as a Council minute phrased it. Fortunately his widow was to prove no less staunch a benefactor and friend. Charles J. Heywood became the new honorary treasurer. Lees had, with Behrens, been one of the two trustees in whose hands the College was vested. After his death a new trust deed was drawn up in the names of Behrens, Dunderdale, Eller and Murray.

The College entered its second year with 135 students, nearly double the first intake, and Hallé instituted two further obligatory classes, in sight reading and musical dictation, and a new class for organ students in extemporisation and score-playing. This rapid expansion created an urgent need for extra accommodation. Other drawbacks of the building also kept coming to light. Hallé reported that the students complained of 'a bad smell'[1] and the House Committee allowed Willy Hess to have a coal fire in his classroom and a sandbag to keep out the draught. The need for sound-proofing became ever more obvious and Withers was asked to write to a music-seller in Sydney, N.S.W., whose acoustical treatment of his offices had caught Hallé's interest when he visited Australia in 1891.

---

[1] The College is in the Greenheys district which used to be known as 'Frankfurt-on-Odour' because of the smell from a brook which flowed through it and because of the number of its German inhabitants.

Arrangements were also made for Hallé to visit Manchester board schools to inspect their sound-proofing methods. This question was given extra urgency by the decision to build five extra classrooms as an upper storey fronting Ducie Street. No. 28 Ducie Street was offered as an annexe at a price of £625, but the Council decided that any separate accommodation would be impracticable because of 'the difficulty of preserving order and discipline', even though the building work would cost up to £1,000. This sum was defrayed by Mrs Charles Lees. Another internal addition to the College facilities was a library, in the formation of which Dr Henry Watson played a leading part.

Changes in the staff began towards the end of the first year. Miss Shaw retired from the piano teaching, Azeglio Valgimigli joined to teach Italian. Most far-reaching, however, was the departure of the principal violin professor, Willy Hess, in July, 1895, to take up a similar post in Cologne. This meant that Hallé not only had to find a new college professor but a leader for his orchestra. For both posts he suggested the name Adolph Brodsky, then aged 44 and one of the outstanding soloists of the day. Brodsky was accordingly offered the College posts of violin professor and conductor of the College orchestra at a salary of £500 for 15 hours' tuition a week, from 30 September.

Brodsky was a Russian Jew who was sent, as a youthful prodigy, to study in Vienna under Joseph Hellmesberger. After a spell in Paris, he became an assistant professor at Moscow under Nicholas Rubinstein. He made a year's special study of Tchaikovsky's violin concerto, which had lain unplayed since its completion in 1878. Its dedicatee, Leopold Auer, had declined the dedication and had declared the work to be 'unplayable'. Sauret and Kotek had similarly shied away from it. But Brodsky, who picked up the score in a music-shop in Leipzig, saw its possibilities, went into seclusion to improve his technique and played it at a Vienna Philharmonic concert, conducted by Hans Richter, in November, 1881.

How this came about Brodsky himself recounted in an autobiographical talk he gave on a Saturday evening in the Albion Hotel, Manchester, on 7 February, 1903. The custom in Vienna at that time made the orchestra the judge of which new compositions were to be played. 'An oboe player who perhaps had to play only a few notes could prevent the performance of any piece which did not please him.' Richter was willing that Brodsky should play the Tchaikovsky, but was powerless to arrange it unless the orchestra agreed. Brodsky played it to the orchestra who said: 'Yes, it's very fine and you play it very well, but—play something else.' This he agreed to do, but changed his mind a few days later, went to Richter and said he would play the Tchaikovsky or nothing. With pressure from Richter he had his way.[1] Even so the audience and critics were violently divided in their opinion of the concerto, and Hanslick wrote his notorious criticism which Tchaikovsky knew by heart, so wounded was he by the extravagance of the language. (It has to be taken into account that Russia and Austria were unfriendly towards each other at this time.)

Tchaikovsky's gratitude to Brodsky, however, was unbounded and was signified by the dedication to him of the revised edition of the concerto. 'I know only too well', Tchaikovsky wrote to a friend, 'that for him, whose position is still not established in Vienna, it would not be easy to appear before a Viennese audience with a concerto by an unknown composer, and in addition a Russian. So I doubly prize his service to me.'

Almost as remarkable was the performance Brodsky gave of Brahms's concerto while he was violin professor at Leipzig. With Nikisch conducting, he played this concerto at a concert of the musical society of which Liszt was president at a time when the disciples of Wagner regarded Brahms as antichrist. This performance also was a triumph and, again, won Brodsky the composer's friendship. Yet it was Bach's A minor concerto that he admitted he loved best and by his performance of which he wished to be judged. From 1890–4 he spent, not very happily, in New York as leader of Walter Damrosch's Symphony Society orchestra. It has been said of Willy Hess that no finer orchestral leader has been known, his only drawback being too powerful a tone and a tendency to force the pace so that, in quartets, the impression was given of a solo part with string accompaniment. His personality was restless and his playing fiery and energetic. His style was at the opposite extreme from Brodsky's. Brodsky subordinated himself, was more concerned with interpretation than with technical display. It says something for the reputation which Hallé had built for music in Manchester that men of the calibre of Hess

---

[1] *Manchester Guardian*, 9 February, 1903.

and Brodsky could be persuaded to settle there. Brodsky's arrival, however, was to be providential. He appeared first as leader of Hallé's orchestra at a Liverpool Philharmonic Society concert on 22 October, 1895. Three days later the orchestra opened its Bradford season, but Hallé was tired and asked Brodsky to conduct the programme. The Manchester season was due to begin on 31 October but on the morning of the 25th Hallé died from a stroke.

Hallé had spent the late summer of 1895 on a concert tour of South Africa with his wife. While he was away, the Council had a brush with Lancashire County Council who had decided —'because of lack of suitable competitors'—to award only one musical scholarship and had further reported that the successful candidate was very anxious to hold the award in Germany. The College in vain protested that this was 'most injurious' to its interests. Hallé attended his last Council meeting on 16 October, when he recommended that Brodsky should be allowed to organise chamber concerts to be performed in the hall of the College. Wherever he had worked Brodsky had formed a quartet, and his Manchester quartet was to become a glory of Mancunian music-making. When the Council next met, on 30 October, it was to pass a special resolution recording its deep sorrow over Hallé's death and adding these words:

That in the judgment of the Council, while the foundation of this College was made possible chiefly by the artistic fame of the late Sir Charles Hallé and by the powerful influence of his personality, the measure of success already reached has been largely due to his energy, tact and devotion, and that the Council feels assured that his name will always remain inseparably associated with the history of an institution called into life and established on a solid foundation by himself, as well as with the noblest artistic memories of the city where he spent so many laborious and fruitful years.

The Council offered the Principalship to Brodsky at a salary of £300 a year in addition to his salary as violin professor. He accepted, on the basis that at the end of two terms both he and the Council would review the appointment. He was to stay for another 34 years.

3
Brodsky takes over

It is reasonable to suppose that Hallé selected Brodsky not only as leader of his orchestra and violin professor but, in view of his previous experience in conservatoires, as a potential successor as Principal. If so, it was a wise choice, because it is rare to find disciplinary gifts combined with superb musicianship as was the case with Brodsky. He was authoritarian but he was conscientious and he cared deeply about good musicians. Time and again he was to recommend the Council to pay the fees of some promising student whose parents could not afford the money for an extra year of College tuition. As soon as he took over he threw himself with gusto into the running of the College and into Manchester's musical life. Though he soon relinquished the leadership of the Hallé Orchestra, he conducted several of its concerts in the season after Hallé's death, including a famous occasion when Joachim played the Beethoven concerto. Perhaps his finest asset, as man and musician, was his great humanity. Music was a way of life for him, not an abstract exercise. He had considerable sympathy with the underdog, and was as happy giving recitals at Charles Rowley's Ancoats Brotherhood—a famous example of work for the arts in a depressed area—as he was at a Hallé Concert. As Neville Cardus wrote in the *Manchester Guardian* on the day after Brodsky's death, 'he made himself part of Manchester and in all the city's places, the richest and the poorest, his name and genius were admired in that intimate way which is the measure of a large democratic affection.'

Brodsky's rages with his pupils became legendary but were no myth, as several of them have confirmed. He was strict and would not tolerate carelessness or slackness. It was a fairly common sight for the door of his room to be flung open and stand, music, violin, bow and finally pupil to be shot out into the Lees Hall. Once he bit clean through his pipe and threw the portion that broke off at his pupil; on another occasion he seized the hapless student's bow and smashed it across his knees like matchwood; and one of his women pupils has told me how he tore her copy of the Brahms concerto in half. What angered him most was any attempt by a pupil to deceive him into thinking that he or she had been working hard when they hadn't. His method of teaching followed accepted paths using studies, pieces, concertos and other material as he thought them best suited to the individual's needs. He had no time for 'dumb' teaching incorporating photographs which showed every conceivable position of arms, wrists, hands and fingers—such methods he regarded as 'cranky' because they ignored the mental processes involved in violin-playing. Clifford Knowles asked him how to improve a certain form of technique and the reply was a terse 'Practise it'. Of course, the temper was only one side of him and was only roused by indolence. If pupils were doing well, Brodsky, who was a sociable person, would ask them to visit him and his wife in Bowdon and perhaps play some chamber music. There the favoured pupils discovered his charm and his peasant humour.

One of Brodsky's first acts as Principal was to call an informal meeting of the teaching staff on 13 November, 1895, at which he expounded his views and was reassured that 'there was every disposition on the part of the teachers to work in harmony and fellowship with their new chief'. His first task was to find a new chief professor of the piano to replace Hallé, to find another piano teacher in place of Frederick Dawson, who resigned because of increasing public engagements, and to find a substitute for Andrew Black, another whose growing professional commitments made his continuance at the College difficult. Santley was again approached for the singing post, but again refused. Preliminary approaches concerning the piano post were made to Max Pauer, Alexander Siloti and Leonard Borwick. Eventually in March, 1896, the post was offered, on the same terms as Hallé's, to the Belgian virtuoso Arthur de Greef, who at this date was 33, but was declined. In June Brodsky suggested William Humphreys Dayas, professor at Cologne and a pupil of Liszt. Dayas was a member of an old Bristol family, but was born in New York. There was again some delay and Brodsky was given authority, if Dayas declined, to negotiate with Joseph von Slivinski (1865–1930), a pupil of Leschetizky and Anton Rubinstein. But, after Brodsky had gone to Cologne, Dayas accepted and joined the staff for the beginning of the College's fourth year. Meanwhile David Bispham, the baritone (1857–1921), agreed to become

professor of singing but said that he would be in the United
States until May, 1897; Black, therefore, was prevailed upon
to stay another year.

Brodsky lost no time in instituting his quartet concerts in
the College. He was first violin, Rawdon Briggs second, Simon
Speelman viola and Carl Fuchs cello. The leader gave his
services; and the proceeds not only of these but also of his
public chamber concert series always went to the sustentation
fund. He also took in hand the orchestra class which had for
the first two years been of string players only, there being then
little encouragement for students to learn wind instruments.
Realising that if the orchestra was to be of any value it must
be able to play the symphonic repertoire, Brodsky persuaded
the Council to buy instruments and to allow the wind professors to play in the orchestra. Another popular feature from
almost the first days of the College was the students' monthly
Open Practice—specifically not called concerts because, as
Hallé said, 'we wish the students to take a modest view of their
own performances'. Some of the programmes of these evenings
will be discussed in Chapter 6. By the end of Brodsky's first
year in office the College had 161 students, comprising 58
piano students, 55 of singing, 34 violin, 12 organ and one each
of cello and harp. Women predominated. During 1896 new
diploma regulations were approved providing, as at the R.A.M.
and R.C.M., a teachers' diploma in addition to that for performers. Possession of either entitled the holder to be called
an Associate. In July, 1896, the first 17 students to complete the
full three-year course became the first A.R.M.C.M.s. Their
names will be recorded here, historically, and as token of all
who were to follow them:

Performer's diploma, with distinction: Edith L. Webster (pianoforte), John C. Bradshaw (organ), Minnie L. Grime (singing).

Performer's diploma: Henry Mozart Sheaves (organ), Rosa
d'Armin Blumberg (pianoforte), Ethel M. Wood (singing).

Teacher's diploma: Edith Bardsley (singing), Muriel M. Blydt
(piano), Annie B. Stevenson (piano), Mary H. Entwistle
(piano), John C. Bradshaw, Ethel M. Booth (piano), Minnie
L. Grime, Mary Gordon (singing), Harriet Burrows (violin),
Marion Garnett (piano), Evelyn Child (singing), John Holme
(violin), Mildred Byrne (singing), Ethel M. Wood.

A curiosity arises in the case of the 23-year-old Miss d'A.

Blumberg, one of Hallé's pupils. For some reason she did not receive her diploma; so, when she was 86, in 1959, she attended the diploma ceremony at the invitation of Frederic Cox, the Principal, and graduated among her juniors by 60 years, surely a classic case of better late than never.

John Holme, later to become the College Registrar, was the first of many R.M.C.M. students to become a member of the Hallé Orchestra.

A year later numbers had dropped to 151, but for the first time the Council report gave a breakdown of age and sex of the students. Of the 39 men and 112 women, 24 were under 16, 43 between 16 and 18, 41 between 18 and 20 and 43 over 20. Of these, 47 lived in Manchester and, of the 104 remaining, 65 came from distant localities including two from the United States, one from Canada and two from Germany. Specially encouraging was an improvement in the availability of scholarships. Cheshire County Council increased theirs to three, Lancashire to four, Ashton and Oldham provided one apiece and the Meadowcroft Trustees provided one of £30 a year for male students of the organ (first holder, Frank Radcliffe, of Stalybridge). In addition, the Hallé Memorial Committee instituted a pianoforte scholarship, open only to students of the College (its first holder was Edith Webster); and the Rev. C. A. Wellbeloved, acting trustee of the late Mrs Elizabeth Read, gave £1,100 to found the Read Scholarship for women students whose means were insufficient for payment of fees. The first holder was a singer, Frances Baguley, of New Brighton. A new four-manual organ for the large hall, built by Wadsworth and Brother of Manchester to replace the temporary Burne-Jones organ, was presented to the College by Miss Dorothy Lees in memory of her father, Charles Lees, and to mark her coming-of-age. The College architect, Edward Salomons, designed a case for it. A tangible memorial to Hallé was a bronze medallion portrait, executed by his daughter Elinor Hallé, which was presented to the College by past and present students. It was placed above the entrance to the Principal's room, where it was unveiled by Olga Neruda during the 1896 annual examination.

The year 1897 saw some changes in personnel. Dr Adolphus Ward resigned the chairmanship of the Council in anticipation of his resignation from the Vice-Chancellorship of the Federal University because of his appointment as Master of Peterhouse.

His successor as chairman was George R. Murray and his place
on the Council was filled by Alfred Hopkinson, Q.C., Professor
of Legal Jurisprudence, his successor as Principal of Owens
College. The Council placed on record its special indebted-
ness to Ward[1] for his work in establishing the College, framing
its constitution and regulating its diplomas. Henry Simon, the
head of the engineering firm and one of the three men (Behrens and James Forsyth were the others) who took over the
running of the Hallé Concerts in 1895, also joined the Council.
Madame Lemmens-Sherrington retired from the post of senior
Professor of Singing. The post was offered to Anna Williams,
whose name had from the first appeared on the College prospectus but who never taught, but she refused and the job
went to Cecilia M. Hutchinson.[2] Andrew Black's resignation
became effective at the same time and, as Bispham no longer
wished to take up the offer, his place was taken by Walter
Ford, a baritone who was later to play a part in the revival
of the Folk Song Society and to co-operate with Cecil Sharp
and Vaughan Williams. In this year, too, an old students'
association was formed, electric lighting was installed, and the
Council took a dim view of their president's name appearing
among the patrons of the Manchester School of Music—and
they told him so. Sir William Houldsworth responded with a
cheque for £50 for the sustentation fund.

The new organ was inaugurated by Kendrick Pyne on
11 May, 1898. There had been trouble with Wadsworth, the
builders, who had departed in several cases from the approved
nomenclature of the stops. The platform had been altered and
further changes were made in the large hall because of the
numbers who attended the open practices. A partition wall
which had been erected in 1893 to make temporary cloakrooms
was removed, giving room for extra seating. New cloakrooms
were built in the basement. All this cost money and a new
£1,000 appeal for subscribers was made. Sixty new subscribers

[1] Ward (later Sir Adolphus) had been Professor of English Language
and Literature and of History at Owens College. He was Principal from
1889–97 and had two terms of office as Vice-Chancellor, from 1887–91
and from 1895–7.

[2] Anna Williams's was, in fact, a 'prestige' appointment. It was she
who, when a young soprano, had been commanded to sing in the Royal
Albert Hall for Queen Victoria when the Queen visited the building six
months before it opened. 'No one', she complained, 'can sing properly at
nine o'clock in the morning, except in the bath, when we all *think* we
can.'

came forward and £900 was promised within a very short time. In its first five years, the College received benefactions amounting to £17,600. In the one year 1897–8, subscriptions to the guarantee fund alone came to just short of £2,000. It was clear that the experiment was a success. Financial matters were eased in 1898 by a successful application, under an Act of 1843, for the College's exemption from payment of local rates on the building. It is worth recording, also, as an early example of a civilised outlook on cultural affairs, that the City Art Gallery (to which admission was not then free) and Thomas Agnew & Sons allowed College students into their exhibitions free of charge. The College was indeed fortunate in its friends; to read through the names of the early subscribers is to discover many names that have played so large and beneficent a part in the history of Manchester's civic, commercial and cultural life: Mather, Platt, Simon, Behrens, Taylor, Scott, Lees, Rylands, Grommé, Heywood, Armitage, Horsfall, Donner, Tootal Broadhurst, Gaskell, Eckhard, Godlee, Forsyth, Harwood, Hecht, Charles Rowley and the Ancoats Brotherhood, Worthington, Dehn, Broadfield, Crossley, Kendal Milne and Company, Hime and Addison, Houldsworth, and Sidebotham.

During 1898 and 1899 Brodsky made some changes in his staff. He brought in Giulio Tartaglione to teach *solfeggio* in the vocal classes, strengthened the harmony and composition by the addition of a lecturer in the person of Thomas B. Keighley, the first former student to join the teaching staff, and dispensed with Lalande and Knight as bassoon teachers, the post going to Violla Akeroyd. The requirements for diplomas in 1899 are interesting. For the performing diploma, pianists were required to play one of these works: J. S. Bach's Chromatic Fantasia, Beethoven sonatas, op. 53, 57, 101, 106, 109, 110 or 111, Liszt's edition of Schubert's *Wanderer Fantasy* and Chopin's B minor sonata, together with one of the '48'. They also had to play selections from Chopin's studies, Czerny's studies, op. 365, Kessler's studies in B minor and E major from op. 20 and Liszt's Transcendental Studies, op. 2 and op. 5. For the teaching diploma the works were Beethoven's op. 31 sonatas, Bach's partitas, and selections from studies by Cramer, Clementi, Moscheles and Bach. Violin performers had the choice of six concertos—Spohr's 9th, Beethoven, Mendelssohn, Bruch's G minor, Wieniawski's 2nd, Vieuxtemps's D minor, no. 4—and parts of studies and caprices by Gavinié and Dont. For teachers the concertos were Rode's 7th and 8th, Viotti's 22nd, de Bériot's 7th and 9th or Spohr's 2nd and 11th, with studies by Kreutzer and Rode. Cello performers' six concertos were Romberg in B, Haydn in D, Schumann, Davidoff in D, Lalo in D and Dvořák, and studies by Dotzauer (op. 35), Kummer, Piatti, Cossmann and Servais (op. 11). For teachers the choice of concerto was from Romberg No. 4, Arnold in C, Grützmacher (*Fantaisie Hongroise*), Saint-Saëns in A, or Bruch's *Kol Nidrei*, and selected exercises from Dotzauer (op. 54), Merck (op. 11), Schröder (op. 45), Franchomme (op. 7, book 1), Lee (op. 31, book 2) and Bach's Suite in D, no. 2. Organ performers' prescribed choice was from Bach's Prelude and Fugue in D major, Capocci's Capriccio in B flat, Lemmen's offertoire *Hosanna*, Rheinberger's sonata in A major or Mailly's sonata slow movement, with studies by Clemen (pedal), C. Loret, J. S. Bach (chorales), Wesley in C sharp minor. The organ teaching diploma required Bach's Toccata in D Minor, Rheinberger's seventh sonata or Guilmant's second sonata, with studies by Lake (pedal), Bach (chorales) and Bach (Trio in E flat no. 1).

After that of Hallé, the name associated with the College staff in its first years which still lives daily on the lips of Mancunians is Henry Watson. Anyone remotely connected with musical matters in Manchester has cause to be grateful to the Music Library which bears his name. He was an organist and choirmaster, born in Burnley in 1846. Although of modest means, he began to collect books on music and scores with the specific intention of founding a free reference libary; it had always seemed to him iniquitous that all other students could consult books on their chosen subjects in a free library, but the music student had to buy what he needed. Over the years he accumulated books to the value, at that date, of nearly £20,000 which in 1899 he handed over to Manchester Corporation with the idea that they should form a branch of the reference library but should remain in his control and under his roof during his lifetime. He died in Salford in January, 1911, and his library, which by then contained 5,000 bound volumes (including complete standard editions of Handel, Bach, Mozart and Beethoven) and a vast collection of sheet music and some rare books, was transferred to the city reference library. By then Watson, knowing the difficulties and expense facing choral societies, had allowed for a lending branch as extension to his original idea. It was Watson who campaigned for a College library, of which he was chairman. He gave many books to it, and in the autumn of 1900 presented to the College his valuable collection of musical instruments. This included examples of the dulcimer, virginal, clavichord, spinet, harpsichord and square piano, a set of old English viols, and instruments from France, Germany, India, China, Japan, Africa and the South Sea Islands. Some of the exotic items are a gunibry (tortoiseshell guitar from Algiers), a Dahomey harp, and a Tibet trumpet made from human leg-bone. In 1909 a number of duplicate instruments was transferred to Manchester Corporation. Watson was a good lecturer on such subjects as 'Contemporary Composers', 'Some curiosities of music' and 'Music in Shakespeare's day'. When he died the annual report singled out 'the exceptional geniality of his nature, which made a friend of every student who passed through his hands or came within the sphere of his influence'. An inscription on his memorial tablet in the College says: 'He sought not riches but the common weal'.

As the 19th century ended, the changes at the College mainly affected the Council. Henry Simon died and George Murray handed over the chairmanship to Alfred Hopkinson, the Principal of Owens College. Edith Webster, one of the College's first Associates, joined the pianoforte staff. But perhaps the most important change was one not officially connected with the College although its influence was to be felt: in October, 1899, after four years of difficult, frustrating and occasionally comical negotiations, Dr Hans Richter settled in Manchester as conductor of the Hallé Orchestra. This great figure, friend and protégé of Wagner, first interpreter of symphonies by Brahms, Bruckner, Dvořák and others, was one of the most illustrious names in music, and his decision to work in Manchester could hardly fail to enliven and illumine the city's culture. Behrens and Simon had been determined to win him for Manchester, and although his 12 years in the city were eventually to be marred by bitter controversy over the conservative outlook of his programmes, he attracted to his concerts nearly all the great soloists of the day, he became the foremost champion of Edward Elgar's music (having given the first performance of the *Enigma Variations* four months before he opened his first Hallé season), and he introduced the music of Sibelius and Bartók to Northern audiences.

Like Brodsky,[1] he lived 10 miles outside Manchester, in the pleasant Cheshire suburb of Bowdon which in Edwardian days was at the height of its distinction as a residential centre for the business and intellectual élite. Richter had been 19 when he first met Brodsky in Vienna in 1862: Brodsky remembered a performance of the *Tannhäuser* overture in which Richter played the horn, cymbals and triangle. Richter made it clear from the start of his time in Manchester that he had no aptitude for teaching, so he was never officially connected with the College. But he was its benefactor in several ways, as will be seen, and the very fact that he was in the city, that students could attend his rehearsals and concerts, was a boon and a privilege. Not only could Edwardian Manchester boast of Richter at the Hallé, Brodsky at the College, Miss Horniman running the Gaiety, and Scott at the *Manchester Guardian*, it also had its musical events in those years recorded by three writers of outstanding calibre, Arthur Johnstone, Ernest Newman and Samuel Langford.

[1] Brodsky and his wife lived first at 41 Acomb Street, Manchester. They moved to Bowdon at some time late in 1903 or early in 1904.

Plate 1

(*a*) Willy Hess

(*b*) W. H. Dayas

(*c*) Max Mayer

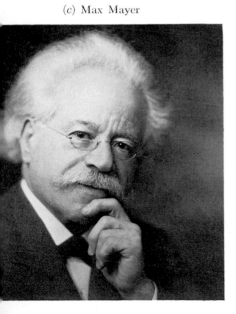

(*d*) Wilhelm Backhaus

Plate 2

(a) (L to R) Carl Fuchs, Edward Isaacs and Arthur Catterall

(b) R. J. Forbes and Dr Adolph Brodsky

(c) Sir Charles Hallé

Plate 3

May 1962 (L to R) Sir William Mansfield Cooper, Claud Biggs, John Ogdon and Frederic R. Cox, looking at a Tchaikovsky letter presented to John Ogdon by the College

A.G.M. November, 1967. A student (Anthea Jane Robb) receives a prize from the Earl of Harewood who is flanked by Frederic Cox (L) and Michael Brierley (R)

Plate 4

(*a*) Sir John Barbirolli led forward by Judith Quine (L) and Eiddwen Mair Harrhy (R) to receiv
Honorary Membership, May, 1969

(*b*) Sir John Barbirolli rehearsing past and present students at the Free Trade Hall in Apri
1964, during his 21st Manchester season

Plate 5

(*a*) The College exterior from Oxford Road

Plate 6

(*a*) Verdi's *Otello*, 1964. (L to R) Alan Ward (Iago), Janet Jaques (Emilia), Dianne Matthew (Desdemona) and Edwin Fitzgibbon (Otello)

(*b*) Beethoven's *Fidelio*, 1964. (L to R) Patrick McGuigan (Rocco), Alan Ward (Pizarro) Rhiannon Davies (Leonora) and Kenneth Langabeer (Florestan)

Plate 7

(*a*) Egon Petri

(*b*) Dora Gilson

(*c*) Lucy Pierce

(*d*) Iso Elinson

Plate 8

(*a*) (L to R) Vilmos Schummy, Endre Wolf and Rudolph Botta

(*b*) Frederic R. Cox

(*c*) J. H. Thom

4
Consolidation

The College approached and passed its tenth anniversary with advanced prestige. The new queen, Alexandra, became its patroness; Brodsky was made an honorary Doctor of Music by the Victoria University, and he and three other professors were in 1904 appointed to lectureships in the University Faculty of Music. During 1901 the College had agreed to admit students of Owens College to lectures and classes even if they did not take the full course. It should be explained that the independent Victoria University of Manchester did not come into being until 1903. Owens College had been founded in March, 1851, and became in 1880 the first constituent college of the newly created federal university, the Victoria University, when it received its charter.[1] In 1903 the Victoria University shed its constituent colleges and the following year, under Act of Parliament, Owens College became the Victoria University of Manchester. The College Council in 1902 lent strong support to the university's claim for independence, passing a resolution that 'a charter should not be granted for creating a separate university in Liverpool unless at the same time provision is made for the constitution of an independent university in Manchester' and that it was 'very desirable that a prompt decision be arrived at'. From July, 1904, the College became part of the University as far as the teaching of music was concerned.

Looking back on its first ten years, the Council could with justice boast that the College had supplied a need. By 1903 there had been 650 students, of whom 105 had taken the diploma. Already a dozen instrumentalists had found places in Richter's Hallé. But the financial position was unsatisfactory. Fees received and staff salaries cancelled each other out, leaving running costs of over £1,000 a year to be met by other means, usually voluntary subscriptions. But, because of the deaths of some original benefactors, subscriptions in 1902 had been the lowest known, leaving a deficiency of over £750. The

[1] The other two constituent colleges were University College, Liverpool, from 1884, and Yorkshire College, Leeds, from 1887.

3

Council therefore approached several county and borough councils for financial help which they were empowered to give under the 1902 Education Act. Most of the voluntary subscribers lived in Manchester, but this was held to be unfair because the city itself had never supplied more than a quarter, and at some points only an eighth, of the total number of students. 'By its constitution', the Council pointed out, 'the College cannot under any conceivable circumstances distribute its funds or be worked for private profit. . . . In due time it is hoped that State aid may also be vouchsafed to it.' This was looking ahead, indeed. Their enterprise was rewarded and during 1904 Manchester City Council made a grant of £300, Lancashire County Council of £200, Oldham £50 and Cheshire County Council £50.[1] These were the first grants ever made by Education Committees to an English institution giving systematic courses of nothing but musical education. Encouraged by this success the Council then decided to approach the Treasury, which at this date gave £500 a year each to the two London Royal Colleges and £300 to the R.A.M., Dublin, but the Chancellor of the Exchequer refused even to meet a delegation.

Just before its tenth year, the College experienced another piece of generosity from the Lees family when Mrs Lees gave £2,000 to form the nucleus of a permanent endowment. More scholarships were also sought especially for wind instruments. Lack of them had meant that poor but gifted pupils had been turned away. 'Few things are more deplorable', the Council said, 'than the wholesale waste to the community, through the lack of facilities for placing systematic education within the reach of the artistically gifted.' The sustentation fund did what it could in this respect, but its resources would rapidly have been exhausted had not Brodsky contributed £700 in seven years from his quartet concert receipts. At the end of the first 10 years there were 170 students: 67 singing, 54 pianoforte, 38 violin, three cello and eight organ. Of these 127 were women. One male student (Catterall) was entering his 10th year of attendance.

Another example of progressive ideas at the College at this

---

[1] The councils to whom approaches were made by the College were: Manchester, Oldham, Bolton, Rochdale, Burnley, Accrington, Ashton-under-Lyne, Stockport, Hyde, Preston, Blackburn, Blackpool, Southport, Bury, Warrington and Wigan.

date was the suggestion to the Council by the Board of
Professors that a junior department should be instituted. It
was felt then, as it is still felt today, that the thorough training
of musicians begins too late. The Council passed the matter
to the House and Finance Committee for examination, and no
more was heard of the idea. Other serious matters occupied
the time of the Council besides 'the provision of a suitable
hatstand' and the recovery of £3 2s. 1d. from the Corporation
because the electricity meters were faulty. From the day the
College opened, it had been the fortunate recipient of generosity from the piano firm of John Broadwood and Sons who
had lent eight of twelve grand pianos *gratis* and had kept them
tuned. Late in 1902, however, Broadwoods said that they could
no longer continue this arrangement because they had become
a limited company. Later the firm offered to hire out the pianos
at a fee of £12 a year for grands and £6 for uprights if the
College would undertake the tuning and regulating. The College refused this and asked Broadwoods to remove all the
pianos by the end of the year. A letter had been received from
John Brinsmead and Sons offering the free loan of one grand
piano and eight or nine pianos at the rate of £6 a year including tuning. This was rejected because Steinway, Erard and
Bechstein had each offered the free loan of a grand and Ibach
had offered nine grand pianos for not less than two years at
£6 a year. This was accepted but Ibach then decided they
could send only four grands. So Brinsmead's offer finally won
the day and the Council, as well they might, thanked Withers,
the Registrar, for his 'vigour, tact and discretion' in the
negotiations.

The year 1903 was eventful in other respects than the tenth
anniversary. The Manchester High School for Girls decided to
give three musical exhibition scholarships tenable for two
years at the College; and the Council's oft-repeated invitation
for the establishment of a scholarship in wind instruments was
at last accepted. At the December meeting it was reported that
'an anonymous donor' had offered a three-year bassoon scholarship worth £30. The Council decided that there should be two
scholarships each worth £15 for one year but renewable for a
second or third year at discretion. At the same time fees of all
wind instrument students (including brass) were reduced from
£30 to £15 a year. Three years later the anonymous donor
was revealed as being Dr Hans Richter, who then renewed

the scholarships for a fourth year. British music should be specially grateful to him for this gesture because one of the first two holders of the bassoon scholarships was a 16-year-old boy from Sale, Cheshire, named Archibald L. Camden. Within two years Archie Camden was bassoonist in the Hallé under Richter, later achieving great distinction under Harty, and from 1933 was principal bassoonist of Sir Adrian Boult's B.B.C. Symphony Orchestra and, from 1946, held the same post in Beecham's newly formed Royal Philharmonic Orchestra. As orchestral player, soloist and chamber music player, Camden shone equally brilliantly, continuing to play with almost undiminished skill and verve after he had passed the age of 80. His first teacher at the College, appointed by Brodsky to coincide with the foundation of the scholarships, was Otto Schieder. Another major staff change was necessitated by the sudden death on 3 May, 1903, of the senior pianoforte professor, William Dayas. In the seven years since he had succeeded Hallé, Dayas had made his mark in the College: the Council minute recording his 'untimely death' was unusually fulsome, speaking of 'one whose ability, earnestness and enthusiasm were not less exemplary than the spirit of self-sacrificing devotion in which he fulfilled the duties of his office'. Arthur Johnstone, the music critic of the *Manchester Guardian*, himself to go to an early grave 18 months later, wrote that Dayas's death 'can only be described as a disaster for musical Manchester'. He had established a high standard of pianoforte teaching and was a 'most learned theorist' but was 'unequal' as a public performer. 'He was singularly wanting in business ability', Johnstone wrote, 'and never understood how to turn his remarkable talents to any sort of worldly advantage.' His pupils had learned to recognise 'the sterling qualities of mind and heart beneath the disguise of his somewhat unconciliatory manner'.

The successor to Dayas was another Liszt pupil, Arthur Friedheim, born in St Petersburg in October, 1859, of German parentage. He studied with Anton Rubinstein and in addition to being Liszt's pupil was for some years his secretary and companion in the 1880s. Later he worked in New York, where it is possible that Brodsky met him. It is said of Friedheim that his hero-worship of Liszt led him to copy many of his teacher's mannerisms including the tiresome ones. According to Busoni, 'he bows in such a way that his hair covers his face. . . . During the tuttis ... he examines his nails, considers the audience, thrusts his hands into his hair, and does other silly things.' But he *could* play the piano and was good enough as a conductor to be offered the New York Philharmonic post. He died in New York in 1932. Of more significance for the future of the College was the appointment in October, 1903, of a former student, Robert Jaffrey Forbes, as accompanist at the students' fortnightly open practices at a fee of one guinea per evening. Forbes, born at Stalybridge in 1878, entered the College from Leigh in 1897 as a pianoforte student on a Lancashire County Council Scholarship which he held until 1900. He never became A.R.M.C.M. but was made a Fellow of the Royal College of Organists in 1897.

The year 1904 was equally eventful, principally because of the closer ties with the University and the financial grants from local authorities, both of which have been detailed earlier in this chapter, and also because of a large crop of staff changes. Dr Hiles, who had been harmony and composition professor since 1893 and was now 77, retired to Worthing at the end of the summer term and died there three months later. He was succeeded by Dr Walter Carroll, but Brodsky, anticipating Hiles's departure, had earlier been trying to attract a 'big name' to the College in the person of Edward Elgar, whose music was at this time rapidly achieving the acclaim which had been denied to it fully even after the *Enigma Variations*. In this overdue recognition no one had played a bigger part than Richter and the Hallé who, in March, 1904, travelled to London to play at the three Elgar Festival concerts given in the Royal Opera House, Covent Garden. Elgar had paid several visits to Manchester since Richter's arrival, notably for the first Hallé performance of *The Dream of Gerontius* on 12 March, 1903, after which Brodsky wrote to him of the 'greatness and sincerity' of the work adding, 'Then only you begin to realise that it is also a great masterwork from the technical point of view. Only a genius and a pure practical soul could have created such a work.' In February, 1904, Elgar was in Manchester for a performance of *The Apostles* and Brodsky went to see him to put certain proposals to him. Nothing further happened, so on 5 April, 1904, Brodsky wrote this letter, which is reproduced here in its entirety and its rather charming Russian-English:

3 Laurel Mount,
Bowdon, Cheshire

Dear Dr Elgar,

As such a long time passed without having heard from you I am afraid you have quite forgotten about the interview you granted me at the Grand Hotel, Manchester. Allow me to recall to your memory what has been said at that interview.

1st. The Royal Manchester College of Music offers you the post of Professor of Instrumentation and Composition.

2nd. The Victoria University offers you the same post at its Musical Faculty.

3rd. The "teaching" for both (the College and the University) will take place in the building of the R.M.C.M.

4th. As little as we would expect Franz Liszt to be a piano teacher, as little we are expecting from you to be a "teacher" in the common sense of the word. It is your great personality we want to secure. Your name would give glory to the Institutions and attract, I am sure, all the talent of the country. In Dr Carroll we have a very good and experienced teacher in harmony and counterpoint who will be proud to prepare the students for you. You would only admit them in the mysteries of modern instrumentation and you would criticize their compositions and develop their taste by which to be guided when composing.

5th. The both Institutions can offer you £400 a year.

6th. You will have at your disposal all the time you happen to want for composing your immortal works.

7th. Any time you may require for a journey abroad or in this country will be certainly granted to you.

8th. If you could give us some popular lectures at the Victoria University on any subject you like, we should certainly be quite happy.

9th. I feel certain that you and Mrs Elgar will find many friends here devoted to you and still have all personal freedom you may require for the time you would like to be left to your work.

Hoping to receive a favourable answer, I am

Yours most sincerely,

Adolph Brodsky

Mrs Brodsky joins me in heartiest greetings to you and Mrs Elgar.

Elgar refused this generous offer and Brodsky wrote again on 15 April: 'I am not surprised at your refusal. I scarcely dared to hope that you would accept. ... Still I am very thankful to you, that you have found it worthwhile to give it full consideration before saying a final "No".' Later that year, Sir Edward, as he had by then become, accepted the specially created Peyton Chair of Music at Birmingham University where he gave the series of controversial lectures which brought him much personal unhappiness and worry.

Another long-serving member to retire from the staff was Mrs Hutchinson, who had been Professor of Singing for seven years. She was succeeded by Marie Fillunger, a soprano singer of German Lieder and of oratorio, who was born in Vienna in January, 1850, and had studied at the Conservatorium there under Marchesi and later, on Brahms's advice, at the Hochschule, Berlin. In 1891 and 1895 she had accompanied the Hallés on their tours of Australia and South Africa, Friedheim, after only a year, resigned the piano professorship and returned to America. His successor, from 1 January, 1905, was Wilhelm Backhaus, then aged 20, who had already made an international reputation and had appeared at the Hallé Concerts with Richter in the 1901–2 and 1902–3 seasons. He, too, was to stay only for a year, for he soon found (as might easily have been anticipated) that his concert work left him little time for teaching. But in that year he enriched Manchester life with several memorable recitals. In May, 1965, when he was 81, he returned to the College to receive the highest honour it can give to non-students, Honorary Membership. Finally Hallé's sister, Anna, resigned as teacher of German because of failing health, and was succeeded by Miss Margaret Jordan. It should perhaps also be mentioned that 1904 was the year when a 'low-pressure heating apparatus' was installed in the College at a cost of £227 and the Registrar (who had been allowed the telephone in 1903) was 'empowered to purchase a type-writing machine'. It was also the year when the large hall of the College was re-named the Lees Hall in commemoration of 'its ever-remembered first treasurer', Charles E. Lees. This decision was taken at a Council meeting on 19 October, 1904. On 15 March, 1905, Mrs Lees unveiled a brass tablet in Lees's memory. The year 1905 had begun on a memorial note, with the receipt in January of a letter from Mrs Arthur Johnstone offering to the College the library of books and music which had belonged to her husband, the *Guardian* critic, who had died in December, 1904, at the age of 43, after an operation. This gift necessitated enlargement of the library and the creation of the new post of Librarian, the first holder of the office being John Holme, who since October, 1896, had assisted Withers in management of the library. Also during 1905 past students contributed £74 for endowment of a medal in memory

of Dayas, to be awarded triennially to the best pianoforte
student on the register. Its first recipient was Ellen Arthan,
and subsequent winners have included Lucy Pierce (1909),
John Wills (1915), David Wilde (1952), John Ogdon (1956),
Anthony Goldstone (1964) and Christian Blackshaw (1969).

These events apart, 1905 was a year of little moment unless
we include the presentation of a Loyal Address—'very uncon-
ventional in design and colour scheme, its chief ornamental
feature being the figure of St Cecilia and the interweaving
of musical symbols, viols, etc., in a girdle round the text'—to
the King and Queen when they visited Manchester on 13 July.
Edward VII, in his reply, said that the Queen was very pleased
to be the College's patroness 'and feels confident, as I do, that
the College will continue the admirable work it is now doing'.
On 1 December the treasurer, Charles James Heywood, died.
He had been in office for 11 years, and was one of the College's founders and most devoted friends 'to whom it has from
the first been indebted for unremitting personal services and
generous material support'. This support was continued by his
widow, who gave £1,000 for an open or entrance memorial
pianoforte scholarship of £30 a year. The first holder was
Dorothy Cole (1907–8) and among her successors have been
Dora Gilson (1908–12), Edith Halliwell (1938–41) and Maureen
Challinor (1954–9).

In finding a successor to Backhaus, Brodsky again selected a
young virtuoso from abroad—this was the time when it was
still natural to look to the Continent for musical eminence.
His choice fell on Egon Petri, a 25-year-old Dutch pupil of
Carreño and Busoni who had also in his youth studied violin,
organ and horn. He had begun his career as a recitalist in
1902 and had at once won international fame. Brodsky fixed
his first contract at 18 months and it appears that Petri threw
himself heart and soul into his teaching activities. Within a
few weeks of taking up his appointment he was one of a sub-
committee of the Board of Professors who decided to re-
examine the College diplomas 'in the light of the practice
prevailing in other similar institutions at home and abroad'. A
later meeting, with Carl Fuchs in the chair, recommended that
the teacher's diploma could not be retained in its present
form but should be re-modelled and that final year candidates
should attend a short course of demonstration lessons in their
subject. The Board also recommended the appointment of

external examiners[1] and it also passed a resolution preventing any teacher from being an examiner of his own students in the diploma examination. The Council refused to accept this latter resolution. The sub-committee of professors—Rawdon Briggs, Dr Carroll, Petri and Fuchs—then urged the Council to abolish the teacher's diploma 'with distinction', suggesting that the words 'with honours' be marked upon the diplomas of candidates who obtained 95 marks in their principal study and 90 in each other part. This was approved by the Council, but it is interesting to note that in January, 1907, the diploma 'with distinction' was reinstated by the Council. Other recommendations which the Council accepted were:

(1) The performer's diploma should be retained but made gradually more severe.
(2) There should be three examiners, two of them members of the staff, but the teacher of the candidate should not be one of them. The teacher should be asked to provide the examiners with a brief report on the general peculiarities and aptitudes of the candidate.
(3) There should be a lecture each term to all students on 'the principles of teaching'.
(4) In preparing for the teacher's diploma, the teacher should shape the lessons with a view to giving students a practical knowledge of how to teach elementary pupils.
(5) That verbal questions on teaching should form an essential part of the examination, the candidate being required to answer 'searching and well-prepared questions on the subject, each question to be put by the examiner who may require the candidate to illustrate his answer by performing a short passage'.

A later meeting of the sub-committee laid down further regulations for demonstration lessons for final year candidates, to all of which the Council gave its agreement. They were:

(1) The professor should be prepared to answer questions and should invite questions from his class, and should be prepared to illustrate his answers verbally or by examples with voice or instrument and to comment generally upon the difficulties encountered in teaching the average pupil.

---

[1] Among the first external examiners at the College were Leonard Borwick and Fanny Davies (pianoforte); Henry Blower, Edward Bairstow and Francis Harford (singing); and Alfred Gibson (violin).

(2) The pupil to whom the demonstration lesson is given should be provided by one of the professors in the subject in consultation with the Registrar and that any small expenses should be paid by the College.

(3) The pupil concerned should be of an elementary grade, and the student giving the lesson should be informed beforehand of the approximate stage of the pupil's advancement.

(4) Candidates for the teacher's diploma should be 18 or over.

(5) Every candidate for the teacher's diploma should be prepared to give a model lesson, examiners having the right to hear the whole or a part of any lesson they thought advisable.

(6) Candidates should be required to write a paper on the teaching of the principal subject; the questions asked should be general; the papers should be set by the external examiner; the paper work should cover two hours and the percentage for a pass should be 70.

This greater emphasis on the teaching diploma was placed at the chief insistence of Dr Carroll, whose principal interest it was. The logical conclusion to this first step was the creation, in March, 1909, of a new department of 'The Art and Practice of Teaching' with Dr Carroll as Professor at a salary of £120 a year. It was plainly understood that the Principal had over-riding power to excuse such students as he thought proper from attending lectures in the new department. The new department—'somewhat of an innovation in the equipment of a college of music'—was a success. In those days, teaching of music was regarded as a respectable profession but performing it in public as a professional was still 'not quite the thing' as far as most middle-class families were concerned, so it is not surprising to read that 'the great majority of students' became teachers after leaving College and that many teachers unconnected with the College applied for admission to the new classes.

Returning to 1907, several staff changes became necessary after a comparatively stable period. Miss Lemmens-Sherrington, one of the original members, retained direction of the Opera Class but gave up her individual pupils to other teachers. A year later she resigned. The Opera Class was taken over by John Acton, another of Hallé's appointments, but he too resigned 'because of uncertain health' during 1909. A third surviving member of the first staff, Olga Neruda, also retired in 1908 because of increasing ill-health (she survived for many more years) and the need to change residence as a result of 'the severe winter of Manchester'. In her final weeks at the College the Council allowed her pupils to have their lessons at her home, 38 Clyde Road, Didsbury, instead of from her substitute, R. J. Forbes. During 1907 two vacancies had occurred on the violin staff with the resignations of C. Rawdon Briggs (leader of the Hallé since 1905) and T. W. Poulter. Their places were taken by Edith Robinson and Arthur Catterall. Miss Morden Grey took over elocution classes from Miss Lemmens-Sherrington, Helena McCullagh became an accompanist for the open practice in company with Forbes and in place of Kate Coates. Miss Neruda's professorship was filled by Max Mayer, who had lived in Manchester for several years as private teacher and public recitalist. As long ago as 1895 he had written to Brodsky applying for Hallé's vacant piano professorship but negotiations had failed because of the College's inability to guarantee a fixed number of students. The piano staff was increased to six in 1909 by the appointment of Forbes (only one accompanist then remained, a newcomer, Isidore Eisenberg). Forbes's appointment was the result of a fracas with Egon Petri; once again the demands of a concert career and those of teaching were found to be incompatible. Early in 1908 Petri gave four recitals (to students and the public) in the University's Whitworth Hall. He played 20 Beethoven sonatas, in chronological order, all from memory, including the *Hammerklavier*, and the audiences for each recital never fell below a thousand in number. The Council were overjoyed and voted him £25 in recognition of the event. Six months later the tone was rather different. At the start of the winter term a special meeting of the House and Finance Committee was called at which a letter from Petri was read. He asked for extension of his leave of absence until 9 November and announced that he would withdraw from the College in July of 1909. The Committee refused his request and asked Brodsky to order him to return for 15 October. On 16 October a special Council meeting sent a telegram to Petri saying that he should either return or resign. He wired back his resignation. Brodsky gave most of Petri's pupils to Forbes, who was not at this date a member of the pianoforte teaching staff. All the students agreed to this with the exception of one who preferred to go to Mayer and another (Clara Fischer) who asked to leave and to have her fee returned. At the November Council meeting two explanatory and apologetic letters from Petri were read and he was reappointed to his post as from 12 November on the understanding that his engagement terminated in July, 1910. This was a year later than his original notice, and the matter was clinched by a legal contract.

Staff changes and gifts comprise the history of the next few years which saw, in 1911, Richter's departure from his Hallé post. He had been a good friend of the College, continually giving money to the sustentation fund, giving former College students a chance to make their professional debuts under his mighty auspices, and finally presenting several scores to the College Library. In 1910 Mrs Lees put the College once again in her debt by giving £200 to cover the cost of installing an electric blower for the organ. John Cassidy's life-size bronze bust of Hallé, which stood in the Lees Hall, was presented to the College by Mrs Walter Beer. Miss S. F. Scott, daughter of the first Principal of Owens College, gave the College a death-mask of Chopin and a cast of his hand (both of which can today be seen in the Henry Watson Music Library). The mask was taken by the French sculptor Chesneau on 17 October, 1849, the day after Chopin's death, for Chopin's Scottish pupil Miss J. F. Stirling. She bequeathed it to A. J. Scott who was collecting material for a biography of Chopin. This gift was made to mark the centenary of Chopin's birth. Rietschel's portrait medallion of Liszt, also now in the Henry Watson Library, was given to the College by Max Mayer who succeeded Petri as Chief Professor of Pianoforte. An Amati violin, to be allocated to advanced students on special occasions at the discretion of Brodsky, was bequeathed to the College by the Misses Leo, descendants of the textile merchant Hermann Leo who in 1848 had persuaded Charles Hallé to settle in Manchester.

John Acton's resignation from the singing staff in October, 1909, led to the engagement of the English bass, Francis Harford, on terms which included a free railway ticket between London and Manchester, a guaranteed six hours' teaching weekly at a guinea an hour, and 18s. for additional hours. Harford was one of the finest singers of his day, especially notable as an exponent of the Lieder of Wolf, Brahms and

Schubert. In January, 1910, Tartaglione, the teacher of sol-feggio, died. He was not replaced, but in 1911 Lillie Wormald left to be married and was succeeded by a former student, Sarah Andrew. Frank Merrick joined the pianoforte staff in 1911 to fill Petri's vacancy. Henry Watson's death meant that Dr Thomas Keighley became choir trainer and Kendrick Pyne took over as curator of the Watson collection. It is pleasant to record that the Council's differences with Petri left no rancour. The annual report for 1911 specially mentioned his 'high ideals of work and the strenuousness with which he carried them out', and paid tribute to his recitals of the Beethoven sonatas 'as well as of a great variety of music seldom heard, which ranged from classical to ultra-modern and displayed no less catholicity of taste in selection than interpretative skill in performance. Mr Petri takes back to Germany the sincere good wishes of the Council for his future success'. This great pianist played again at the Hallé Concerts between the two world wars and in 1938 received an honorary degree from Man-chester University. A link between the College of Edwardian days and of the 1960s, the 'space age', is forged through Petri, for he taught John Ogdon and shared with him admiration for the music of Busoni and the virtuosity to play it. Those who knew Petri still speak of his charm and nobility with impres-sive reverence. Of his piano-playing, gramophone records give some idea. His art was described to me by one of his distin-guished colleagues as 'monumental'. Like many foreigners with a good command of English, he relished making puns. This was known to his students, hence the following authenticated exchange: 'The thought of having lessons with such a great pianist as you has petrified me'—'How Egonising for you.'

Finally, a last link was broken in the early summer of 1911 when the Council recorded its 'sense of the great loss sustained by the musical profession and the art of music generally by the death of Lady Hallé, an artist of the loftiest ideals and of pre-eminent accomplishments, and desires, further, to express its more intimate feeling of regret at the severance of the long and valued association which existed between the College and the distinguished lady who, as the wife of the first Principal and virtual founder, was herself one of the inspiring influences in the creation of the College'.

5
Coming-of-age

The College reached its 21st year in 1914 and in 1912 a joint committee of Council members and professors was formed to plan the celebrations. This committee had four stated aims:

(a) The provision of an endowment fund;
(b) Clearing of debts;
(c) Foundation of a hostel for women students;
(d) Establishment of scholarships and bursaries.

It was also decided to take advantage of the occasion to make the College better known by giving concerts by past and present students in towns near Manchester for the benefit of local charities, and Stanley Withers, the Registrar, was asked to write a short history of the College for publication as a booklet. (This did not materialise for another four years.) Gustav Behrens was chairman of the Celebrations Committee, and its other members were Lady Donner, Mrs Lees, Miss Gaskell (who later withdrew because of ill-health), E. J. Broadfield, Brodsky, Carroll, Mayer, Eller, Fuchs, E. W. Grommé and Dr Perkin (University representative).

As the College grew, its financial difficulties grew alongside. At the end of its 20th year, in July, 1913, it had 167 students, of whom 124 were between the ages of 16 and 21. Fifty were men and 117 women. There were 62 singing students, 49 pianoforte, 36 violin, seven cello, three clarinet (Harry Mortimer had joined Edward Mills as teacher of this instrument in 1910), two flute (teacher V. L. Needham since 1906), three organ, and one each for double bass, oboe, trumpet, trombone, and composition. The number of students had held fairly steady round the 160 mark since the turn of the century. The staff had increased and some of them were receiving slightly more pay (professors' fees in 1894 were £4,333 a year and in 1912–13, £4,525), but the number of people both willing and able to subscribe generously to the College costs was an ever-dwindling factor. Three figures in the revenue account are of special importance. Subscriptions, which had run in 1898 at a figure of £1,916, were in 1912 down to £546. In 1912, too,

the revenue from students' fees was £4,198, and in 1898 it had
been £3,976 when there were 148 in the College. By 1912 the
annual grants from Manchester, Lancashire, Cheshire and
Oldham came to £570, whereas in 1906 they had amounted to
£650. In 1909 Oldham reduced its grant by establishing a
scholarship tenable at the College. The Council regretted this
move, although they welcomed the extra scholarship. Constantly they stressed the need for some kind of State grant and
continued to feel bitterly that London and Dublin were
favoured in this respect. In January, 1913, a delegation led
by Sir Alfred Hopkinson saw Charles Trevelyan, President of
the Board of Education, and presented once again the College
case for a capitation grant for all students. They had a sym-
pathetic hearing. Later the matter was passed to the Chancellor of the Exchequer, Lloyd George, but still no money
materialised. However in May, 1913, Mrs Lees gave £3,000
to the new endowment fund and Sir William Houldsworth
gave £1,000. Gustav Behrens, too, was generous in support
but, as always, did his good by stealth; and in 1912 the name
of his son Leonard appeared for the first time among the
subscribing members. This was still the age of the private
patron, the generous private patron, but it was an age in its
death throes, with 1914 waiting in the wings.

As if to clear the decks for the new world that was to come,
death removed in 1913 two founder-members of the College,
Edward J. Broadfield, Vice-Chairman of the Council for many
years, treasurer of the University since 1908, and Chairman
of the Hallé Concerts Society since 1899. 'Warm supporter,
wise counsellor, willing helper,' a believer in the 'elevating
and refining influence of the art of music', one whose life was
dominated by 'disinterested devotion to the highest interests
of the community'. Who could wish for a nobler epitaph than
these words from the Council minute recording his death?
Later the same year, Miss Gaskell, daughter of the author of
Cranford and *North and South*, died. She had served on the
Council for 14 years and was mourned as one 'whose hand was
never closed to the appeal for aid'. Broadfield was succeeded
as Vice-Chairman by Mrs Lees. The Chairmanship also fell
vacant during 1913 when the Vice-Chancellor, Sir Alfred Hopkinson, resigned (though retaining his seat on the Council)
because he was to undertake a prolonged educational mission
in the Far East. The office was left open.

The major staff change during 1912 was caused by the resignation of Marie Fillunger from the Chief Professorship of Singing. In 1911 her guaranteed salary of £400 a year was reduced to £300 for the next two years, and she asked to go at the end of July, 1913. She was succeeded by Marie Brema, at a salary of £400 for 12 hours' teaching weekly, a first-class railway ticket between London and Manchester and extra hours at 18s. an hour. The singing staff was further enlarged by the engagement of a former student, Hilda de Angelis, as a second studies teacher. Brema was one of the best-known singers of the day, born in Liverpool in 1856 of American-German parentage. She was a mezzo-soprano with a range wide enough to bring Brünnhilde among her rôles, and she was the first English singer to be asked by Cosima Wagner to sing at Bayreuth. She sang all the great Wagnerian rôles in New York under Damrosch and she had had experience as an actress-manager of opera, putting on Gluck's *Orfeo* at the Savoy Theatre, London, in 1911, singing the title-rôle herself. Her operatic rôles included Ortrud, Brangäne, Fricka, Kundry, Amneris and Delilah; and in English musical history she has a special place as creator of the rôle of the Angel in Elgar's *Dream of Gerontius* in 1900. On appointment to the College she also took charge of the Opera Class (at an extra £20 per term) and added Richard Evans to her staff to bring its complement up to five, its highest for some years. The piano staff was raised to seven by the addition of two former students, Ellen Arthan and Lucy Pierce. One of these was a replacement for Miss Julius, who retired after 19 years on the staff. Miss Bretey, who had been appointed by Hallé, at the same time had her fee raised from 5s. to 6s. an hour! In February, 1913, Dr Keighley and Dr Carroll wrote to the Council urging the appointment of a junior teacher in harmony. There were the seeds here of impending friction between these men. Keighley probably already felt that the new teaching department was taking up most of Carroll's time. At any rate in May another former student, H. Baynton-Power, was appointed a harmony teacher, on Carroll's recommendation, the Council adding that 'further diminutions of the number of students in the harmony classes is not desirable'. Keighley in any case had taken on an extra burden by persuading Brodsky and the Council to authorise two experimental weekly classes in the Dalcroze system of rhythmical gymnastics for students who had the Principal's permission to attend them. Keighley was the teacher. In 1914 the class gave a demonstration which drew a doubting letter from Mrs Gustav Eckhard, wife of a Council member, and led to her being reassured that Keighley's use of the description 'based on the eurhythmics of Dalcroze' had the approval of the head of the Dalcroze College in London.

An important reform in the government of the College was started in February, 1914, by a deputation (Carroll and Mayer) to the Council from the Board of Professors suggesting that the Board should be represented on the Council. This point was conceded the following month and in May Carl Fuchs and Max Mayer were elected. At the same meeting Professor F. E. Weiss, the botanist and new Vice-Chancellor, was elected Chairman of the Council. In June, 1914, Kendrick Pyne became the College's first professor emeritus when he resigned his organ post. Sydney Nicholson, then Manchester Cathedral organist, was offered the post but declined, and the organ pupils were passed to R. J. Forbes until some other candidate was found.

Meanwhile the coming-of-age celebration went its way, and concerts were given in the autumn of 1913 and spring of 1914 in Stalybridge, Bolton, Burnley, Rochdale, Bury, Leigh, Crewe, Preston, Blackburn and Southport. At Rochdale, the new town hall organ was inaugurated by Pyne, but at the Bolton concert, in aid of the blind school, on 22 October, there was 'an unfortunate contretemps' and the Registrar was asked to inform the hapless new harmony teacher, Baynton-Power, 'that he had failed in his obligation to the College by not taking proper steps to secure an adequate performance'. Nevertheless the concert raised £82, over £30 more than the next most successful financially. Although the proceeds of the concerts went to charity, students solicited contributions to the endowment fund appeal and by March, 1914, had obtained promises of £2,000 for this fund and £46 for the women's hostel. Mrs Lees, as might be expected, had offered to buy the Gaskells' home, 84 Plymouth Grove, and present it to the College as a hostel in memory of the novelist and her daughters. A subcommittee inquired into administrative costs of such a purchase, and the matter was dropped.

In July, 1914, the College year ended. The students dispersed for their holidays, Brodsky went to Vienna to fulfil solo

4

engagements, Fuchs went to Jugenheim to visit his mother. On 4 August war was declared. Brodsky was detained in Austria, now enemy territory. Fuchs was interned at Ruhleben. The Council met specially on 16 September and read a letter from Brodsky in which he made suggestions for the continuation of his work while he was away. His violin pupils were shared between Arthur Catterall and Anton Maaskoff. The quartet class went to Rawdon Briggs, the orchestral class alternately to Keighley and Forbes, the ensemble class alternately to Mayer and Merrick, and Fuchs's pupils were handed over to Walter Hatton. This hiatus in its affairs, while its Council faced a war most people thought would be all over in a few months, seems an opportune moment to review the musical activities of the College since its foundation.

6
The music, 1893–1914

The first music publicly performed in the College was at the Conversazione on its first Saturday of existence, 7 October, 1893. The programme was:

Quartet in D minor . . . SCHUBERT
  (two movements, Andante con moto and Presto)
  (Willy Hess, Rawdon Briggs, Simon Speelman and Ernest Vieuxtemps)
Song: Young Dieterich . . . HENSCHEL
  (Andrew Black)
Kol Nidrei, for solo cello . . . BRUCH
  (Carl Fuchs)
Duet: Giorno d'orror (*Semiramide*) . . . ROSSINI
  (Mme Lemmens-Sherrington & Miss Lemmens-Sherrington)
Traumeswirren . . . SCHUMANN
  Novelette in E . . . SCHUMANN
  (Frederick Dawson, pianoforte)
Songs: Serenade (*The Pearl Fishers*) . . . BIZET
  Biondina No. 5 . . . GOUNOD
  (Miss Lemmens-Sherrington)
Romanza in A minor, for violin . . . BRUCH
  (Willy Hess)
With Verdure Clad . . . HAYDN
  (Mme Lemmens-Sherrington)
Songs: When thy blue eyes . . . LASSEN
  Cradle Song . . . GRIEG
  (Andrew Black)
Intermezzo in E flat, op. 117, no. 1 . . . BRAHMS
  Barcarolle in F sharp, op. 60 . . . CHOPIN
  (Sir Charles Hallé)

It was a typical miscellany of the time, obviously designed to display the accomplishments of the staff. The *Semiramide* duet is unusual, and it was characteristic of Hallé that he should have played a recent work by Brahms, who was still alive; the three Intermezzi op. 117 had been composed and published only the previous year, 1892.

In the summer of 1894 the students gave three end-of-term recitals open to the public. These became known as Examination Concerts, from Hallé's remark that the College had examined its students, now it was the public's turn to examine the College. The first of them was on 16 July and included Grieg's *Holberg Suite*, Bach's double violin concerto in D minor (soloists John Platt and John Holme), a C minor sonata for violin and piano by Beethoven, some operatic and oratorio arias, Chopin's *Grande Polonaise* (played by Rosa d'A Blumberg) and 'Master Catterall' in the first movement of Rode's A minor violin concerto. On 17 July, works for full choir and for women's voices were sung, there was an aria from Sullivan's *Ivanhoe* and the 'Jewel Song' from Gounod's *Faust*, and a vocal quartet by Sir Michael Costa, 'Ecco quel fiero istante'. In this and in 'O God Have Mercy' from Mendelssohn's *St Paul* the bass was one of Andrew Black's pupils, Charles Walton, of Oldham. Eight years later he was to become the father of a son, William, who grew into one of England's greatest composers. On 18 July an interesting choice was Dvořák's Terzetto for Two Violins and Viola, op. 74, the last movement of Kreutzer's violin concerto in D minor, and the op. 110 sonata by Beethoven.

On 30 October, 1894, Hallé instituted the students' musical evenings, or open practices, as a way of giving the students experience of public performance before a friendly audience of College subscribers and staff. The choice of music varied greatly, showing the least taste in the vocal items. A string quartet in E flat by Dittersdorf, Handel's G minor organ concerto and a movement from a Hummel piano concerto are more encouraging. An aria from Massenet's *Hérodiade* and Hiller's Capriccio fugato for Four Violins were performed on 30 November and on 13 February, 1895, one of Olga Neruda's youngest piano pupils, Master E. Isaacs, who was to make a considerable mark on Manchester's music as Edward Isaacs, played Beethoven's Variations on an Original Air in G.

The practice on 14 March was attended by Joachim. He heard Catterall in a Handel sonata, Walton in 'Even bravest heart may swell' from *Faust*, and much else. The public examination concerts from 8 to 11 July, 1895, included Edna Thornton singing 'Softly awakes my heart', a movement from Beethoven's first piano concerto, Catterall in a violin piece by de Bériot, an aria from Meyerbeer's *Dinorah*, Walton in the Prologue from *I Pagliacci*, an impromptu in B minor composed by Hallé, the scherzo from Dvořák's Serenade for Strings, and songs by Korbay and Goring Thomas.

Charles Walton sang Rossini's 'La Danza' at the first practice of Brodsky's era, on 29 November. A movement from Bruch's G minor violin concerto, the first movement of Schumann's piano quintet, and a vocal duet by the 17th-century composer Clari were also performed.

The Brodsky Quartet made its debut on 24 February, 1896, when the programme was Haydn's op. 76, no. 5, in D major, Schumann's op. 41, no. 3, in A major and Beethoven's op. 59, no. 2 in E minor. A month later it played Mozart's C major quartet, Schubert's D minor and Beethoven's op. 59, no. 3. The first orchestral evening by the students, with assistance from the staff on wind instruments, included Beethoven's eighth symphony and Gluck's overture *Iphigenia in Aulis*. The adagio from Brahms's piano quartet in C minor and the first movement of Dvořák's piano quintet were played on 8 May, 1896, and on 21 May the Brodsky Quartet was enlarged for Mozart's G minor quintet, Brahms's C minor string quartet, op. 51, no. 1, was played and Brodsky and Olga Neruda played Grieg's sonata. On 6 July Beethoven's second symphony was performed, and the College's first operatic essay was Act III of Gounod's *Faust*, with William Wild[1] as Faust, Minnie Grime as Marguérite and Charles Walton as Mephistopheles. The first Wagner to be sung at the College was 'Elisabeth's Prayer' from *Tannhäuser*, by Ethel M. Wood on 20 November, 1895, and Wotan's 'Farewell', sung by Charles Walton on 27 January, 1897. Under Brodsky's influence in the quartet class, the students now began to play movements from Beethoven quartets.

The orchestral concert on 1 February, 1897, was remarkable for the inclusion of Brahms's first symphony, at that date still regarded as a very tough nut to crack (it had not been played for 20 years at the Hallé Concerts) and Mozart's 41st symphony. Of the great composers, Schubert seemed least popular at this time, although a movement of his E flat Trio was played on 20 May, and a contralto pupil sang 'Grief for Sin', the first extract from J. S. Bach's *St Matthew Passion* to be included in a students' concert. Dayas encouraged one of his pupils, Edith Webster, to play Brahms's *Variations on a Theme by Schumann*,

---

[1] Wild later was a soloist in Richter's notorious Hallé performance of Berlioz's *Romeo and Juliet*, when Ernest Newman wrote of him in the *Manchester Guardian*: 'Men do not go through tragic, feverish scenes like that at the end of *Romeo and Juliet* with an air as if they were posing for a statue of Morpheus.'

and on 5 July, 1897, Brahms's second symphony was played, followed by Act I of *The Magic Flute*, with William Wild as Tamino, Charles Walton as Papageno and Edith Bardsley as the Queen of Night. This was followed by Beethoven's *Leonora No. 3* overture. Presumably Brodsky conducted. Walton left at the end of this term, his final solo being 'Non più andrai' from *Le Nozze di Figaro*. Elgar's name appears on a College programme for the first time on 6 July when his part-song 'The Snow', for female voices, was sung by Dr Henry Watson's choral class. Liszt's second piano concerto was played by a pupil of Dayas (Irene Schaefsberg) on 7 July, and on 25 February, 1898, three of Fuchs's ensemble class performed the first movement of Beethoven's triple concerto, by no means a common choice, then or now. Tchaikovsky's Serenade for Strings and Beethoven's fourth symphony were in an orchestral concert on 18 March and Saint-Saëns's G minor piano concerto was shared between two students on 1 April.

The inaugural recital on the new organ, given by Kendrick Pyne on 11 May, 1898, began with Handel's fifth organ concerto, followed by an arrangement of the andante from Beethoven's septet. Widor's fourth organ symphony (F minor), a Romance by the organist's father, Bach's Prelude and Fugue in A minor, a traditional Scottish air, a Fantasy by Guiraud and S. S. Wesley's Choral Song and Fugue in C major completed the programme.

Henceforward the programmes of the open practices become rather more interesting. Movements from Lalo's *Symphonie Espagnole* and Schumann's piano concerto were played on 20 May, an evening which ended with the Toccata in F of J. S. Bach played on the organ by R. J. Forbes, the first mention of him in a College programme. Mendelssohn's music to *A Midsummer Night's Dream*, interspersed with readings, was performed in full on 4 July, 1898, and 27 January, 1899, by a cast which included Sarah Andrew and Lillie Wormald. The piano quartet in E flat by Rheinberger was performed several times, and the vocal trio, 'Le faccio un inchino', from Cimarosa's *Secret Marriage*. Catterall several times played movements from concertos by Vieuxtemps and de Bériot, and Dayas's pupils played the Liszt and Chopin first concertos. Brodsky's pupil John Lawson played the first movement of Tchaikovsky's concerto on 7 December, 1898, having studied it with its first interpreter, and it is delightful to find that Walter Ford taught one of his pupils, Frances Baguley, to sing Scarlatti's delicious 'Le Violette'. Sarah Andrew seems to have had inordinate affection for Somervell's 'Home they brought her warrior dead', but if this sort of thing still occurred fairly often it was offset by a concert as adventurous as that on 22 March, 1899, when Brahms's fourth symphony was played and the first (and last?) performance in Manchester was given of Reinecke's Serenade for Strings in G minor (op. 242). The second and third movements of Brahms's first piano concerto were played on 18 May, 1899, by Irene Schaefsberg, and the first movement on 14 June.

Edith Webster, also a Dayas pupil, played the adagio and finale of the *Hammerklavier* sonata on 13 February, 1900. An organ pupil played the first movement of Elgar's sonata on 27 February. On 23 March there was a concert performance of *The Marriage of Figaro* conducted by Brodsky, with Sarah Andrew as the Countess, Fowler Burton as Figaro, Frank Barker as the Count and Lillie Wormald as Susanna. The Cherubino was Millie Jones, who also sang Berlioz's 'Absence' on 15 May. Past and present students aided the sustentation fund on 30 May, when Liza Lehmann's *In a Persian Garden* was sung, and a young cellist, William Warburton, played a movement from Goltermann's concerto in D minor. For the first time, the first movements from Brahms's B flat major and Beethoven's G major concertos were attempted on 10 July, the former by Edith Webster and the latter by Edward Isaacs. 'The Swimmer' from Elgar's *Sea Pictures*, which had only just been published, was sung on 16 November. Liszt's B minor sonata made its first College appearance on 14 December, played by Dayas's pupil Augustus Mayhew. Catterall, who was now 18, played the Paganini concerto on 26 March, 1901, and another Brodsky pupil, Clara Kloberg, was the first to tackle Brahms's concerto, playing the first movement on 27 March, 1901. Spohr, Raff, Sinding and Sauer were composers whose music was frequently played. Haydn's string quartet, op. 64, no. 1 in D, was played by a quartet led by Catterall on 28 March. The following evening Brodsky conducted Beethoven's *Fidelio*, with Blanche Cooper as Leonora and William Wild as Florestan. A trio from Verdi's *Attila* on 23 May is a rarity worth noting. The concert-performance opera in 1902, on 22 March, was of *Don Giovanni*, sung in Italian, with Frank

Barker as the Don, Blanche Cooper as Anna and Charles Walton returning to sing both Masetto and the Commendatore. (His son William was born exactly a week later.) On 5 December, Dr Watson conducted Schumann's *Paradise and the Peri*. Extracts from *Carmen, The Flying Dutchman* and *Hiawatha* now begin to occur in programmes, and it was surely enterprising of Brodsky in 1903 (28 March) to conduct Nicolai's *Merry Wives of Windsor* in the new Whitworth Hall of the University. Lucy Pierce's name first occurs on 28 May, 1903, when, as 'a pupil of the late W. H. Dayas', she played Rheinberger's Toccata. Harold Dawber, too, another great College personality of the future, appears as organist at the practices at this date, and Isaac's quintet for piano and strings was played on 9 July by a quintet which included Catterall and himself. On 26 March, 1904, the opera performance was of *The Magic Flute*. That the students were also encouraged to sing modern opera is proved by the inclusion of 'Vissi d'arte' from Puccini's *Tosca* (first produced 1900) at an open practice on 16 June, 1904. *Figaro* was again sung on 25 March, 1905, and the name of Richard Strauss was admitted into the open practice programmes on 8 June, 1905, when Lucie Gratama sang the 'Serenade'. At the same recital Alfred Barker played a de Bériot concerto, and Blanche Mackie sang Aïda's 'Ritorna vincitor'. This was the period of Backhaus's professorship and his pupils included Ellen Arthan, who played two movements of Beethoven's C minor concerto, and Lucy Pierce, who played the Schumann—and anyone who heard her play it in later life will not easily forget its poetry. By 1906 she had become Petri's pupil[1] and played Franck's Prélude, Chorale et Fugue on 7 March. Brodsky chose Weber's *Der Freischütz* for the opera performance on 2 April, with Hamilton Harris as Caspar. Petri's influence is discernible in the practice on 24 May when one of his pupils played a Busoni arrangement of Bach and another played two studies by Alkan. Lucy Pierce played Beethoven's op. 109 sonata on 12 July and Brodsky's pupil Anton (Tony) Maaskoff played the Saint-Saëns violin concerto on 13 November.

Hugo Wolf's 'Verborgenheit' was the first of his songs to be included in a student's repertoire at the College (Annie Knowles on 5 December, 1906) and the soon-to-be-famous

[1] Lucy Pierce was the pupil successively of Dayas, Friedheim, Backhaus and Petri.

name of the clarinettist Harry Mortimer appears in Brahms's
clarinet quintet on 5 February, 1907. In later years Samuel
Langford was to write of Mortimer in this work thus: 'Mr
Mortimer has certainly sought out every avenue of beauty and
poignancy by which the heart of the listener may be moved;
and many a listener must have been surprised, first at him and
at the insight which he displayed, but yet more at the abound-
ing beauty which this music at every turn reveals.' Brodsky
conducted Verdi's *Un Ballo in Maschera* on 15 March, 1907,
with Richard Evans as Renato and Norman Allin in two small
parts. Gertrude Barker, a pupil of Rawdon Briggs and Edith
Robinson who became a Hallé player and survived, as her
friends gratefully remember, into Barbirolli's time, played a
movement of a Mozart concerto on 16 May—dear Gertie, a
'character', a kindly soul, a good fiddler. Alfred Barker and
Maaskoff were Brodsky's star pupils at this date, playing Bruch,
Tchaikovsky, Wieniawski, Saint-Saëns, Sarasate, and in chamber music. The Franck piano quintet, first movement, was
played on 9 July, and two days later George Whitaker, Olga
Neruda's pupil, played Richard Strauss's *Burleske*. Two other
famous Brodsky pupils, Hélène (Lena) Kontorovitch and Naum
Blinder, first played at an open practice on 30 October, 1907,
the former in Ernst's F sharp minor concerto and the latter in
a movement from Vieuxtemps's first concerto.

The year 1908 was remarkable in Manchester's musical history for the legendary series of four recitals of Beethoven
piano sonatas given in the Whitworth Hall on 27 January, 10
February, 24 February and 9 March by Egon Petri. The programmes were:

First recital: Sonatas in A flat major, op. 26; op. 27; no. 1, in
E flat major; op. 27, no. 2, in C sharp minor; op. 28 in D
major; op. 31, no. 1, in G major.
Second: Sonatas, op. 31, no. 2, in D minor; op. 31, no. 3, in
E flat major; op. 53 in C major; op. 54 in F major; op. 57 in
F minor.
Third: op. 13, op. 78, op. 79, op. 81a, op. 90, op. 101.
Fourth: op. 106 in B flat major; op. 109 in E major; op. 110 in
A flat major; op. 111 in C minor.

In a note on the programme of the second recital, Petri cites
Czerny on Beethoven's use of the right pedal, especially the
holding of it down throughout the recitative of the D minor

sonata, and adds: 'The student looking into his music for these marks will be surprised not to find them there, except in very early editions of the sonatas. Subsequent editors changed them, remembering only too well the iron rule that whatever happens you must not let two different harmonies run into one another.' He played the *Hammerklavier* with the metronome marks given by Czerny as Beethoven's own, i.e. in the allegro $\boldsymbol{\int} = 138$; scherzo $\boldsymbol{\int} \cdot = 80$; adagio $\boldsymbol{\int} = 92$ and finale $\boldsymbol{\int} = 144$. Two nights later Siloti played Bach, Chopin, Rachmaninov and Liszt.

At the open practice on 4 March Norman Allin sang 'Honour and Arms' from Handel's *Samson* and the players in Beethoven's Septet included Blinder, Kontorovitch, Maaskoff, Barker (on viola), Mortimer, Archie Camden and Otto Paersch. For the opera on 30 March Nicolai's *Merry Wives* was sung again, with Allin, Harris and Richard Evans in the leading male rôles. Petri's pupil Joseph Percival played the first movement of Tchaikovsky's B flat minor concerto on 30 June. The next now-well-known name to occur among the students is that of John Wills in Franck's Symphonic Variations on 16 February, 1909. The College again was host to Siloti on 25 February, when he played D'Albert's arrangement of Bach's Passacaglia, Chopin's B minor sonata, a group of smaller Chopin pieces including the D flat Nocturne, and Bach's Chromatic Fantasia and Fugue. Nor should we overlook Brodsky's own solo recitals, usually accompanied by Forbes. To quote Langford again: 'Mr Forbes is always just something a little more than himself when he plays with Dr Brodsky. It is past admiration how he scents the challenge of a style so daring and is so unfailing in the way he lives up to it.' And this is Langford on Brodsky in the *Kreutzer* sonata:

> There was the characteristic energetic vigour which bites itself into the music at the first note and never leaves hold until the work is ended. There is no room in such a conception of music for the half-man or the declining man. The wrestle with the music is to the death, and the invisible entity of the composer's mind is something as tangible as an opponent in the ring.

Gluck's *Iphigenia in Aulis* was conducted by Brodsky on 6 April, 1909, with Allin as Calchas and Richard Evans as Agamemnon. Dora Gilson's name first occurs at a practice on 26 May when she played Chopin's Ballade in G minor. She was a pupil of Petri. Brodsky's beloved A minor concerto of Bach was played complete by Alfred Barker on 16 June. He, Blinder, Clarice Dunington and Lena Kontorovitch were the Principal's leading pupils at this date; Catterall was now on the teaching staff. Blinder became the first to be allowed to attempt the Beethoven concerto (at a practice on 15 March, 1910) probably because the College orchestra took part on this occasion. Petri's pupils included Wills, Pierce, Gilson and Dorothy Crewe. Norman Allin, whose teacher was now Francis Harford, in place of John Acton, sang seven of Schumann's *Dichterliebe* on 5 July.

Curiously most of the student composers of those days, from Dr Carroll's class, seem to have been women, Alice Dill (a violin pupil of Brodsky) and Enid Grundy being two names, but H. Baynton-Power's chamber works were several times performed by his fellow-students. The orchestra class, now strengthened by student wind players, could tackle works like Beethoven's eighth symphony (29 March, 1911), and Max Mayer's pupils betrayed a leaning towards Reger's music which reflected their teacher's enthusiasm. On 6 July, 1911 (within eight months of its first performance), the first movement of Elgar's violin concerto was played at an examination concert by Lena Kontorovitch. Would a modern concerto today pass so quickly into a College repertoire? Another Brodsky pupil, Frank Tipping, who went into the Hallé Orchestra and was killed in action in the 1914–18 war, played two movements of the Mendelssohn concerto on 6 February, 1912. On 1 April of that year Brodsky conducted Baynton-Power's dramatic scena 'A Passion on the Deep', with Norman Allin as one of the soloists. The synopsis explains that 'a man and a woman are left alone on a storm-tossed and foundering barque. His desire is that their last hour should be spent ignobly, but she, strong in faith and purity, resists his entreaties.' Readers will be sorry to hear that her faith and purity were of no avail and she drowned anyway. After which, Dora Gilson (now Frank Merrick's pupil) playing Mozart must have been classic relief. On 20 June May Burton, another Merrick pupil, broke new ground by playing three pieces by Debussy. Richard Strauss's sonata, op. 18, was played by Blinder and Alwyne Browne on 2 July, and Blinder played the Elgar concerto complete two days later. Harford, who had given first performances of several songs by Vaughan Williams (including 'Silent Noon') in the early 1900s,

introduced two of the *Songs of Travel* ('Youth and Love' and
'The Vagabond') into a practice on 19 November, when his
pupil Alfred Grant sang them. Songs and piano music by Max
Mayer, including the song-cycle *Maeve*, were performed on
26 February, 1913. Carl Fuchs's pupil Carrodus Taylor played
the first movement of the Dvořák cello concerto on 2 April,
Gertrude Barker and Lilias Dunlop played the D minor concerto for two violins (Bach) and John Wills played a Schumann
rarity, the beautiful Introduction and Allegro Appassionato,
op. 92, rediscovered for our own day by Benjamin Britten.
Marie Brema's women pupils, none of whose names have any
significance today, gave a very mixed programme on 3 April,
in which MacDowell and Somervell predominated; Harford's
taste seems to have been superior, for songs by John Ireland
and Richard Strauss were sung by his pupils instead of the
royalty ballads hitherto much too prevalent.

The last peacetime musical activity of the College was the
Dido and Aeneas performances on 16 and 17 July by Marie
Brema's opera class accompanied by John Wills at the piano.
The Cummings edition was used, with a few alterations by
Mme Brema. Dido was sung by Mabel Hirst and, on the
second night, by Olive Brown. The Belinda was May Till and
Aeneas Alfred Grant. It seems extraordinary that the College
orchestra was not used.

Although they do not strictly come within the scope of this
survey, the Brodsky Quartet concerts were in their 18th season
in 1913–14. This was the heyday of chamber music in Manchester, when you could hear Siloti and Brodsky playing Bach
together, the *Trout* quintet played by the Brodsky Quartet with
Max Mayer as pianist and John Hoffman double bass, the first
performance (7 March, 1914) of the C major quartet by Nova-
cek, Fauré's piano quartet in C minor with Frederick Dawson
as pianist, Brahms's sextet and his piano quintet with Karin
Dayas (a relative of the former pianoforte professor). Manchester's music was dominated from 1900 to 1914 by Richter,
Brodsky, Petri and Michael Balling. The war was to sweep
away this foreign domination, only Brodsky remaining as a
link with what now seems to have been a golden age.

7
Beecham's song contest

Before their curtailment by the war, the festivities to mark the College's 21st year had brought in £2,710 for the endowment fund. This money was to prove doubly valuable because of the inevitable hardships which were to be faced. With Brodsky and Fuchs away and Harford joining the Army, where he was soon promoted to the rank of captain, the reorganisation of the staff was considerable. Harford was allowed three guineas per week per term during his absence on military service. The Board of Professors suggested engaging either Campbell McInnes or Herbert Brown in his place, but the Council preferred to leave the vacancy open and his pupils were shared between Marie Brema, Sarah Andrew and Dora Gilson, who had acted as his assistant. In November Archie Camden was appointed bassoon professor and in December, when it seemed that Brodsky's absence might be prolonged, Withers was appointed Acting Principal.

Wartime problems in plenty awaited the College Council, but in that first winter their attention was diverted by a battle nearer their own doorstep. In 1913 at the December annual meeting it had been decided to invite distinguished civic and other guests to attend and to speak. The Mayor of Oldham and Richter's successor as Hallé conductor, Michael Balling, were the first of these VIP guests. The College report for 1915 blandly states that at the annual meeting on 4 December, 1914, 'the Lord Mayor and Mr Thomas Beecham took part in the proceedings', a classic example of understatement if ever there was one. Beecham's own account of what follows can be found in his autobiography,[1] but it should be explained that he has his dates wrong (he says it all occurred in the spring of 1915) and he gives the impression that the invitation to him to speak was given on the eve of the meeting, whereas the Council decided on 18 November to ask him to do so. The facts are these, and they are amusing enough to need no fictional decorations: on 3 December Beecham conducted a Hallé Concert at

[1] *A Mingled Chime* (Hutchinson, London, 1944), pp. 137–8.

which some of Delius's music was played in the presence of the composer. Beecham and Delius dined 'at the house of the principal patron of the College of Music', probably Donner or Grommé, and Delius, who like Beecham had a contempt for academic training based on almost total lack of experience of it, 'entertained the party with a magnificent effort of abusive condemnation'. His host apparently asked Delius if he would like to address the College meeting next day on this subject, but the composer declined. Beecham, however, decided to make this the point of the speech he had promised to deliver, but, he wrote,

since I knew that to create a lively interest and provoke any useful reaction over a wide area I should have to employ the tactics of an out-and-out offensive, I thought that I should first ask our local Maecenas if they would be likely to injure the interests of the especial object of his protection. He answered that the more out-spoken my criticism the better, as there was far too much self-satisfaction in the place for his own liking.

So the next evening, with Mrs Lees in the chair and the Lord Mayor and Delius present, Beecham spoke and in the *Manchester Guardian* and *Manchester Courier* of 5 December there were full reports of what the former called his 'extremely energetic' criticisms. He began by proclaiming his contempt for musical academies and asserting that the war 'had accomplished what he had been vainly attempting for years, the expulsion of all the accomplished foreigners'. British composers and musicians were now being 'welcomed as great geniuses by the gentlemen of the Press' and the younger generation had the chance to

continue the fight that some of them had been fighting for ten or fifteen years. There is no place in music today for anyone who is not profoundly competent and efficient. The kingdom of music is less like a republic than anything else in the world—it is an aristocracy, and everyone going into the profession should make up their mind to be a musical and mental aristocrat.

The Manchester College was only 21 years old. If it were one of the 'old-established perfectly useless institutions like those in London' he would not have troubled to say a word about it. He never troubled to listen to singers who applied to him from the London colleges—'especially that great bazaar the Guildhall School'—because he knew they would be bad. 'But you are young and enthusiastic, and though you have up to the present time accomplished absolutely nothing there is still plenty of time, and you will probably not make the same mistakes as your hopelessly effete, played-out and useless brethren in London.' He then went on to pay tribute to Delius and to compare the British advance in instrumental playing with the German decadence. Germany had not, in the previous 40 years, produced a single pianist or violinist of the first rank, but in England the advance in this respect had been enormous —though he remembered himself in time to add that none had come from the colleges of music. But it was singing that was 'hopeless and tragic'—

I really don't know how many students are studying singing in this college. Very few I hope ... I have one question to ask schools of music in England. How many artists have you produced in the last ten years? And I make this statement with all severity and solemnity: in the last ten years you have produced not one artist of first or second rank. In all the colleges and academies of this country there is not one great artist. Out of all the singers in England today I should have the greatest difficulty in getting together a second-rate opera company.[1]

The Manchester and Birmingham colleges, he added, were the only ones for which there was hope of salvation. But if he thought that rider would save him he was soon disillusioned. On 7 December Withers came to the College's defence in a letter to the *Guardian*. What about the 30 ex-College members of the Hallé Orchestra, he asked. Was it 'nothing' to have turned out them? What about Arthur Catterall and R. J. Forbes? As for the singers, when Beecham had conducted *The Ring* in Manchester in 1913, two of his principal singers had been former College students. If he had seen Miss Brema's students in *Dido and Aeneas* in July, 1914, he would have witnessed an exhibition of the very qualities he denied. In the same issue the *Guardian* had a leader, no doubt written by Samuel Langford, supporting Beecham's 'explosive and extravagant' speech and urging that it should not be taken 'sourly' because it was 'manifestly intended to be as much invigorating as devastating'.

Beecham returned to the attack in a letter to the *Guardian* of 11 December. Withers's reply, he said, made him wish he

---

[1] Eighteen months later, in Manchester, he gave the first of three seasons of opera, with English singers, which many good judges think have yet to be surpassed.

had hit out more strongly. Young as the College was, it was 'beginning to show unmistakable signs of premature decline and decay'. It was 'insular ignorance' or 'parochial megalomania' for the College to claim in its report that it could challenge comparison with any similar institution at home or abroad. With the possible exception of Catterall, said Beecham, no College student had any reputation outside this country. He then made an onslaught on the students' performance of *Dido and Aeneas*, 'a work performed in Europe perhaps once in 100 years and of a character entirely different as regards style and stage movement to anything else they may ever be called upon in the future to take part in'. A year had been wasted on this 'archaic' piece which could have been spent on Verdi, Massenet, Mozart or Wagner, simply

to gain for the College a reputation for exoticism and antiquarianism in taste, to exploit the fad of a celebrated artist [Brema], and to obtain a laudatory notice in a certain London newspaper [*The Times*] which . . . has always been the sturdy champion of musical reaction in England. *Dido and Aeneas* is a work which may be played by a company of gifted amateurs or mellow and experienced professional singers for their own amusement; it is absolutely the last thing in the world to give to a company of unsophisticated students. One does not engage as leader-writer on a paper a man who is able to write only in the style of Chaucer. . . . How, then, in the name of goodness can anyone expect a singer to be engaged for any opera written during the last fifty or one hundred years who has been brought up exclusively on such toast-and-water musical fare as *Dido and Aeneas*?

More uproar. Brema gave an interview to the Press justifying herself; and William Eller, a Council member since 1893, wrote from his home in Knutsford that Purcell would be honoured long after Beecham's name had been forgotten. But he admitted that the Continental conservatoires would 'beat' the College when it came to opera singers because no one would support opera in Britain so no students could expect to make a living by singing in it. Withers had another go, rather ill-advisedly, in the *Guardian's* column and Edith Robinson, the violin teacher, made a disastrous intervention by writing that the public would receive just what it was willing to pay for. 'We may not be getting the best out of the College, but we are certainly getting the best the public is prepared to receive.' A lady from Rusholme, however, agreed that the singing at the College was 'remarkably poor'. Beecham then fired his final shots in a letter published on 16 December. He demolished Edith Robinson with these words:

It is terrible even to try to imagine what must be the influence on the unhappy student of anyone imbued with such ideas as these. . . . I would still say it is one of the duties, perhaps the principal duty, of a college of music, to stand four square to the ill winds of fashion and caprice, resolutely to resist all corruption and backsliding, and if it cannot exist by upholding a fine tradition without making vile concessions, then let it perish fighting gloriously.

After this burst of rather excessive rhetoric, Beecham came to the real point of his letter:

Mr Eller seems to think that my denunciation of English singers is intended to be directed against opera singers only. Nothing of the sort; I included opera singers, concert singers, and every other existing kind of vocalist. Now, I have in my library three works which contain parts of not more than average difficulty for a soprano, a tenor and a baritone. I do not believe for one moment that the Manchester College has, within the last few years, turned out a single student who can do justice to these pieces, and I challenge the College to produce them. I will begin with baritones. . . . One of these works is a composition of Mr Frederick Delius which the Hallé Concerts Society are anxious to perform at one of their concerts next March. For this work a baritone is required, not a great artist such as Sir Charles Santley, Mr Chaliapin, or certain others, but simply an ordinary efficient singer of which, if Mr Withers is to be believed, there must be hundreds in the near vicinity of Manchester.

The Hallé Concerts Society have most kindly placed their organisation at my disposal for the purpose of discovering new talent, and authorised me to say that if any young baritone can satisfy Mr Delius that he can competently sing this rôle he will be engaged for the Hallé Concert next March.

He then gave the conditions for his 'modern tournament of song'. Eligible candidates must have been on the College books for a period not longer than ten years before 1 January, 1915; six weeks would be allowed for the study of the work; Delius alone would decide the winner, whose name would be the only one published.

Beecham concluded:

No one will be more delighted than myself if, as the result of this little trial, there should be discovered some new singers of talent; if, on the contrary, the seemingly impossible were to happen and Mr Delius were to find himself 'non-suited', I should proceed

5

to pursue my inquiries as to the probably unfortunate state of
things in respect of sopranos and tenors. But in any case I should
like some of the College authorities to know that I am only just
beginning my investigations.

Appended to his letter were letters from J. Aikman Forsyth,
honorary secretary of the Hallé, confirming the Society's part
in the affair and from Delius agreeing to act as judge and
adding: 'I do not think you should have any difficulty in finding a singer for my work; it has been frequently done in
Germany where I could easily find twenty or thirty baritones
to give a good account of themselves.'

The name of the work had not been mentioned by any of
these three correspondents. It was *Sea Drift*, and it is astonishing to find Beecham and Delius evidently in agreement that
it could be properly performed by 'an ordinary efficient singer'.
My experience of it is that only a sensitive and poetic interpreter can penetrate to its secret. There could, of course, be no
question of a refusal to take up the challenge, as the *Guardian*
pointed out, and the Council happened to be meeting on the
day the letter was published. They decided that Withers
should write to the *Guardian* stating that the College could
put no pressure on its students past or present, but that it felt
sure Mr Beecham's challenge would be taken up. As indeed
it was. Five baritones entered but only three went on to the
final contest on 26 February, 1915. Beecham described the outcome:

I knew that eventually I should have to choose someone to sing
the work, but I hoped that the argument would drag on long
enough for me to extend it to a much wider domain of debate, to
create a pleasantly dramatic tension, and that by spinning out the
trials I would be enabled to make the ultimate verdict all the more
gratifying to local pride. But I had reckoned without the incalcul-
able element of Frederick Delius, who, at the opening audition,
forgetting entirely the real purpose of the whole adventure,
approved the first singer who presented himself. It availed nothing
that in aesthetic endowment the fortunate vocalist was far from
being a fitting selection for this particular piece; the decision was
given, and the triumph of the College complete. For if the very
first candidate who appeared had proved acceptable, then it followed as a matter of course that there must be many more of equal
eligibility. My discomfiture was as total as the elation of the other
side, and I vowed never again would I entrust the casting vote
of decision in any other of my carefully calculated projects to the
unaccountable impulse of a composer, however eminent.

The winner was Hamilton Harris, of Ashton-under-Lyne, who had won the Curtis Gold Medal for singing in 1908. He sang in *Sea Drift*, as promised, at the Hallé Pension Fund concert on 18 March. Langford thought that he sang it powerfully and with richness of sentiment, and that, like the composer, he was finest of all in the lovely closing pages. The hall was full for a by no means popular programme (Stravinsky's *Three Japanese Songs*, Debussy's *Nocturnes* and Delius's piano concerto were also performed). As Beecham had prophesied, the publicity had ensured that the successful candidate would make his Hallé debut on a great occasion. So all ended happily, and everybody benefited from the furore. It was, of course, all part of Beecham's campaign of revivification of English musical life which he had been waging in the opera house and concert hall since about 1907. This was the most fruitful and worthwhile part of his career, and the College episode was a typical example of the splendid and good-humoured panache with which at that time he made his assaults on complacency and reaction.

8
An era closes

While Beecham was providing such entertaining diversions, the College had to replace a singing teacher when Hilda de Angelis left to be married. In her place came Paul L. Vallon. The Board of Professors recommended that in future vacancies on the staff should be advertised and this was done when a reorganisation of the organ department was undertaken. Choir training and singing were included as constituent parts of the organ professor's duties and the new post went to Dr Keighley. At the same time the fee for the course was reduced by £10 to £20 a year.

The chief event of 1915—apart from *Sea Drift*—was the release from internment of Dr Brodsky, mainly through the efforts of Frederic C. Penfield, American Ambassador in Vienna, efforts, as the Council minuted, which were 'the more gratifying inasmuch as they were voluntary and disinterested, Dr Brodsky as a Russian subject having no claim upon the helpfulness of the American Embassy in Vienna'. He returned to Manchester, where a reception was held in the Lees Hall on 21 April to welcome Mrs Brodsky and him. Contributions to the Sustentation Fund while the Brodsky Quartet were silent had been made by the Rawdon Briggs Quartet, Edith Robinson's Quartet and sonata recitals by Forbes and Catterall. Brodsky's first gesture on return was to give a solo recital in aid of the fund and then to re-form his quartet. Fees in 1915 fell by £400 because many students were given leave of absence until the end of the war. Women students outnumbered men by nearly three to one. By midsummer, 1916, 25 former students and staff were serving in the Forces. Economies had to be made. Marie Brema was told she could have no extra money for her annual opera performance and Brodsky was asked to take the absent Fuchs's two ensemble classes. But £900 was received and invested as the endowment of a scholarship in memory of Will Pearce, and the executors of Miss Ida Freund, a niece of Ludwig Straus (leader of the Hallé, 1875–88) gave £500 to the Sustentation Fund. Thus the College's good fortune continued from private sources; but there

was consternation in January, 1916, when Lancashire Education Committee decided to withhold the grant of £200 from
their estimates for 1916–17. This amount had been forthcoming
for the past ten years, and the College Council pointed out
that the R.M.C.M. suffered a considerable annual loss on
Lancashire County Scholarship holders and that it trained for
a professional musical life 'the sons and daughters of residents
of the Lancashire County area for whom the Lancashire Education Committee makes no educational provision whatever'.
The force of the argument was acknowledged and the grant
restored in 1917.

Early in 1916 it was decided to insure the College against
damage by aircraft (Zeppelin raids). The war impinged in
other ways and there was a personal reminder of its effects in
the sympathy expressed to Gustav Behrens when one of his
sons was wounded. Three members of the teaching staff,
Forbes, Catterall and H. Baynton-Power (appointed a piano
teacher in 1915), were due for military service and the College
appealed to the Military Tribunal for their exemption. Brodsky
himself appeared before the tribunal to plead the College's
case for retaining important members of the staff. The tribunal
exempted Catterall and Forbes on condition that Baynton-
Power's appeal was withdrawn. Baynton-Power was called up
early in 1917. Another absentee was Frank Merrick, who went
to prison as a conscientious objector. He offered to resign his
professorship but the Council refused to accept it, and engaged
his wife, Hope Squire, to deputise for him. (It was Merrick's
pacifist views, or his championship of women's suffrage, which
had led to his rebuke by the Council in July, 1914, when the
chairman was asked to seek a pledge from him that 'neither
within the College nor without will he attempt to influence
any of the College students on matters unconnected with their
studies'.) By 1917 three former students had been killed in
action—Herbert Taylor, Frank Tipping and Sydney Wilson—
and a further 61 were serving, plus two staff.

There were also non-military casualties. Two famous
teachers died, Charles Reynolds, Richter's favourite oboist,
and V. L. Needham, the flautist. (They were succeeded by
Arthur Nicholls and E. S. Redfern.) Council members who
died were Alderman Thewlis, who had represented Manchester Education Committee for 13 years, Archdeacon
Fletcher and Herbert Smith-Carrington. The last-named had

served actively for 15 years. Then on 22 April, 1917, the College's first president, Sir William Houldsworth, died. At the end of the year Beecham was elected his successor for a period of five years. At the beginning of 1917 Professor Weiss resigned the chairmanship of the Council in favour of the new Vice-Chancellor, Sir Henry Miers. Mrs Lees was re-elected vice-chairman, and the Council rejoiced later in the year when she was appointed D.B.E.

Of the 187 students at the College at midsummer 1917, only 34 were male. This inevitable disproportion, combined perhaps with the arrival of two more women on the Council, led to improved accommodation being provided during the long vacation. Better cloakroom facilities were built, the basement was concreted, the walls tiled, the ground floor remodelled and the heating apparatus overhauled. Women students were provided with a small rest-room. Needless to say, the cost of the work (over £7,000) was met by Dame Sarah Lees. The absence of men had a serious effect on the opera performances; Marie Brema's 1917 offering merely comprised scenes from *Cavalleria Rusticana, Lohengrin* and *Orfeo*. All the students of the opera class took part in the Elysian Fields scene of the O'Mara Company's production of *Orfeo* at the Gaiety Theatre. This was conducted by Forbes.

A notable event during the 1916–17 period was the foundation of the College's first permanent wind instrument scholarship in the capital sum of £500, the gift of Mrs Elwell and her sister Miss Elsie Bishop in memory of their uncle, Lt.-Col. H. J. Candlin. Each year in the annual report the Council besought a wind scholarship but, apart from Richter's bassoon scholarship, which had not been maintained, nothing had ever materialised.

The year 1918 saw the College's 25th anniversary, but no special celebration marked the event except for the writing by Stanley Withers of a short history. The end of the war was celebrated with Dvořák's *Song of Thanksgiving*, Elgar's *Carillon*, some Belgian music and the peace prologue from Rameau's *Castor et Pollux*. Peace brought its problems, too, and the first of them was the position of Francis Harford, the professor of singing who had served in the Army throughout the war and at the end of 1918 was on indefinite leave awaiting demobilisation. The College had allowed him £36 per term while he was away and agreed to continue this for another term on the understanding that if he could obtain his release and return to his teaching he should repay a proportion of the sum for so much of the term as he worked. Harford refused these terms and sent in his resignation in February, 1919. The House and Finance Committee were asked to re-open the question and to invite Harford for an interview. The committee offered him re-appointment on terms of one year's guarantee of eight hours per week at 15s. an hour; or four hours at a guinea an hour; or six hours at 15s. an hour. He refused to consider the alternatives and was reappointed on his pre-war terms, less the grant of a season ticket from London, for one session only. He resigned in October, 1919, leaving the College at the end of the Easter term of 1920. Harford was an exceptionally artistic singer and a generous teacher. On one occasion he was one of an examining board which awarded 100 marks to a candidate. Withers thought this should never be done and engineered a reduction of two or three marks, much to Harford's indignation. Another returning member was Carl Fuchs, who was released from Germany, where he had been given a certain freedom to play in orchestras during the war. He was reappointed on his old terms in May, 1919, but such was the anti-German feeling in the country that, sensing it, he resigned a month later 'on the grounds that by remaining a member of the staff he might injure the College which he loved'. This decision was accepted with regret, and it was to be two and a half years before this beloved musician returned to his post.

May, 1919, was also the month when a long-brewing pot of trouble came to the boil. Dr Carroll's prime interest was in the training of teachers and in 1918 he became England's first full-time music adviser when he was appointed to this post by Manchester Education Committee, an appointment sponsored by Councillor Will Melland, who represented the committee on the College Council. Carroll did not see eye to eye on College policies with Dr Keighley and with Forbes. With the former he had a major difference of opinion which led to his resignation from the Council, in company with Mrs Norman Melland, in 1919 and his resignation from all his College posts in 1920. Keighley succeeded him, and Carroll went on to do famous work in Manchester in the realm of school music. His daughter Ida was also to play an important part in Manchester educational life as Principal of the Northern School of Music.

It was decided also in May, 1919, that six members of the

staff should receive higher pay and that students' fees should be raised to £12 per term. Over the next year the College register was to rise to 350 students. This put a severe strain on accommodation. The College was bounded on three sides by streets and on the fourth by small houses which, at a time of acute shortage, could not be interfered with. Several members of the staff eased the position by placing rooms in their private homes at the disposal of the College for certain classes. The number of students was artificially inflated by the admission of 88 ex-Servicemen who had been awarded Government grants. The annual report for 1920 commented somewhat tartly: 'The College has never refused admission to any ex-soldier who could satisfy the conditions of entry, but several have already been withdrawn by the Board of Education on the grounds of unsatisfactory attendance or inability to comply with the conditions prescribed.' Of the 350, the piano class numbered 127, singing 115, violin 54, cello 19 and organ 15, with the remainder in single figures. One good result of the extra fees and higher attendance was a surplus on the year of £1,431. There was encouragement, too, in the establishment by the borough of Nelson of an external scholarship worth £60 tenable at the College. The Council report commended Nelson's example to 'other large towns in Lancashire, most of which are equally distinguished for their love of music and also for their entire absence of any provision for its cultivation upon advanced and systematic lines'. The year 1920 was also the 25th year of Brodsky's Principalship. In offering him its warmest congratulations the Council recognised 'with special gratification that Dr Brodsky has founded a School of Violinists imbued with his own serious spirit and with the authentic classical traditions of interpretation'. Whatever delight Brodsky himself took in this anniversary must certainly have been diminished by the death early in 1920 of Simon Speelman, who had been the violist in the Brodsky Quartet since its foundation, had taught the viola at the College since its inception and had been principal viola of the Hallé Orchestra for over thirty years. Besides being a great instrumentalist he was also a renowned wit, about whom many affectionate stories were once told. His successor in the Hallé, Frank Park, also succeeded him at the College in the Quartet. Death also removed two other members of the staff in 1921: the horn player, Franz Paersch, and the flautist Stanley Redfern. The former was succeeded by his son Otto and the latter by Joseph Lingard. Both these players were members of the Hallé Orchestra which at this date was in process of being returned to its former eminence by the inspired and mercurial Hamilton Harty, appointed conductor in 1920. Brodsky's staff in 1921 was still distinguished, with himself and Catterall as the chief violin professors. Of the eight pianoforte teachers, if there was no longer a Petri or a Backhaus, at least there were Max Mayer and Frank Merrick, with Forbes and Jeanne Bretey and, representing the younger element, Lucy Pierce and John Wills. Among the singing teachers still the most dynamic personality was Marie Brema whose principal virtue was her ability to infuse dullards with life even if the effects were sometimes unduly, even grotesquely, exaggerated. (It was she who told a pupil whose interpretation of an aria from Bach's Mass in B minor had been too enthusiastic, 'My dear, people will think you are coquetting with the Almighty.') Her chief assistants were Sarah Andrew, Richard Evans, Dora Gilson and Paul Vallon. A newcomer early in 1921 was Elsie Thurston, who had been called in to take Miss Andrew's pupils when she was seriously injured in a motoring accident. All other instrumental teaching was in the hands of Hallé Orchestra principals and included such famous names as Arthur Nicholls (oboe), Harry Mortimer (clarinet), Archie Camden (bassoon), Willem Gezink (timpani) and Charles Collier (harp). Possibly the weakest department was the harmony and composition, where Dr Keighley's influence seems from all accounts to have been baleful.

During 1921, impelled perhaps by the extra zest for life and its fuller meaning which seems usually to follow a war— though, equally usually, the spirit soon evaporates—several education authorities followed Nelson's example and endowed musical scholarships tenable at the College. And, for the first time, Manchester Education Committee included music in its scholarship scheme and awarded a pianoforte scholarship. With this extra outside interest in mind, the College lent its support to renewed pressure for the foundation of a Chair of Music at Manchester University and decided also to renew its petition for a Royal Charter. At a meeting on 24 November, 1920, Charles Dunderdale, the College solicitor, was requested to apply to the Privy Council for the grant of a Charter. Bearing in mind the importance attached to the success of this petition, one can understand the Council's dismay when the new president, Beecham, made adverse criticisms of the College's work which were regarded seriously by Manchester Education Committee's representative on the governing body, Will Melland. Sir Thomas was invited to visit the College 'and personally ascertain the quality and nature of its work or, failing that, to put into writing the substance of the adverse criticisms verbally reported to the Council'. The grants sub-committee of the education committee meanwhile recommended withholding of the £300 grant to the College. Although the main committee referred this back for further consideration, the sub-committee dug its heels in and in October it met a College delegation. The Council agreed to invite a report from an independent outside authority on the work and efficiency of the College. This task was accepted by Professor Granville Bantock, then Principal of Birmingham School of Music, for an honorarium of fifty guineas. He spent a week at the College in December and quickly reported favourably. He suggested closer connections with the University and the Hallé and proposed institution of an accompaniment class. (The latter was speedily started, under Forbes.) The College, Bantock said, had obtained 'a really national position' and there was every reason to believe that its usefulness would be increased. The education committee was pacified and renewed its grant. When the five-year renewal of the presidency came up in 1922 Beecham's name was not put forward again. The post was offered to Dame Sarah Lees who declined. It was then offered to the Duke of York (later King George VI) who accepted.

Throughout 1921 Charles Dunderdale rallied support for the Charter petition. Many leading public figures and musicians signed it and, most important of all, it was not opposed by the heads of the Royal Academy of Music and the Royal College of Music (Dr J. B. McEwen and Sir Hugh Allen) provided that a clause was inserted stating that the R.M.C.M. did not propose to hold external examinations or award diplomas to non-students. Alas, Dunderdale died in the Spring of 1922 and his partner and successor John Galloway was elected to the Council as honorary solicitor. A strong pointer to success was contained in a report of the Standing Joint Committee on Secondary Education (the Burnham Report) which named the College with the R.A.M. and R.C.M. as the only 'recognised institutions of music'. The charter was granted on 5 May, 1923, and was laid on the table at a Council meeting on 10 May. To celebrate this event, which strengthened the College's claim for an annual Treasury grant, and to mark the 30th anniversary, the Council, on the recommendation of the Board of Professors, created the award of Honorary Fellowship of the College. This title would be conferred on distinguished past students, whether associates or otherwise. The first ten Fellows, who were admitted on 7 December, 1923, were Norman Allin, Sarah Andrew, Dr J. C. Bradshaw, Arthur Catterall, Richard Evans, R. J. Forbes, Edward Isaacs, Dr Keighley, Edna Thornton and Lillie Wormald. The Council was elected at this meeting, under the terms of the Charter, and its membership was proposed by C. P. Scott.

Early in 1924 a composition prize of unusual character was instituted, known as the 'Mrs Leo Grindon Shakespeare Prize'. Its value was two guineas and it was to be awarded for an original composition, song or male voice quartet, with words from Shakespeare. Its first winner in 1925 was Thomas B. Pitfield. In 1927 it went to Alan Rawsthorne, who in 1928 also won the Chappell Gold Medal for students of the piano. Rawsthorne's later career lay wholly in the realm of composition, but his teacher, Merrick, said that he could have been a fine concert pianist had he wished. When he and Harry Blech played Beethoven's C minor sonata, Fuchs declared that 'they could play it anywhere'. Rawsthorne was 21 when he entered the College, having abandoned dental training to concentrate on music.

In the decade from 1913 to 1923 the College's intake had doubled from 167 to 384. The strain on accommodation was eased by the purchase for £1,500 in 1921 of a house in Oxford Road, No. 330, which had a large double room suitable for lectures, and five smaller ones. Also in 1921 Carl Fuchs was reappointed to his old post as Professor of Cello and Harty, conductor of the Hallé, became conductor of the College Orchestra. This latter appointment was short-lived because pressure of other work forced Harty's resignation during 1923. Over the next year or two there were to be several important staff changes. Sarah Andrew had never fully recovered from her car accident and died in the winter of 1924, in her forties. She had entered the College as a student in 1895 and, as the Council minute of her death said, 'won step by step to a leading place in the ranks of professional musicians. . . . The College has lost a teacher whose gifts and enthusiasm can ill be spared, and one who was a true friend and helper of her students.' She had appeared as soloist at Hallé concerts and sang the Angel in *The Dream of Gerontius* under Richter. A memorial scholarship was instituted in her name in 1925, on an endowment of £850 from Miss Ethel Johnson.

Max Mayer, who had been Professor of Pianoforte for 16 years, resigned in May, 1924, because of poor health, and the vacancy was filled by Claud Biggs, who came to Manchester from the Royal College of Music. Mayer and Olgar Neruda were appointed Professores Emeriti by the Council. Max Mayer was a lovable man, slightly resembling Grieg in looks. He had been a pupil of Liszt and told many stories about his teacher, notably of an occasion when another pupil had played the march from Schumann's Fantasy in C with scrupulous care but with his eyes glued to the keyboard. 'You must not play it like that', said Liszt, who seated himself at the pianoforte, gazed fixedly at the ceiling and played the passage with faultless and effortless brilliance. Mayer's wife, Alice, had studied singing with Stockhausen and he himself composed several beautiful, if Brahmsian, songs, some to German texts and several settings of English poems by his friend Eva Gore-Booth. He was elected a member of the College Council in 1925 when Ludwig Aron, a member since 1907, died.

Marguerite Swale was appointed to the vacant position on the singing staff in February, 1925, but almost immediately another vacancy was caused by the death of Marie Brema. She was 69 and had been taken ill on one of her regular visits to the College to direct the Opera Class. In the autumn of 1926 Sir Henry Miers retired from the Vice-Chancellorship of the University and consequently from the chairmanship of the College Council, being succeeded in both offices by Dr (later Sir) Walter H. Moberly. The new chairman took over at a period of comparative stability in College affairs. Apart from the slight disruptions caused by the General Strike in May, 1926, the mid-twenties were a comparatively uneventful period in College history. Yet, looking round him, he must have realised that many changes would shortly be inevitable. Many of those who had run College affairs for most of the century were old. Gustav Behrens was 80 in 1926, Dame Sarah Lees was two years older. William Eller and George Murray were, with Behrens, the only surviving members of the first Council. Stanley Withers, the Registrar since 1893, was in increasingly poor health and Brodsky himself was now nearing 75. Brodsky was still, however, an active and autocratic Principal and teacher (he could still perform Paganini caprices admirably). He was much exercised during 1927 by the falling-off in the singing department. The deaths so close together of Sarah Andrew and Marie Brema had been severe blows and the appointment of Miss Swale under an arrangement whereby she did not live in Manchester had not proved successful. She was offered reappointment on terms which required her to move from London, but she preferred to resign. The teaching staff now comprised Richard Evans, Paul Vallon, Dora Gilson and Elsie Thurston, and efforts were made to persuade Norman Allin to join it but his professional commitments, especially those with the British National Opera Company, prevented his acceptance. However, Forbes took over direction of the Opera Class. He had experience of conducting opera with the excellent small professional touring companies which were then a welcome, and generally underrated, feature of the musical scene in Britain, and he rapidly transformed the College singing to the extent that in June, 1928, four splendid performances of Mozart's *The Marriage of Figaro* were given in the Lesser Free Trade Hall which received acclamation from Press and public. Humphrey Procter-Gregg, at this time on the opera staff of the Royal College of Music, produced it and the costumes were specially made by Mrs Lawrence Haward, wife of the director of the City Art Gallery, who was thereupon made an Honorary Member of the College and elected to the Council.

New blood had been injected into the Council at the annual meeting in December, 1925, when two of the new members were W. R. Douglas, the distinguished surgeon, and Philip Godlee. The latter, then aged 35, was a textile manufacturer, a keen and talented amateur musician and a man of forceful personality and considerable personal charm with the streak of ruthlessness which often accompanies the ability to lead and take decisions. In January, 1928, he was appointed deputy treasurer, since it was clear that Gustav Behrens might soon wish to resign from the post he had held for 23 years. At the same time John Holme was appointed deputy registrar as well as secretary because Withers became seriously ill during the late summer of 1927. A few months later he died. A well-read man with a distinct literary talent, Withers had administered the College since the day it opened its doors with unfailing zeal and pomp. Holme was appointed to succeed him, but not until October, 1928, when Forbes was appointed Assistant Principal on the proposal of Gustav Behrens, seconded by Brodsky. It was a prudent move, for at the Council meeting of 9 January, 1929, the chairman reported the serious illness of the Principal. Brodsky had abdominal cancer and on 22 January he died—'a performer of such eminence, a teacher of such enthusiasm and an artist of such lofty and noble ideals'. . . .[1]

With the death of Brodsky an era in Manchester musical history ended. Stanley Withers, writing in the *Christian Science Monitor* on the occasion of Brodsky's retirement from solo playing (at a Hallé Pension Fund concert on 13 January, 1921) said: 'No one has such a repugnance for mere showiness and everything savouring of the meretricious; he is one of the few remaining artists in whom dwell the rich traditions of a riper age, when depth was not sacrificed to brilliance or interpretation to display.' It was something for College students to know that their Principal had walked and talked and worked with Tchaikovsky, von Bülow and Brahms. While he was in Manchester the performances of Brahms's chamber works by College staff—Catterall, Forbes, Merrick, Fuchs and Brodsky himself —had, from all accounts, an authenticity which must have stemmed directly from association with the composer himself. Withers thought Brodsky was at his best in chamber music, an opinion shared by many other critics. Langford was full of praise for him and his quartet; Bonavia, in *The Daily Telegraph* of 11 March, 1933, wrote of Brodsky in the late Beethoven quartets as giving 'the full measure of their depths'. Brodsky's colleague Carl Fuchs, in his book of memoirs,[2] recalled the 'soul-searching way in which Brodsky played the Cavatina of Beethoven's great B flat quartet'. Neville Cardus, too, considered him 'the best player I have known in a late Beethoven quartet; his violin seemed to receive the music, not to play it. He did not make a god of technique; nowadays he might be called uneven and thin of tone.'[3] Another of his

[1] R.M.C.M. 36th annual report.
[2] *Musical and other recollections of Carl Fuchs, Cellist*, Sherratt & Hughes, Manchester, 1937.
[3] *Second Innings*, by Neville Cardus, Collins, London, 1950.

College colleagues, Frank Merrick, told me that he had in his personality something of 'what might be called peasant-mentality, with no appreciation of the courtliness of Mozart; it was a great surprise to me that anyone could be splendid in Haydn and totally unsuited to Mozart'. Brodsky's sympathies were for the classical composers, but he once played the Debussy sonata with Merrick: 'He said he regarded the task as that of an actor playing a rôle, and he gave as fine an account of the violin part as you could ever hope to hear.'

Yet there was one contemporary work which he loved above all, Elgar's concerto. 'I never get tired of it', he wrote to the composer. 'I play it to myself almost dayly [sic] as other people do their prayers. It is a wonderful inspiration which grows upon you as time goes on. My only wish now is, if I dare to express an opinion, that you could revise the instrumentation of the orchestra in a few places where it seems to me to be heavy.' Another of his letters to Elgar (18 April, 1919) throws revealing light on Brodsky's own attitude to solo work and his entire lack of professional jealousy or ambition to be 'first' in the field with new works.

I am not a record hunter! and hearing your works performed by others saves me a great deal of brainwork. When I heard Kreisler play your magnificent concerto I first of all used the experience I got from his excellent performance for teaching purposes. I taught it to Anton Maaskoff, Naum Blinder, Alfred Barker and Helena Kontorovitch and having acquainted myself with the depth and the innermost structure of that wonderful work I then only began to study it myself and I think I got a thorough grasp and understanding of its innermost meaning.

In January, 1927, the year of Elgar's 70th birthday, Brodsky came out of retirement to pay tribute to his friend by playing the concerto with Elgar conducting, at a Hallé concert. 'Dr Brodsky sought his strength in the expressive features of the work', Langford wrote next day in the *Manchester Guardian*, 'and played them with so much depth of feeling that the question whether he played all the bravura passage work with the strength of a player in his prime never seemed to matter.'

Elgar, in 1918, fulfilled a long-standing promise to write a work for the Brodsky Quartet when he dedicated his E minor string quartet to them. Brodsky was overjoyed and went to London to hear the first performance by the British String

Quartet in May, 1919. Writing to Elgar ten days later he apologised for seeming

a little reserved in my judgment about the 2nd and 3rd movements. I am happy to be able to tell you now that my opinion has been thoroughly changed after the magnificent performance . . . by the Catterall Quartet. I don't know now which of the movements I like best although my inclination is still towards the first movement, which is a wonderful work of art. I am now quite cut off from my quartet colleagues; especially Speelman is tied fast to the North Pier at Blackpool. For me it will be only possible to play *the* Quartet first opportunity next season. But does it matter? In a sense —yes. But after all it matters most that your Quartet should be played and admired no matter who plays it provided the players do justice to the beautiful work. I am therefore thankful to the younger Quartets to do now the pioneer work. In due time I hope to join them and (once having thoroughly grasped it) to play it all over the North of England and in Ireland. . . . With love, your grateful and affectionate Adolph Brodsky.

In 1921 Brodsky's wife Anna had a severe illness which paralysed her left limbs and made her helpless for four years. During this time she wrote some charming and naïve reminiscences from which it is possible to gain a touching picture of Brodsky in his last years:

This terrible calamity has been a great blessing; for it has revealed to me the depth of my husband's love and devotion. No sacrifice was too great for him, no service too tiresome or trivial. When I could not sleep he would sit up with me far into the small hours of the morning and read himself hoarse. When I grew a little better and was longing for music he would play for me piece after piece. . . . The final joy and surprise came when my sister, who had been lost to our sight in Russia, opened the door of my room one morning and appeared as if she had fallen from heaven. . . . My husband by incredible exertions had managed to get her out of Russia. She arrived in Bowdon on 11 November 1924. Our circle was soon joined by another of our dearest friends—our beloved Toni Maaskoff. . . . We never had children of our own. Toni became our dear son. . . . Toni's violin was also brought, then my husband opened a parcel he had brought from the College containing the music of Bach's concerto for two violins and now—to our unspeakable delight—they both played this concerto so familiar and so dear to us all. . . . Then my husband gave us another treat—he played Elgar's concerto. . . . He was in a very happy mood and put all his heart into this beautiful work. . . . Toni was completely carried away. . . . The whole atmosphere of the room seemed to be full of love and happiness.

'A rare spirit made wise through long devotion to life and to art.' So Neville Cardus wrote of him on the morrow of his death.[1]

Manchester will remember always the way Dr Brodsky would lead his quartet, how he would lie back and give himself up to a noble phrase; how, in a slow movement, you could see his very soul turning upon itself, retiring to the music's peaceful sanctuary. Then, with the advent of a quick movement, how he would relax genially as though saying to us 'That was a very solemn music, now let's have a happy bit.'... At the College his good ghost is bound to linger, touching young students in countless mysterious but heartening ways.

This, then, was Adolph Brodsky. One day he was talking to some friends about Tolstoy, whom he knew and venerated, and something he said alarmed Anna. 'But Adolph', she said, 'do you not believe in God?' He replied: 'Anna, have you not heard me play?'

[1] *Manchester Guardian*, 23 January, 1929.

6

9
The music, 1914–29

Brodsky's death provides the breathing-space for a further look in detail at the College's musical programmes since the outbreak of the First World War when, it will be remembered, the Principal himself was interned in Austria. The open practices were held as usual in November, 1914, with one of Merrick's pupils, Sydney Seal, playing Debussy preludes. He was eventually to serve in Palestine when conscripted, and helped in the foundation of a college of music there. The staff, filling the gap caused by the absence of the Brodsky Quartet, gave several concerts, at one of which, on the day of the annual meeting, Marie Brema sang Saint-Saëns's *La fiancée du Timbalier* and songs by Stanford and Franck, Catterall played violin solos by Gluck and Arensky, and Ellen Arthan and Lucy Pierce played Saint-Saëns's *Variations on a Theme by Beethoven*. This was the recital to which Beecham listened on the day of his onslaught on College standards. On 29 January, 1915, Forbes and Catterall played violin sonatas by Busoni (op. 36a), Pierné and Brahms (op. 108), and on 27 February the Rawdon Briggs Quartet played Ravel's quartet, and Cherubini's in D minor. Edith Robinson's Quartet on 13 March played Franck's string quartet, were joined by Merrick for Mozart's piano quartet in E flat and by Harry Mortimer for Brahms's clarinet quintet.

Brodsky's concert to mark his return from internment was on the evening of 18 May, 1915. He was accompanied by Forbes and the College Orchestra and began by playing Elgar's concerto. After the interval he played Grieg's G major sonata, Chausson's *Poème*, Bach's A minor concerto, and a 'Little Suite' for violin and piano by Mensenkamff, a Russian aristocrat interned in the same camp at Raabs with Brodsky, who asked him to write this suite and promised to play it when he returned to England. The programmes of the open practices have many fewer trivial items, such as ballads, by this date. Gertrude Barker and Frank Tipping were still the most prominent violin pupils and John Wills the best piano student. Tipping played the concertos by Goldmark and Brahms during the examination concerts of July, 1915, and John Wills played the *Appassionata* sonata and Brahms's D minor concerto. Delius's piano concerto was played by Forbes's pupil, Arnold Perry, and an enthusiasm at this date for the music of Nováček is reflected by a performance of his string quartet no. 3 in C major, at which only the cellist remained constant in the four movements, the other three players exchanging places. Reger's music, too, had several exponents among the students. On 14 and 15 July Brema's opera class sang the Magic Garden and Good Friday scenes from *Parsifal*, and an extract from *Samson and Delilah*, while 'gestures to music' were superimposed on songs by Schumann, Schubert, Grieg and others. The resumed Brodsky Quartet concerts for 1915–16 included the string quartets by Verdi, Nováček (in C major), Schubert (*Death and the Maiden*), Beethoven (op. 130) and Haydn (D major). Brodsky and various pianists (Mayer, Merrick and Wills) played sonatas by Brahms (D minor, no. 3) and Fauré (in A).

Kathleen Moorhouse's name occurs in the examination concerts of 1916. One of Sarah Andrew's pupils sang three songs by Reynaldo Hahn and two others a duet from Délibes's *Lakmé*. There are several similar indications that Miss Andrew tried to steer her pupils away from exclusively Germanic songs, and two movements of Debussy's string quartet were performed by four of Edith Robinson's quartet class on 20 July. Debussy's cello sonata was played by Forbes and Walter Hatton at a Brodsky Quartet concert on 16 December, one of its earliest British performances for it was written only in 1915, and repeated on 17 March, 1917, because the earlier concert had been 'interfered with by the fog'. Scenes from Gluck's *Orpheus*, Wagner's *Lohengrin* and Mascagni's *Cavalleria Rusticana* were sung by the Opera Class on four evenings of March, 1917. Elsie Thurston, a pupil of Sarah Andrew, sang Wolf's *Ganymede* and the aria 'Justice, Justice' from Massenet's *Le Cid* on 27 March and 24 May respectively. Albert Hardie appeared as an organ student of Dr Keighley at this date. The College had a distinguished ensemble class during 1917, with several performances of string quartets and trios shared between Phyllis Greenhalgh, Gertrude Barker, Christian Orford and Kathleen Moorhouse. Miss Moorhouse was often invited by Brodsky to be the second cellist when he enlarged his quartet for performances of Schubert's quintet and Brahms's sextet.

Among the first outstanding pupils to emerge after the war was Philip Newman, a Brodsky protégé who later settled abroad and in 1950 appeared at a Hallé concert with Barbirolli when he gave an extraordinary performance of Beethoven's concerto—extraordinary not only because of its idiosyncrasies but also because of the flashes of remarkable playing which fitfully illuminated the interpretation. At an open practice on 18 November, 1919, he played a movement from the seventh concerto by de Bériot. Another Brodsky pupil in 1919 was Ellie Spivak, and Don Hyden was studying with Catterall. The 1920 season of Brodsky Quartet concerts included Elgar's sonata (Brodsky and Forbes, 15 January, 1920) and his E minor string quartet a fortnight later.[1] Langford wrote later of the 'broken and swift energy' of Elgar's quartet as played by the Brodsky Quartet and of its coldness, adding curiously 'the music is rich in English hardness'. On 18 March the piano quintet was played, with Lucy Pierce. The last two movements of Elgar's cello concerto were played by Vyvyan Lewis, a pupil of Walter Hatton, at an examination concert on 6 July, nine months after the work's first performance. It cannot be said that the College was slow to perform these Indian-summer works of England's greatest living composer, nor several by Delius. Patrick Ryan, later to be better known simply as Pat Ryan, was the clarinettist in Mozart's quintet on 7 July, 1920, and Leonard Hirsch played part of a Spohr concerto on 9 November, at an open practice that included Albert Voorsanger playing the slow movement of Elgar's violin concerto and Stephen Wearing playing Schumann's Toccata. Some of George Butterworth's *Shropshire Lad* songs were sung on 23 November by J. Dale Smith, a pupil of Brema. Max Mayer's French pupil Yvonne Tiano (Tiénot) was also a distinguished student during the immediate post-war years and others were Louis Cohen (Brodsky), W. J. Rees (Catterall), Norman Andrew and George Armstrong (Keighley) and Maurice Johnstone (Carroll). Noel Walton, son of Charles and brother of William, and a piano pupil of Forbes, played Liszt arrangements of Schubert songs on 22 June, 1922; Haydn Rogerson, pupil of Fuchs, played a Sammartini sonata on 31 October; and Albert Hardie,

[1] The constitution of the Quartet for this performance was still Brodsky, Rawdon Briggs, Speelman and Hatton (vice Fuchs); by the time Brodsky played it again, on 22 November, 1920, the 'new' Quartet was Brodsky, John Bridge, Frank Park and Hatton.

now a piano pupil of Jeanne Bretey, is a constantly recurring recitalist throughout 1923 and 1924. The College Orchestra was good enough by 1925 to play the *Enigma Variations* under Forbes and to accompany Haydn Rogerson in the first movement of Dvořák's cello concerto. The name of Gordon Green first appears at an examination concert on 8 July, 1925, when he played the first movement of Brahms's F minor sonata. On 24 November of that year Clifton Helliwell and Michael Collins (cello) played two movements of Brahms's E minor sonata and on 8 December the last student to play was Alan Rawsthorne, in Mozart's E flat concerto. On 9 March, 1926, he and Green played Bach's double piano concerto in C minor. Two songs by Thomas Pitfield, a composition student of Dr Keighley, were sung at the open practice on 23 March, and on 22 June Clifford Knowles played a movement of Wieniawski's D minor violin concerto. Muriel Liddle, a piano pupil of Claud Biggs, played Harty's piano concerto at several College practices. On 2 November another Merrick pupil, Denis (Michael) Brierley, played a movement from a Mozart piano concerto. On 15 March, 1927, three songs by Rawsthorne— 'The Sunken Garden' (De La Mare), 'Shall I compare thee to a summer's day' (Shakespeare) and 'Lay on plustost rondeau' (Villon)—were sung by Marjorie Lyon, pupil of Richard Evans. It is possible that these were the first Rawsthorne compositions to be performed in public. Later that year, on 5 July, Rawsthorne and Maurice Ward played the first movement of his sonata in E minor, at an examination concert at which Norah Winstanley played the slow movement of Elgar's concerto and Hilda Singleton played Delius's piano concerto. Opera had lapsed in these years, but scenes from *Madam Butterfly*, *Mastersingers* and *Faust* on 2 June, 1927, were sung by Margaret Collier, Dorothy Pearce, Sara Buckley, Clifford White and others. On 29 November Rawsthorne, Evelyn Thornton and Leonard Baker played the first two movements of Brahms's trio in E flat, op. 40, for piano, violin and cello. Rachel Monkhouse, a pupil of Miss Thurston, sang two songs from Wolf's *Italian Song Book* on 13 December. Charles Meert appears among the cello pupils of Walter Hatton in 1928 and Brodsky's pupil Philip Hecht played the Brahms concerto (first movement) on 12 June, 1928. Rawsthorne and Norah Winstanley played Debussy's sonata on 30 October, and Brierley the first movement of Glazunov's piano concerto at the same concert. (From 22 May 1928 the open practices were re-named simply 'Students' concerts'.) On 5 July and for the following three evenings the College staged *The Marriage of Figaro* in the Lesser Free Trade Hall, its first wholly theatrical presentation. Forbes conducted, Procter-Gregg produced, and the two assistant stage managers were Michael Brierley and Alan Rawsthorne. John Greenwood was Figaro, Clifford White the Count, and Susanna and the Countess were shared, the former by Margaret Collier and Dorothy Pearce, the latter by Evelyn Duke and Gladys Morton.

At the students' concerts in November five pieces for piano and strings by Eugene Goossens were performed by Muriel Liddle, Doris Smith and Leonard Baker, and Christian Orford played the first two movements of Busoni's violin concerto. Busoni was still a god to the Manchester musical hierarchy. He had been dead for four years and Langford had written of how he was attracted to Manchester by 'powerful personalities' such as Richter, Brodsky and Dayas. He wrote:

> Some notion of what terrific things the analytical notes on music might become if composers condescended to tell us all their mind was once shown in the notes by Dayas to a sonata for violin and piano by Busoni, played at a Brodsky concert by Dr Brodsky and the composer. No wonder, if such thoughts were in Busoni's mind, that the power of climax in this outwardly calm music was tremendous.

A curiosity rarely heard today was Backhaus's arrangement of the Serenade from *Don Giovanni*, played by Clifton Helliwell on 27 November. Two other students on this date played a movement of a violin sonata by Wolf-Ferrari. Delius's sonata, played by Muriel Liddle and Norah Winstanley, and Scriabin's Prelude and Nocturne for Left Hand (Phyllis Eley) were novelties on 11 December. By the time students gave another recital Brodsky had died and Forbes presided in his stead.

10
Forbes as Principal

The Council, at its emergency meeting on 31 January, 1929, appointed Robert Forbes to be Acting Principal and set up a sub-committee of E. W. Grommé, Gustav Behrens, Philip Godlee, Max Mayer and Professor Arthur Lapworth to inquire into the appointment of the next Principal. As was to be expected, they recommended that Forbes should be confirmed in the post and this was done at the Council meeting of 30 April. His salary was fixed at £500 a year, with extra payments for his work in the Orchestra, Opera Class, Ensemble Class, Accompaniment Class and piano teaching 'it being understood that, as soon as practicable, Mr Forbes reduces the time devoted to these classes to approximately 16 hours per week'. He faced the tricky problem of following a legendary figure who had been both feared and loved.

It would be idle to pretend that Forbes, who was 50, inspired devotion comparable with that which had been accorded to Brodsky. Loveableness was not his most apparent characteristic, for he was a man who successfully concealed his feelings, and his enemies regarded him as a past master of intrigue. He was highly principled, a shrewd administrator, wise investor and a first-class musician. Nor did he suffer fools gladly. Whereas Hallé and Brodsky had been musicians of international fame and stature who came to the College with laurels already won, Forbes had spent most of his life at the College and in Manchester. He was, so to speak, the first home-grown Principal and not everybody liked the idea. It was certainly no coincidence that as soon as his appointment was inevitable, Frank Merrick resigned and took a post in London. Other staff changes were among the first problems Forbes had to face: Edith Robinson resigned from her violin professorship because of ill-health. This left only Catterall on the violin staff: he was appointed senior professor and Laurance Turner, John Bridge and James Matthews joined him. In place of Merrick, Forbes appointed Frederick Dawson, Hallé's pupil, who had been on the original staff from 1893–6. Within a year Claud Biggs accepted the post of senior professor at the Royal Irish

Academy in Dublin: his pupils were taken over by Dawson, who undertook to stay at the College for at least another two years. Perhaps the biggest blow was the resignation at the end of the Michaelmas term, 1929, of Arthur Catterall, who had been appointed leader of the newly formed B.B.C. Symphony Orchestra. Thus, within 12 months, all the members of Brodsky's violin staff, who had produced such splendid results, had left the College. Two alternatives were put forward as Catterall's successor: Naum Blinder, a Brodsky pupil who was in New York after holding professorships in Moscow and Odessa, and Henry Holst, at that time leader of the Berlin Philharmonic Orchestra. It was decided to appoint Blinder, with a guarantee of a first-year income of not less than £600. Unfortunately the Ministry of Labour held up the grant of a work permit and Blinder had to decline the invitation. Thereupon the post was offered to and accepted by Holst, who could not take up his duties until April, 1931. In the interim period another of the original staff, Willy Hess, returned from the Berlin Hochschule to take charge of the advanced violin students and the quartet class. Catterall was appointed professor emeritus.

Forbes started auspiciously and with considerable energy. He reorganised some classes, chiefly on the theoretical side, and visited both the London Royal colleges for talks with his fellow Principals. He conducted Verdi's *Falstaff* with such success, despite poor public attendance, that in February, 1930, the same cast performed it at the Royal College of Music, thanks largely to a grant of £100 from the Palmer Fund for opera. This was a notable feather in the College's cap. He also conducted a Brodsky memorial concert in the Free Trade Hall, with Catterall and Norman Allin as soloists, the funds of which went towards endowment of a memorial scholarship. Another scholarship, for the pianoforte, with endowment of £1,000, was a result of a bequest in the Will of Miss Johanna Julius, a member of the staff from 1894–1913, who died in Holland. It should also be recorded that the Council, in April, 1929, voted a personal gift of £300 a year to Mrs Brodsky. However she died during the summer.

One serious problem with which Forbes had to contend was the steady decline in the numbers of students attending the College. This had begun in earnest in 1927 when there was a drop to 320 from 335 in 1926. In 1928 the attendance was 298, in 1929 261, and in 1930 it fell to 216. By 1931 another 40 had left and not been replaced, taking the figure to 176, of whom 64 were men and 112 women. The annual report made no mention of any reasons until 1930 when, with numbers down to 146, it blamed partly the acute industrial depression—for this was the period of appalling unemployment in Lancashire and elsewhere—and 'very largely the mechanisation of music which has, for the time being, materially altered the prospects of so many professional musicians, especially orchestral players'. Whether broadcasting and the gramophone really had this effect is very much open to question, but it was certainly Forbes's view and also that of Sir Hamilton Harty, who had been elected to the Council in 1930. Harty was a major opponent of the B.B.C. at this time—'the amiable bandits of Savoy Hill' was one of his descriptions of the Corporation—and Forbes considered that the B.B.C. had deliberately starved the North in order to establish its new symphony orchestra in London 'for the delectation of a comparatively small number of people' (eventually, millions of listeners). Nevertheless if numbers had declined, the report was justified in claiming high quality among its students. It is always invidious to select names by reason of later achievements—for many brilliant students devoted themselves to teaching—but among those still on the College register in 1930 were some remarkable individual talents. Norah Winstanley, Clifford Knowles, Philip Hecht, Jessie Hinchcliffe, Harry Blech and Sydney Partington all became leading orchestral violinists in the Hallé and other orchestras; Alan Rawsthorne, Michael Brierley, Gordon Green and Clifton Helliwell were among the pianoforte students; Leonard Baker and Charles Meert, cellists; Norman Walker, the bass; Leonard Regan, clarinet; Sydney Coulston and Frank Taylor, horn; and Geoffrey Gilbert, flute. Outstanding students in the earlier part of the 1920s had been the pianists Stephen Wearing and Albert Hardie and the violinist Leonard Hirsch.

The greater stress on opera, to which Forbes attached considerable importance, meant an annual production, and, alas, an annual financial loss because of public apathy. In 1931, there were four performances of Puccini's *Suor Angelica* and of Acts II and III of Gluck's *Orfeo* resulting in a deficit of nearly £61. This was wiped out by a gift of £100 from Mr Joseph Shore. Later the same year the production of *The Magic Flute* lost £55 and that of *The Marriage of Figaro* in 1933 only £12 because of better attendances.

One of Forbes's first changes was to institute an enrolment fee of 10s. per term for the elocution, French, German and Italian classes and for the new class (under Madge Atkinson) for gesture and natural movement. These important subsidiary classes were always given special care and were in good hands: Italian, still Signor Valgimigli; elocution, James Bernard; German, Mrs Addis; French, Dorothy Simpson. The class in appreciation of English literature had been Withers's personal enthusiasm and had ended in 1923. Dr Keighley's art and practice of teaching classes were broadened to include lectures by specialist teachers, for instance by Edith Robinson on strings, Frederick Dawson on the piano, and on singing and class teaching by Harold Dawber, organist and chorus-master of the Hallé, who had joined the staff to take charge of the aural training and musical appreciation classes. The advent of Harty to the Council was followed by his gift of a three years' scholarship for the French horn and by his offer to give practical experience to the advanced wind students by allowing them to take part in Hallé rehearsals and sometimes in concerts. This ended in 1933 when Harty left Manchester. The teachers' training course was reorganised to meet new conditions laid down by the Burnham Committee and to enable students to qualify for salaries on the graduate scale. Another scholarship followed the death in 1931 of Max Mayer. A memorial fund raised only £200, undoubtedly because its launching coincided with the worst of the 'dole' era, and the organisers hoped that this would form the nucleus of a travelling scholarship. Forbes pointed out that the amount was inadequate for the purpose and there the matter rested until October, 1934, when Oscar Beer gave £1,000 to the College 'in memory of the late Mr and Mrs Max Mayer', for the endowment of a Mayer scholarship and also offered reversionary interest in a further sum of between £3,000 and £4,000 provided it was used for a travelling scholarship tenable for one year by a student who had completed at least three years at the R.M.C.M. These conditions were accepted with gratitude. In 1932 because the number of students under Henry Holst was below that required to make up his guarantee the College decided to offer two entrance scholarships for competition, tenable for a year and only to be awarded to candidates of exceptional promise. The first examination was held on 16 April and the scholarships were awarded to Henry Hinchcliffe and

Olive Zorian. Miss Zorian was later awarded a Lancashire County Council scholarship and therefore became ineligible for the violin award. Incidentally 1932 was remarkable for there being no staff changes. Rutland Boughton, the composer, who had given several lectures at the College and whose *Moon Maiden* had been performed by Miss Atkinson's 'gesture' class, applied to become a singing teacher, but a sub-committee, perhaps having heard something of his unorthodox mode of life, decided that they could not recommend the appointment 'under present conditions'. The stringent financial situation was responsible for an increase in the fee for new organ and wind students from £30 to £36 a year in 1932, and when, in the following year, the diploma regulations were revised the fee for both diplomas if taken concurrently was raised from four to five guineas. Ways of swelling the Sustentation Fund for assisting needy students had constantly to be devised. (A major source of income to this fund had been the proceeds of the Brodsky Quartet concerts, but this ceased after the 1920–1 season when economic difficulties in promoting chamber concerts put an end to generosity which had contributed £2,048 18s. 7d. in 23 years.) During the winter of 1932 members of the staff gave a series of 'Five o'clock Chamber Concerts' in the Lees Hall. The proceeds paid the fee of one student, a contribution, as the annual report said, 'disproportionate to the efforts of the performers, all of whom gave their services. . . . The public apathy towards chamber music is one of the most distressing features of the present-day musical life of the city.'

In May, 1933, Jeanne Bretey resigned from the pianoforte teaching staff because of poor health. She had served continuously for 40 years and, with Fuchs, was the last survivor of Hallé's original appointments. She was elected professor emeritus and succeeded by Annie Lord, a former student. Dr A. W. Wilcock, of the harmony and composition staff, left on his appointment as organist of Exeter Cathedral and was succeeded by a pupil of Hindemith, the English composer Arnold Cooke. This was the most progressive appointment for some time and a belated acknowledgment of the new forces abroad in composition. Another vacancy was caused by Archie Camden's departure to join Catterall in the B.B.C. Symphony Orchestra, and his place as Professor of the Bassoon was filled by his Hallé successor and former fellow-student Maurice Whittaker.

Three other changes in 1933 and 1934 are of great sentimental significance. On 22 November, 1932, Leonard F. Behrens was invited to join the Council in place of Charles Lord, who had died. He first attended a Council meeting on 24 January, 1933, and thus began a long and distinguished association with the College which culminated in the conferment of Honorary Membership in 1969.

His father, Gustav, was now in his 88th year and on 23rd January, 1934, he failed to attend a Council meeting—an exceptionally rare occurrence—but instead sent a letter asking to be relieved of the honorary treasurership. This was received with great regret and the Council recorded 'its profound gratitude to Mr Behrens not only for the time and thought he has so generously given to the financial interests of the College during the 28 years he has occupied that position, but also for his unfailing devotion to the welfare of the College, in the foundation of which he played such an important part'. He was succeeded by Philip Godlee and died in 1936 aged 90. On 13 November, 1934, Dame Sarah Lees, who had last attended the Council on 18 July, 1933, asked to resign because she was no longer able to go to meetings. She was 92. She died in the spring of 1935, the most generous benefactor the College had known and a woman who took the most active interest in every aspect of College life, particularly the welfare of the students. Apart from her endowment of funds she was responsible for innumerable generous acts which were never made public. In Dame Sarah, Gustav Behrens and Lady Donner, who died in 1935 after 29 years on the Council, the College had been blessed by three great human beings.

A further resignation, early in 1935, was that of Sir Walter Moberly from the Vice-Chancellorship. His successor, Professor J. S. B. (John Sebastian Bach) Stopford, took office as chairman of the Council on 19 March, 1935. Persistent efforts were again made in 1935 to persuade Norman Allin to teach singing at the College, but his professional commitments were still too many to allow him to accept. Elsie Dove was appointed a piano teacher in 1935 to succeed John Wills, who joined the B.B.C., and Mrs Samuel Langford, widow of the *Manchester Guardian's* great critic, was appointed teacher of German to succeed Mrs Addis. Another long-serving member of the staff,

Dr Keighley, died in the winter of 1935. This caused several staff changes: Harold Dawber became organ professor, Dr Henry Read took over the Art of Teaching and Dr Herman Brearley became teacher of singing, sight-singing and musical dictation. Another change occurred during 1937 when ill-health compelled John Holme to resign as Registrar. Harold Dawber succeeded him, with an honorarium of £100 a year. Forbes's efforts to broaden the structure of certain established features of College life are evident in the Review Week of 1935 when he invited various eminent people to give lectures. The students heard talks from the soprano Agnes Nicholls (Lady Harty), Professor F. S. Shera of Sheffield University, Neville Cardus, and Edith Robinson, the violin teacher.

The years up to the outbreak of the Second World War were comparatively uneventful, unless one singles out a burglary which at least had the result that the Council, as a precaution against a repetition, sent the Chopin death mask to the Henry Watson Music Library on permanent loan. Although the College had still failed to obtain a Treasury grant, Manchester Education Committee increased its grant from £225 to £400 in 1936. This followed increases by Lancashire and Cheshire County Councils which made their grants £800 a year, a total increase of £330. These extra grants—so necessary in view of the diminution of public subscriptions to the College and a ten-year period of deficits which ran at around £300—followed representations to the Board of Education in 1935 in which the College's president, the Duke of York, soon to become King George VI, had interested himself. On his accession to the throne, the King became the College's Patron instead of its President and, after the Duke of Kent had declined the presidency, it was accepted by a Lancastrian, Lord Hewart of Bury, who was at that date the Lord Chief Justice. At the beginning of 1937, after many meetings, a schedule of fees was agreed for students taking a combined course at the College and the University. Forbes greatly strengthened the relationship between the College and the University at this time, principally through his friendship with Procter-Gregg, who had become Head of the University Music Department in 1936. The attendance in 1937 was 113 (a drop of 207 compared with 10 years earlier), but the number of new students at the Michaelmas Term that year was, at 24, the highest for some years.

The Wadsworth four-manual organ which had been installed in the College 40 years earlier was now in an unsatisfactory state. Dame Sarah Lees's daughter Marjory continued a family tradition by giving £100 towards the cost of a replacement. An organ fund was launched and it was decided to install a Compton electronic organ. This gave considerable trouble in its first year and the College withheld final payment until the instrument had been brought up to Dawber's requirements. The old organ was sold privately to a church for £200.

From September, 1938, the fees for new students were raised to fourteen guineas a term. Students wishing to stay for their principal study only, after completion of the three-year course, had to pay nine guineas a term instead of £8, this to include attendance at the Opera Class, for singers, and at an ensemble or quartet class for instrumentalists. The Council then went into the question of scholarships and decided that the annual value of the Hallé, C. J. Heywood, Pearce, Julius, Max Mayer, Sarah Andrew and Brodsky scholarships should be increased to 42 guineas, and that the annual value of the exhibitions for wind and brass should be 21 guineas.

Norman Allin had in 1938 told Forbes that he was now able to consider a teaching post and he was appointed Professor of Singing from the Michaelmas Term, 1938. This great bass, superb in Wagner and Mozart and incomparable in the Elgar oratorios, was a notable asset to the College. Nevertheless his class was not at first big enough to meet his guarantee and Forbes was allowed to admit some male students who would otherwise be unable to take the College course, on payment of half the fee. At the same time Arnold Cooke resigned in order to live in London and his place on the harmony and composition staff was taken by Richard Hall, who was much in sympathy with avant-garde trends. Frank Park resigned as viola teacher in January, 1939, his place being taken by Christian Orford. Later that year Walter Hatton, cello professor for 20 years, died, and he was succeeded by Haydn Rogerson and Leonard Baker. Signor Valgimigli resigned as Italian teacher in 1939 after 46 years' service and was succeeded by his daughter Maria Valgimigli. Dr Kendrick Pyne, professor emeritus since his retirement, died in the autumn of 1938.

One of the last pieces of peacetime business was the sale of the College's 'overspill', 330 Oxford Road, for £450 to the Manchester Royal Eye Hospital and the purchase of Nos. 2

and 4 Ducie Grove for £400, with £150 to be spent on alterations to the new property. The College premises were now all
under one roof, with better accommodation for the canteen,
common rooms and staff. On 16 June, 1939, the College took
part in a reciprocal broadcast with Leipzig Conservatoire.
Forbes exchanged greetings with his opposite number and
each institution contributed half an hour's music. Alas for this
ironically timed example of Anglo-German co-operation. At the
Council meeting on 11 July, 1939, a sub-committee was formed
'to deal with any matters of urgency arising during the summer
vacation'. When the Council next met, on 19 September,
Britain was again at war with Germany and the sub-committee
had ordered the provision of air raid shelters.

11
War and its aftermath

In the uncertainty created by the outbreak of war it was at one moment doubtful if the College would open for the autumn term of 1939. But such a drastic measure proved unnecessary and the wartime motto of 'business as usual' pervaded the College business for the remainder of 1939 and the start of 1940, except for occasional references to wartime regulations and an apology for absence from a Council meeting from the deputy treasurer, Harold Dehn, 'with the B.E.F. in France'. Ninety students were at the College, which was considered satisfactory 'under existing conditions', and at the annual meeting they were regaled by a lecture on 'the enjoyment of music in wartime' by Cardus, before he left for Australia. The deaths of E. W. Grommé, a Council member for 33 years, Harry Mortimer, the great clarinct player and teacher, Edward Stansfield, double bass teacher, Edith Robinson, former violin professor, and Dr Herman Brearley, teacher of singing and harmony all occurred in the 'phoney war' period and during the time of Dunkirk.

During the severe air raids on Manchester in December, 1940, considerable damage was caused to the College buildings and contents, and to No. 2 Ducie Grove, but the new term started on the January date already fixed. The contents were thereafter insured for £4,000 under the War Damage Act, 1941. The worst hardship from the raids was caused by the putting out of action of the heating apparatus—and it was a particularly cold winter. This was not fully repaired for nearly eight months, during which time the University lent electric stoves. During 1942 the College received £300 compensation from the War Damage Commission and £200 for the contents damage.

The College was continuously the object of benefactions from its well-wishers. Ruth Hewitt, a former student who had been killed by enemy action on the South Coast, left £1,000 for a pianoforte scholarship; another pianoforte scholarship was founded with an endowment of £3,000 bequeathed by Jeanne Bretey, who had died in 1941, eight years after her retirement. During this period Godlee, who had steered the College funds to a small surplus in 1940 and 1941 by rigid economies, re-invested the College's holdings of railway stock in 3 per cent Savings Bonds. The last remaining link with Hallé's first teaching staff was broken in May 1942 when Carl Fuchs resigned his professorship of the cello. He was appointed professor emeritus in 1945. Not only was Fuchs a brilliant teacher and performer, he was witty and good-humoured. His was the famous remark to a stubbornly recalcitrant pupil: 'My dear madam, you do not apparently realise that on the cello even an inch makes a difference'. When Lucy Pierce asked him to take part in Prokofiev's *Overture on Hebrew Themes*, op. 34, for pianoforte, clarinet and string quartet, he agreed, adding, 'I have no racial prejudices'.

At midsummer, 1942, the register of students was 109, of whom only 27 were male. Many of the women students left to join the Services or to work in munitions factories but the entry of young students below military age was encouragingly high, a symptom of the wartime interest in music and, as Forbes wrote, a sign of confidence in the future. In an effort to meet the growing demand for experienced class teachers in elementary and secondary schools, Forbes co-operated with Manchester Education Committee, through Dr Griffiths, their music adviser. Griffiths took a class at the College of students who intended to specialise in teaching music in school. In addition to attending Griffiths's lectures, the students were given opportunities of obtaining practical experience, under supervision, of class teaching in schools in Manchester. As a reciprocal gesture, the College Orchestra gave concerts in the schools. These moves were probably dictated by the College's first real taste of competition. In 1920 the Matthay School of Music, specialising in the pianoforte teaching methods favoured by Tobias Matthay, was founded in Deansgate with nine students taught by Hilda Collens. Over the years it had grown, until in 1942 it became a public institution, with a council of management and the title Northern School of Music. It was incorporated in September, 1943, and it too benefited from the growing desire for a richer musical life which was a part of the general feeling that the post-war world would be a better place.

A suggestion of the major changes that were to come over Manchester's musical life is contained in a Council minute of 16 July, 1942, when Forbes was asked to inquire into the

7

possibility of appointing to the staff some of the newly-appointed principals of the Liverpool Philharmonic Orchestra. These included some of the most famous names in British orchestral playing. Early in this year Liverpool Corporation had bought the new (1939) Philharmonic Hall and granted the Philharmonic Society its free use provided that a permanent orchestra was formed. Up to this date the Liverpool Philharmonic had many players in common with the Hallé. Now, attracted by the high rates of pay offered, many leading London players went to Liverpool, and Malcolm Sargent was appointed conductor, thereby depriving the Hallé of his exclusive services in the North. Forbes and Godlee were both members of the Hallé committee, Godlee now being its chairman, and saw these Merseyside moves as a direct challenge. Straightaway Godlee decided to put the Hallé on a new basis and to end, if necessary, the arrangement whereby the B.B.C. Northern Orchestra had a call on the services of many Hallé players. The wartime hunger for music had brought opportunities for expansion such as had hardly seemed possible before the war. So it is no surprise to find that, at the Council meeting on 8 October, 'no further action' on the Liverpool players was resolved.

Forbes, who had known John Barbirolli through his operatic work, at Godlee's behest signed the historic telegram in February, 1943, which brought the conductor from New York to Manchester to re-form the Hallé Orchestra. Barbirolli found several recruits among College students, among them the 16-year-old flautist, Oliver Bannister, who had been admitted to the College in 1942 without fee because of his unusual talent, the oboist Patricia Stancliffe, the trombonist Maisie Ringham and others. Bannister just missed the distinction of being the youngest player ever to join the Hallé—another College student, Raymond Cohen, was 15 when he joined the orchestra in 1937.

Barbirolli himself addressed the College students at the 50th annual general meeting on 14 December, 1943. (Among those who listened to him was a first-year holder of Bolton Education Committee's scholarship, Martin Milner, who in 1958 was to become leader of the Hallé under Sir John.) The war prevented any formal jubilee celebrations, but the College received a present which enabled it to plan ahead with optimism. In the late summer of 1943 Forbes went to London for an interview with the Departmental Committee on Advanced Musical Education, and as a result members of the committee inspected the College on 15 November. On 7 March, 1944, Forbes was able to tell the Council that the Treasury had accepted the committee's favourable report on the College's status and achievement and that an annual grant of £4,000 would be paid to the College as from 1 January, 1944. This long overdue but nonetheless welcome financial assistance relieved various administrative strains, and enabled the Council to extend and improve the curriculum, and eventually to establish 20 Council open scholarships. Five were offered at once. Forbes's salary, which had been raised to £1,000 a year at the beginning of 1944, was increased by £500, making it possible for him to give up his pianoforte professorship without loss of income. Dawber's honorarium as Warden and Registrar, a title he had held since 1941, was also more than doubled. To both men the Council expressed gratitude

for having undertaken more duties than should have properly been allotted to them at remunerations inadequate even to their normal duties. By their generosity they have served the College well and have made possible the maintenance of the high standards and reputation of the College during a most critical period in its history.

The Treasury grant was welcomed especially by the treasurer, Godlee, who knew that the surpluses during the war had been made possible only by drastic wartime economies, by suspension of outlay on decorations, replacements and renewals of equipment, and by the abandonment of opera productions. He also probably foresaw the possibility of reactions to the Treasury grant similar to that of Cheshire County Council which immediately halved its £100 grant to the College.

Staff changes during 1943–4 were many. Allin resigned his professorship of singing and was succeeded by the soprano Stiles-Allen. The vacancy on the singing staff created by the death, after 25 years' service, of Paul Vallon was not filled until December, 1944, when the famous tenor of Beecham's opera seasons in Manchester during the First World War, Frank Mullings, was appointed. Arthur Shaw, of the Hallé, became double-bass professor and Arthur Lockwood took over Harry Mortimer's trumpet class. Evelyn Rothwell (Mrs Barbirolli) replaced Stephen Whittaker as oboe teacher; Forbes's pianoforte work was taken over by Iso Elinson, the very gifted

Russian pianist who had settled in Britain. Additions to the theoretical staff were two former students, Dr Norman Andrew and Dr George Armstrong. Mrs Langford was appointed to the new post of teacher of repertoire for singers. A cello student, John Hopkins, became Librarian—he was eventually to become conductor of the B.B.C. Northern Orchestra in the 1950s and then Director of Music, Australian Broadcasting Commission.

With an eye on post-war development, the Council, in March, 1944, began negotiations for the purchase of a plot of land and its chief rents between the College and Oxford Road. Five months later No. 288 Oxford Road was bought for £275, free from chief rent, and the chief rents on Nos. 290–6 for £1,530. At the same time Forbes told the Council that it would be impossible to cope with a large influx of post-war students and that entries would have to be limited by severe methods of selection and a balance maintained between performers and teachers. He also decided, as a first measure, to discontinue admitting students whose principal study was elocution. During the summer of 1945, Gordon Green was engaged as a teacher of pianoforte, and Iso Elinson's wife, Hedwig Stein, also a brilliant pianist, was given permission to deputise for him on certain occasions. For the first post-war term, beginning in September, 1945, the number of students was 162, the highest for many years. One of them was eight years old. A Council minute for 6 November, 1945, states:

> The Principal reported that he had received a letter from Sir Stanley Marchant, the Principal of the Royal Academy of Music, regarding an eight-year-old boy, John Ogdon, the son of a master at Stand Grammar School. At an audition the Principal had found the boy to possess unusual talent as a pianist—on the Principal's recommendation the Council agreed to admit the boy as a student and to offer free tuition.

Ogdon joined the College at a good time, because the Treasury grant had already enabled a 50 per cent increase in time devoted to personal tuition in all principal and secondary practical subjects, more individual attention in theoretical subjects, and new classes in duet and ensemble playing, pianoforte accompaniment, musical appreciation, transposition and form. Also the Lees Hall had been re-decorated, 250 new chairs provided and fluorescent lighting installed. But the Council well knew that these necessary repairs were no solution of the major problem of accommodation. The end of the war saw a great deal of town planning, much of it destined to be pipe-dreaming, and Manchester in 1945 produced an elaborate new blueprint for a modernised city, with arts centre and educational 'precinct'. In 1946 the College and University authorities had several meetings on this subject and their attitude can best be summarised by this extract from the 1946 annual report:

> It is now obvious that unless a new building, or a large addition to the present one, is forthcoming in the near future the work of the College will be seriously hampered, and not only will a natural expansion of its activities be impossible, but admission will have to be denied to a considerable proportion of really gifted and promising young people. With the present numbers there is not only a shortage of actual classrooms and teaching and practice studios but a regrettable lack of amenities. The overcrowding of such small spaces as are available in the existing building for refreshments and social intercourse has assumed a formidable aspect, and that staff and students contrive to work so cheerfully and effectively under difficult and trying conditions must be taken as a reflection of the admirable spirit of enthusiasm and co-operation that prevails in the College. The Council are very conscious of their responsibilities in this matter and . . . have for a considerable time been negotiating for the acquisition of a suitable site for a new building. . . . As the Corporation recognise in their town-planning proposals that a suitable home for the College should be found in the area set apart for cultural activities, there is some reason to hope that within a measurable period of time it will be possible to proceed with the provision of adequate and dignified accommodation.

Vacant since the resignation of Lord Hewart, the College Presidency was again filled in October, 1945, when Viscount Lascelles, an ardent music-lover and expert on opera, accepted the Council's invitation. He was to prove a valued supporter of the College in all its activities. At the time of his assumption of office he was 22, and had spent part of the war as a prisoner in Italy. Post-war staff changes were many. Henry Holst resigned the violin Professorship in July, 1946, after 15 years. Maurice Raskin and Peter Ryber (concert-master of the Winterthur Orchestra) were approached as his successor but neither was available and the post went to Thomas Matthews. Laurance Turner, who had rejoined the violin staff in 1943 after an interval of 12 years, found (as did Pat Ryan, the clarinet professor) that the new full-time schedule of the Hallé Orchestra, involving well over 200 concerts a year and much travelling, left no time for teaching. He too resigned and, after Raymond Cohen had been approached and declined, Clifford Knowles filled the vacancy. Norman McDonald succeeded Ryan, and there was also a new Professor of the cello, Kathleen Moorhouse, a former student, in succession to Haydn Rogerson, who moved to London. One of his former pupils, Sheila Barlow, took over the elocution classes after the death of the old-world figure James Bernard. In October, 1946, the number of students reached 200 for the first time for 15 years.

The reality of the post-war world differed much from the idealistic visions of 1943—continued international tension; restrictions on building; financial crises; food rationing; general 'austerity'. These were the background of social and cultural life in the period 1946–52. And of these years 1947 was perhaps the darkest. Yet it opened auspiciously for the College, with an invitation from the Associated Board of the Royal Schools of Music (the R.A.M. and R.C.M.) for it, along with the Royal Scottish Academy of Music, to join the Board. This was accepted and meant that the College received £1,000 a year for five years and took its share in conducting the Board's examinations.

Towards the end of 1946 Forbes was asked by the Treasury to submit a report on the College's post-war needs. Having done this, he went to the Treasury on 10 January, 1947, where he was told there was no possibility of a new permanent building for the College 'within the next five or ten years'. The Council was therefore invited to consider erecting some tempory pre-fabricated buildings on the vacant plot adjoining the College. The Treasury would meet the cost—'if reasonable' —but would not be committed to any future expenditure on a permanent building. It was also suggested that the College, like the two London Royal colleges, should raise its fees and perhaps increase professors' salaries, especially those in the lower ranges. The Council quickly followed the Treasury advice, and work began, at a cost of £16,500, on providing six additional classrooms, a library, common rooms for students and staff, extra cloakrooms and lavatories, and a canteen and dining-room.[1] Mr H. T. Seward was the architect. Students'

[1] So that work should not be delayed by haggling the Council condoned a piece of profiteering by acceding to an exorbitant demand by the owner of one old property on the site. He had been offered £350 for what was valued at £225 but refused anything less than £600.

fees were increased from 42 guineas to £60 a year. The pattern of post-war entry was now emerging, with the 20 Council scholarships awarded and an increased number of students at the College on county and borough education committee scholarships and grants. The annual value of scholarships was increased in line with the new fees. Minimum rates of payment for the staff were raised from 10s. an hour to 12s. 6d. an hour, with rates of 15s. and 17s. 6d. for certain individuals. Among new members of the staff in 1947 were Lilian Cooper and Dorothy Donaldson, who took over the singing students of Stiles-Allen; Thomas B. Pitfield, later to be composition professor; Claud Biggs, who returned to the pianoforte staff after an absence from England of 15 years, and Hedwig Stein, also pianoforte staff; Sylvia Spencer as an additional oboe teacher; and Sara Buckley (singing).

Also in this eventful year two new prizes became available. One to the value of £30 was one of six composition prizes offered to individual schools of music by Thomas Wood, then Chairman of the Royal Philharmonic Society, and his wife. The other was a £467 gift from the trustees of the ill-fated Imperial League of Opera (Manchester branch) and was available as two annual £25 prizes for the best male and female operatic singers in the College. New members of the Council were Professor Robert Platt, the distinguished physician (now Lord Platt), who was the University representative and (in 1948) J. H. Thom, a former student who had been constrained to abandon music for a career in business which later proved very successful.

12
Forbes's last years

In the New Year Honours List of 1948 Forbes was appointed C.B.E., a well-deserved honour but one that nevertheless prompts the conclusion that the Manchester College has been unfairly treated in the matter of honours compared with the two London Royal Colleges, where the posts of Principal and Director carry what almost amount to automatic eventual knighthoods. *Who's Who* even ignores the Manchester Principal. Bob Forbes had brought the College through a difficult time and it owed much to his skill and tenacity in negotiations with the Treasury during a period of national belt-tightening. Now the ship was on an even keel and in 1948 he had less with which to contend. He was helped by the decision to return to the appointment of a full-time Registrar, following Harold Dawber's decision, on medical advice, to relinquish his part-time post. Dawber retained the title of Warden and was elected to the Council. A former student, Dr Eric Wilson, became registrar at £600 a year. On the teaching side, James Matthews and Martin Milner joined the violin staff, Paul Ward the cello, Maimie Woods the pianoforte, and Enoch Jackson the trumpet.

Among the students in the years immediately after the war were several whose later careers justify their being mentioned here. Reference has already been made to Martin Milner; Geoffrey Buckley (pianoforte), Eric Chadwick (organ), Ronald Stevenson (pianoforte and composition), Arthur Bevan (horn), Bernard O'Keefe, Michael Winfield and Roger Winfield (oboe), Marjorie Clementi (pianoforte), Ernest Tomlinson (piano and composition), Terence Nagle (trombone), Keith Bond and Norman Kay (organ), Richard Godlee (cello), Susan Tunnell, Keith Swallow, David Wilde (pianoforte) and Doreen Wedgwood (singer) have all added lustre to the College's fame. And Worcester Education Committee sent two great-nieces of Elgar (Patricia Elgar and Margaret Elgar) to the College for pianoforte studies.

Frank Mullings resigned because of ill-health from the post of Professor of Singing at the end of the summer term, 1949.

Forbes immediately tried to persuade Norman Allin to rejoin the staff, without success. Walter Legge then wrote to him urging the claims of Maria Olczewska, principal singing teacher at the Vienna Academy who wished to settle in England. A mezzo-soprano of great achievement, she is best-known as the superb Oktavian in the famous Lotte Lehmann recording of extracts from *Der Rosenkavalier*. Nothing came of this and Forbes then interviewed Dr J. Hutchinson of Newcastle upon Tyne, best known to a wider public as the real discoverer and first teacher of Kathleen Ferrier. Negotiations failed, and Forbes told the Council that, 'through high recommendation', he had seen Mr Frederic R. Cox, of London, who was willing to undertake the professorship. The Council appointed him, at a guinea an hour. Cox came to the College, to quote Forbes, 'with the highest credentials, a wide experience of vocal methods, and a fine background of general musicianship'. Before the war he had spent most of his professional life in Paris and Milan. At the time of his appointment to Manchester he had been working with Joseph Hislop, the tenor.

Another major staff change came at the end of the summer term, 1950, when Thomas Matthews resigned his violin professorship. His work as a solo player, involving visits overseas, had seriously interfered with his teaching duties and although the Council granted him leave they eventually became restless. Naum Blinder and Albert Sammons were offered the post but neither was able to accept. Forbes then persuaded Henry Holst to rejoin the staff.

Revised courses of study, approved and recommended by the Board of Professors, came into operation during 1950, in which year also the Treasury grant was increased by £1,000 to £5,000 a year. Although because of a Government 'squeeze' on incomes and wages no extra pay for the staff was sanctioned, the Treasury urged that the framing of a pension scheme should no longer be postponed, and the Council began to study the matter. The schemes in operation at the two London Royal Colleges were studied and preference was given to that worked by the R.C.M. But the Treasury would not agree to a non-contributory scheme on the lines of that adopted by the R.C.M., preferring the Royal Academy of Music's contributory scheme and emphasising that any scheme for part-time staff required special justification. The Council therefore decided to do nothing about part-time staff but to adopt the

Treasury suggestion of a contributory pension and endowment assurance scheme, worked through an insurance company, for permanent administrative staff. The Treasury was prepared to finance the scheme on the basis of an employer's contribution of 10 per cent, the employee contributing at least 5 per cent. A year later the Treasury promised a £750 contribution to the retirement pension of the Principal but the Council resolved that such a pension should never be less than £1,000 and that when necessary a further payment of £250 or more should be made out of general funds.

Another of Manchester's distinguished doctors, the surgeon Sir Harry Platt, joined the Council in 1949, and at the beginning of 1950 Leonard Behrens became vice-chairman and J. H. Thom deputy treasurer. The Council was smaller now than it had been for some years, its most active members (besides the officials) being Elsie Bishop, Alan Duckworth (who had been elected a member in 1944), Marjory Lees and the architect Gerald Sanville. In 1950 the number of students was 274 and the aim was to stabilise the numbers at around 250. With more students taking strings, wind and brass as their principal study the College Orchestra was now able, without outside assistance, to play large-scale symphonic works.

It is inevitable that the course of College history should be marked principally by changes in staff or by the deaths of old and valued friends such as Carl Fuchs and Dr Henry Read. The latter's successors on the harmony staff were Cyril Crabtree and Shackleton Pollard. At the end of 1950 a former student, Michael Brierley, took over the Opera Class from Professor Procter-Gregg, whose work at the University prevented his regular attendance. He also helped to direct the work of the College Orchestra. During 1951, Sydney Coulston succeeded Otto Paersch as teacher of the French horn and Donald Greed joined the pianoforte staff which now numbered 10 (for 111 students). In 1952, Kathleen Moorhouse, the cello professor, died and was succeeded by Oliver Vella. Lucy Pierce reduced her teaching duties by a day a week and an additional teacher, Derrick Wyndham, a pupil of Moritz Rosenthal and Artur Schnabel, was engaged. He had been a child prodigy before the war but, after service in the R.A.F., had abandoned public performing for teaching. Also in 1952 Lady Barbirolli resigned her oboe post, her duties passing to her assistant Rosemary Wells.

During 1951 an improvement was made in the acoustics of the extension buildings by use of floor covering and panelling. Problems arose, too, from the welcome wider application of local authority assistance. A typical example was of a student who held a College scholarship then being awarded supplementary assistance by the local authority. The Council decided that it could be suggested to directors of education that, as the scholarships were really free places, the maintenance grant should be increased by the amount of the College fees. Scholarship holders in the 1949–51 period included some brilliant names, among them the tenor John Mitchinson, Ludmila Navratil the violist, Jean Reddy the soprano, Joseph Ward the tenor, Catherine Wilson the mezzo-soprano, Elizabeth Walton, pianist and niece of the composer and later to be Mrs Martin Milner, Sheila Bickerdike, oboist, and Robert Elliott, a composition pupil. John Ogdon, who had received free tuition when he was eight, was now 14 and at Manchester Grammar School. His father asked that he might be allowed to resume attendance at the College for part-time tuition but it was decided, in the boy's interests, that no exception could be made to the general rule and that the question of specialised training should be deferred 'until the demands of his general education would be less intensive'.

In September, 1952, Philip Godlee died at the age of 62. He had been on the Council for 27 years, for 18 of which he was treasurer; indeed his service to the College was longer by 11 years than his service on the Hallé Committee. Forbes wrote in the annual report:

Of imposing stature and presence, he suffered, as the result of wounds received during the first world war, from serious and painful physical disabilities, the full extent of which were so gallantly concealed by the unquenchable zest of his ardent and courageous spirit that his sudden collapse came as an unexpected shock to his most intimate friends. . . . The cheerful and breezy manner in which he combined shrewdness, wit and lightheartedness in dealing with financial matters will be greatly missed by his colleagues on the Council and by the general public at the annual meetings of the College.

Cavalier in his attitude to bureaucracy and scornful of obstructive tactics by those whom he considered unnecessarily pedantic in observance of the rules, Godlee was a driving force on any committee on which he served. He was an autocrat, but a charming and disarming one, and no one who knew him and fell under his spell will ever forget him. He was succeeded as treasurer by J. H. Thom, with Alan Duckworth as deputy.

The Council meeting on 8 October, 1952, at which these appointments were made, was also told by Sir John Stopford that for some time Forbes had been contemplating retirement and now, on medical advice, wished to relinquish the Principalship as soon as the Council were agreeable. The Council decided to ask Sir George Dyson, Director of the R.C.M., Sir Reginald Thatcher, Principal of the R.A.M., Sir Adrian Boult, Sir Ernest Bullock, Professor E. J. Dent and Dr H. Middleton to suggest suitable candidates and also advertised the post. Six of the candidates were interviewed on Friday, 13 March, 1953, and at a special Council meeting later the same morning the post was offered to the Professor of Singing, Frederic R. Cox, at a salary of £1,600 a year. The appointment dated from 1 May, 1953, and Forbes's retirement from 31 July. In the transition period the two men acted as Joint Principals.

Forbes, who was now 73, had been Principal for 24 years and three months. The first thing to be said about him is that he had a genius for organisation—he could have had a notable career in business or industry—and a fine natural intelligence. He was something of an enigma, a man with a pronounced dual nature. Neat and precise, with an engaging smile and an affable manner, one soon discovered that he was alert, widely-read, and possessed of a wit almost as keen as that of Beecham and Shaw, both of whom he deeply admired and with whom he shared a streak of vanity. But a darker side sometimes took over, when the wit became caustic and he became unreasonable and said hurtful things about his closest friends, rivalling the worst side of Beecham in his cynical disregard of finer feelings for the sake of scoring outrageous or cheap points. At such times his disillusion and disappointment showed only too clearly. These were perhaps traceable to the course his life had taken and to some indecision within himself about what he was best fitted to accomplish. People who knew him well believed that his dearest wish had been to become a great pianist: he had a splendid technique, a sound intellectual approach and (as his performance of the Delius concerto demonstrated) genuine musical feeling, but he had none of the extra gifts of style and temperament which turn the good craftsman into the great artist. He then turned his attention to conducting, notably of opera, and of course the same deficiencies showed themselves: his stick technique was good, he was an excellent score-reader, but he lacked the most important gift of all—the ability to inspire his players and singers not only to give of their best but to play and sing better than they believed they could. When his efforts did not gain the recognition he thought they deserved he became depressed and also disparaging about those who had won the reputation he craved for himself.

His pupils arc evidence of his ability as a teacher, but one who knew him well believes that Forbes was not born to teach and had no great love for it. His most distinctive work was almost certainly done in chamber music. As a young man he had toured with Kreisler, Elman and Casals: he was particularly expert in violin and pianoforte sonatas where he was nearly always a superb partner. I remember hearing him, an elderly man, in the *Kreutzer*, and he was beyond praise. It is worth remarking that men like Forbes, Beecham and Shaw, outwardly cold men in the public's opinion, shared a passionate devotion to the music of Delius, who was akin to them in temperament. Perhaps in its luscious sounds they—and Delius himself—recognised, fully exposed, the soft centre which in themselves was enclosed by a hard outer shell. Yet Forbes was capable of great delicacy of feeling as an incident told to me by Clifford Knowles reveals. Forbes and Knowles attended some auditions at which an elderly, shabbily dressed man appeared carrying a cheap violin and some tattered music. He explained that he had been forced to earn his living by pushing a handcart round Ancoats, but since his father had taken him as a small boy to hear the Brodsky Quartet at Charles Rowley's Ancoats Brotherhood he had always loved the violin; he had never been able to afford lessons so he had struggled by himself and it had been his life's ambition to win some kind of scholarship to the College and have some lessons. He then began to play, pitifully badly. Forbes let him reach the end of the piece, then there was silence and it could be sensed that Forbes was feeling the pathos of the incident—during his own youth he had tried to learn the violin and had given up in despair. He rose from his chair and spoke very kindly to the man, gently urging him to abandon the idea of lessons and giving him advice on how to make the best use of his limited talents. It was the act of a gentleman.

He left the College, in its sixtieth year, a more efficient, financially healthier institution than when he took over. His whole life had been devoted to it, as student, teacher and Principal, and he gave to it much more than he received from it. He ran the College single-handed in a way that would be impossible today and saw it safely through the Depression and through the Second World War. He more than any man had brought it to equal status with its two London counterparts. That achievement is his memorial, the only one that Bob Forbes would really have wished.

13
The music, 1929–53

The students' concert on 29 January, 1929, a week after Brodsky's death, gave no hint of the sorrow that must have filled the Lees Hall, except that no Brodsky pupil performed. Leonard Regan played part of Weber's first clarinet concerto, and Dorothy Spencer, a Forbes pupil, played the first movement of Rachmaninov's third concerto, its first usage in these concerts. On 13 March, Rawsthorne's song 'Tsu-Yeh', in five sections, a setting of a translation from the Chinese, was sung by Margaret Collier. Two nights later Forbes conducted 100 past and present students in the Brodsky memorial concert in the Free Trade Hall. The list of players reads like a roll-call of all that is best in Mancunian orchestral history: Catterall, Barker, Blech, Hirsch, Hecht, Partington, Park, Warburton, Wright, Moorhouse, Meert, Stott, Shaw, Gilbert, Mortimer, Ryan, Regan, Whittaker, Nichols, Camden, Paersch, Coulston, Holt, Hoyland, Barlow, Liddle, Dawber, Massey, Brierley and Rawsthorne. The programme began with the Elegy from Tchaikovsky's Serenade for Strings. The overture was *Die Meistersinger*; Norman Allin sang Hans Sachs's monologue, 'Wahn, wahn'; Delius's *On hearing the First Cuckoo in Spring* was followed by Tchaikovsky's violin concerto (soloist, Arthur Catterall), Elgar's *Enigma Variations*, the aria 'Il lacerato spirito' from *Simone Boccanegra*, and Dvořák's *Carneval* overture.

At the first of the examination concerts on 3 July, 1929, Rawsthorne and Blech played Beethoven's C minor sonata, a performance to which reference has already been made in Chapter 8, the quartet class played a Dohnányi quartet, and there was also a performance of Franck's quintet. The following evening Rawsthorne was the soloist in Falla's *Nights in the Gardens of Spain*. New names begin to come forward now, for example Norman Walker, that fine bass, singing Handel's 'Hear me, ye winds and waves' on 10 December, and Charles Taylor was the violinist with Arthur Berry in Grieg's sonata on the same evening. Taylor was Catterall's pupil and became leader of the Royal Opera House Orchestra.

A great day in the College's annals was 11 March, 1930, when the Opera Class invaded rival territory and performed Verdi's *Falstaff* at the Royal College of Music, having given four performances in Manchester the previous October. The reactions of the London critics, though slightly condescending as befits the metropolitan attitude to provincial endeavour, were complimentary, with particular praise for the students' teamwork and for Joseph Sutcliffe's Falstaff ('ripely bodied forth', said the *Morning Post*, believe it or not). But the R.C.M. audience came in for some evidently well-deserved strictures from Eric Blom in the *Manchester Guardian*:

> The spectators—they would hardly be called listeners—seemed to think it necessary to furnish the plot . . . with conversational captions, and accepted the music as a mere accompaniment to it and to their incessant comments. Immoderate laughter again and again drowned the most fully scored passages, and the loveliest of orchestral perorations—at the first curtain in the third act—was not safe from a barbarous interruption by applause. . . . Compared with the unruliness on the other side of the footlights, what was seen on the stage was almost the supercilious composure of long experience.

Forbes also brightened Review Week in March, 1930 by arranging lecture-recitals by Frederick Dawson and Lucy Pierce on pianoforte music, Fuchs on the history of the cello, a Catterall Quartet concert which included Richard Strauss's piano quartet (with Forbes as pianist) and a lecture on criticism by Neville Cardus, Langford's successor on the *Manchester Guardian*. 'All students are expected to attend this lecture', the programme said. It is not often a music critic has a captive audience. The students' contributions included the first movement of Sibelius's violin concerto, played by Jessie Hinchcliffe, and Geoffrey Gilbert in Chaminade's flute concertino. Cardus attended this concert and found the Sibelius the finest performance:

> Here was a young student tackling a severe act of musical cerebration [Fie, Sir Neville] by a composer who, whether you like him or not, is not exactly food for babes. . . . She mingled into a true style the composer's drastic contrasts of knotty energy and keen lyrical impulse. . . . Mr Gilbert . . . drew so much winsome melody out of his flute, and so much that was piquant in phrase and rhythm, that we, for the first time in our lives, were convinced that Mr Moddle did not make the flute his very own (as a solo instrument) by using it for the expression of blighted and hopeless love.

And the next evening, writing of a chamber concert in which the students played Beethoven, Brahms (sextet) and Dvořák (piano quintet) Granville Hill had this to say—which proves that attitudes were much the same then as now:

> If among the seven or eight persons (apart from members of the College) who turned up last night at the Houldsworth Hall there were any strangers to the city, they must have been surprised and not a little indignant to find how uninterested the Manchester public is in the work of its chief institution for the training of young musicians. We have attended students' concerts in other towns and never found anything but a lively interest displayed in all that goes forward in educational centres; yet here in 'musical' Manchester there is apparently a mere handful of people who care to listen to such special performances as have been given this week by talented pupils. . . . Perhaps, however, the apathetic attitude in this district is too well known to cause surprise.

The July examination concerts included two movements of Ravel's trio, two of Brahms's clarinet quintet (Regan as clarinettist), and two movements of Saint-Saëns's trio, op. 18. For its next opera venture, the College gave performances at the end of January, 1931, of Puccini's *Suor Angelica* and Acts II and III of Gluck's *Orfeo*. Ann Sholes and Dorothy Pearce shared the role of Angelica, two nights each, and Edith Winston sang Orfeo. This was the first performance of an English version of the Puccini, and Cardus was enthusiastic about the whole evening. He asked:

> Why not a school of Manchester opera of our own? We have the orchestra, the chorus, and judging from last night's performance we have also young singers with the root of the matter in them— and a most beautiful ballet trained by Miss Madge Atkinson. . . . During the Gluck all thoughts of a convenient adjustment of values to suit amateur aspirations had gone from our minds; we sat back and enjoyed an agreeable presentation of one of the world's most beautiful works of art.

(It has always been an exceptional aspect of Sir Neville's criticism that he has never been afraid to sit back and enjoy himself.) On 6, 10 and 13 March, Willy Hess and Forbes gave three Beethoven recitals, playing 10 violin sonatas, and the Review Week again included lectures by Cardus (on 'Music as a Way of Life'), by John F. Russell, Librarian of the Henry Watson Music Library, on 'Books on Music', and by John Booth, of the Royal Academy of Music, on 'Self-help for Singers'. The students' concerts in the week included works

8

for violin and piano by Szymanowski played by Christian Orford and Alan Soulsby.

Forbes and Procter-Gregg again collaborated in December 1931 in staging *The Magic Flute* in the hall of the Church of the Holy Name. Norman Walker sang Sarastro, Margaret Collier the Queen of the Night, Wilfred Firth Tamino and Iorwerth Griffiths Papageno. Between 27 November, 1931, and 18 March, 1932, members of the staff gave six 'Five o'clock Chamber Concerts', devoted mainly to the classics: the *Archduke* trio played by Forbes, Fuchs and Henry Holst; Harry Mortimer in Mozart's clarinet quintet; John Wills as the pianist in the *Trout* quintet; Elsie Thurston singing Schumann. The programmes of the students' concerts are more interesting musically by now, and it is noticeable that Miss Thurston's pupils were encouraged to study a much wider variety of songs, from Senta's Ballad to Delius's 'Twilight Fancies', from Wolf's *Michelangelo Lieder* to Elgar's *Sea Pictures*. Charles Taylor and John Brennan played two movements of a Medtner sonata on 7 June, 1932, and Taylor took part in several performances of Delius's sonatas. For opera in February, 1933, Forbes returned to *The Marriage of Figaro*, in the Lesser Free Trade Hall. On 14 February Neil Barkla, a pupil of Forbes, played his own Three Preludes at a students' concert. Barkla later become the distinguished critic of the *Liverpool Daily Post*. Another new name, appearing on 7 March, is that of Holst's pupil Olive Zorian, who played two movements of Mozart's A major concerto. At a Review Week concert later that month Brahms's C minor string quartet was played by this distinguished class: Charles Taylor, Sydney Partington, Keith Cummings and Alexander Young. Douglas Steele played organ music by Franck on 23 May and Barkla played more of his own piano music on 4 July. Violin and piano sonatas by John Ireland, a quartet by McEwen, a Bach flute sonata and Beethoven's second *Rasoumovsky* quartet were included in the examination concert on 6 July when the players included Taylor, Partington, Cummings, Charles Ellam, Brian Douglas and Dorothy Rice.

In February, 1934, four performances of *Madam Butterfly* were given, with Norah Sinclair as Butterfly, John Caunce as Pinkerton and Edmund Meadows as Sharpless. Review Week of this year included a recital of Busoni's Music for Two Pianos by Lucy Pierce and John Wills; and 'an address by

Sir Thomas Beecham, Bart., on "Influences on Music Past and Present".' The mind boggles. The week began with a recital by Holst's violin pupils. Vivaldi's concerto for four violins was played by Olive Zorian, Ena Whittaker, Eileen Higgins and Kathleen Robinson; Olive Zorian played Spohr's eighth concerto, Keith Cummings played the Bruch G minor concerto and Charles Taylor the *Introduction and Rondo Capriccioso* of Saint-Saëns.

On 17 May there was an early forerunner of the 'public rehearsal' when, sponsored by the R.C.M. Patron's Fund, the Hallé Orchestra conducted by Forbes played at the College, with students as soloists. The works were rehearsed from 2 p.m. until 3.35 p.m. and then played through. In this way Arnold Cooke's *Concert Overture*, which had won third prize in a *Daily Telegraph* competition, received its first performance, Philip Hecht played the first movement of Sibelius's violin concerto, Evelyn Duke and Edith Winston sang a duet from *Aïda*, and Alexander Young played Elgar's cello concerto. Charles Taylor also played the Sibelius at an examination concert in July, Forbes's pupil Nina Papadopoulos, specialising in Ravel, played *Ondine*, Keith Cummings played the first movement of Elgar's violin concerto and Bliss's Concerto for Two Pianos was played by George Mantle-Childe and Robert Keys, both pupils of Frederick Dawson. Holst's quartet 'stars' now comprised Taylor, Olive Zorian, Cummings and Young, who played Delius's quartet on 5 July. Miss Thurston's pupils sang Fauré (Constance Alldritt) and Mahler's *Lieder eines fahrenden Gesellen* (Muriel Ashworth). On 12 February, 1935, another violinist who like Cummings was to find fame as a viola-player—Paul Cropper—played Beethoven's Romance in F, Sheila Barlow (John Wills's pupil) played Debussy's *Reflets dans l'eau* and on 12 March Philip Kendal, a Forbes pupil, played Grieg's concerto, first movement, and Molly Bird, a singing pupil of Dora Gilson, sang two of Bax's best songs, 'The White Peace' and 'Rann of Exile'. One of the principal Review Week items of 1935 was a recital by Frederick Dawson of interest today not for its Beethoven and Schumann but because he championed three pieces (*Labyrinth, Water Pearls* and *Good Night to Flamboro'*) by the Yorkshire composer William Baines, whose music has attracted various intermittent attempts to give it wider circulation, including one by Benjamin Britten. The students' concert the next evening was another extraordinarily enterprising programme: part of Ravel's trio, Tertis's adaptation for viola of Delius's first violin sonata (Cummings and Brian Douglas) and the first movement of Ireland's D minor sonata (Arthur Leech and Philip Kendal). At the orchestral concert on 29 March the soloist in the first two movements of Mendelssohn's concerto was Holst's young pupil Raymond Cohen. His performance of Tartini's G minor sonata (the 'Devil's Trill') became a feature of the students' concerts. Four performances of Humperdinck's *Hansel and Gretel* were staged during the summer. 'Though the orchestral playing was of varying quality', Granville Hill wrote in the *Manchester Guardian*, 'the singing maintained beauty and aptness of style.' Muriel Ashworth, who sang the Sandman, sang Hugo Wolf songs a few days later and another Thurston pupil, Evangeline Harries, sang some love songs by Kilpinen —again an enterprising choice by this teacher. One of Lucy Pierce's enthusiasms, the music of Scriabin, was reflected in her choice of four preludes for her pupil Eileen Foyster to play on 19 November, and Alexander Young on that date played Fauré's *Elegy* for cello, a moving and eloquent work that is still too little known.

On 29 January, 1936, three of the ensemble class played Frank Bridge's Phantasy in C minor for Piano and Strings and Raymond Cohen played the last two movements of Beethoven's concerto. The appointment of Procter-Gregg to be head of the University Music Department was marked on 17 March by a joint concert of the College and University orchestras and the newly-formed university chorus who sang Procter-Gregg's setting of *Jerusalem*, written for the occasion. Brahms's *Song of Destiny*, Wagner's *Siegfried Idyll* and Beethoven's eighth symphony were also performed. Review Week in this year was notable for a competition for a piano prize awarded by Harriet Cohen who herself gave a recital. The students' chamber concert which ended the week was of Brahms's clarinet quintet (Sidney Fell as the clarinettist), Dohnányi's cello sonata, op. 8, and Tchaikovsky's string sextet. Cohen was the foremost pupil at this period, but with him were Nina Papadopoulos, who made a speciality of Saint-Saëns's *Africa*, the violinist Brenda Old, Nancy Harris (especially in Bach), and Zoë Monteanu, a pupil of Forbes. Mary Lingard, daughter of the flautist Joseph Lingard (and later Mrs Richard Lewis), was a pupil of Lucy Pierce and played a Beethoven concerto movement at an open practice on 1 December at which the first movements of Rachmaninov's cello sonata and Richard Strauss's piano quartet were played. Another joint concert with the University on 12 March, 1937, included Vaughan Williams's *Pastoral Symphony*, which had received only one Hallé performance in the then 15 years of its existence. The first movement of Sibelius's concerto was played by Holst's pupil, Arthur Leech, on 15 June and he followed this with the first movement of the Elgar on 5 July. Arthur Bliss's clarinet quintet was played by Sidney Fell, Leech, Cohen, Brenda Old and Peggy Robson at an examination concert on 9 July, followed by Franck's piano quintet. Busoni's violin concerto was revived as a vehicle for Raymond Cohen on 29 November, 1938, and he played the Sibelius on 7 March, 1939. Debussy's Clarinet Rhapsody was played by Frank Reidy, a pupil of Mortimer, on 28 March, 1939, and the last peacetime examination concert for six years, on 7 July, contained another rarity in a performance by Eric Cotton and Nancy Harris of William Y. Hurlstone's bassoon sonata. Norman Allin was singing professor at this time and his pupils Patricia Richards and Minnie Bower were encouraged to sing 'Batti, batti' and Schubert's 'Shepherd on the Rock'.

At the first open practice of the war, on 6 November, Cohen played Székely's arrangement of Bartók's *Five Rumanian Folk Dances*, and Agnes Stephens and Brian Douglas played John Ireland's A minor violin sonata. Organ pupils of Harold Dawber at this date included Ruth Turton and Beryl Dallen, both of whom performed Handel organ concertos, and it is possible almost to detect a friendly rivalry between Elsie Thurston and Norman Allin in finding interesting pieces for their pupils to sing—an extract from Tchaikovsky's *Joan of Arc*, for example, Lieder by Joseph Marx, Liszt's 'Die Lorelei' and the 'Air de Salomé' from Massenet's *Hérodiade*, the last being sung by Edna Hobson, an Allin pupil, on 22 February, 1940. Bizet's 'Agnus Dei', sung by Patricia Coxon (Miss Thurston) on 18 March with the College Orchestra was a real novelty in a concert that ended with Mozart's ballet music from *Les Petits Riens*. Another Allin pupil, Thomas Thomas—now known as Richard Lewis—sang Vaughan Williams's 'On Wenlock Edge', as he has often memorably done since, on 28 May, repeating it at an examination concert on 12 July. A new oboe pupil, Patricia Stancliffe, played in Mozart's oboe quartet on

14 November, in a splendid programme which included the first movement of a trio by Gade, once a favourite composer of Hallé's, two movements of Dvořák's violin concerto played by Gerald Briscoe and the *Liebeslieder* Waltzes of Brahms performed by Flora Kent, Joan Holt and members of the opera class. An extract from Elgar's *King Olaf* was sung by Allin's pupil John Chew on 5 December and on 8 April, 1941, in the Albert Hall, Peter Street, Thomas Thomas sang extracts from Bach's *St Matthew Passion*, Minnie Bower sang Delius songs, and Agnes Stephens and Nina Papadopoulos played Debussy's violin sonata.

Marjorie Thomas, pupil of Elsie Thurston, first appeared at a students' concert on 8 December, 1941, when she sang 'Ombra mai fu'. On 9 June, 1942, Holst's pupil Joan Spencer played the first two movements of Walton's violin concerto, which her teacher had introduced to Britain the previous year. She played it in full at an examination concert on 9 July. Marjorie Thomas sang 'O don fatale' on 4 December and songs by Wolf and Bantock in June and July, 1943. An organ student, Albert Knowles, paid homage to a former College professor by playing the prelude from W. H. Dayas's sonata in F major on 13 June, 1944. Stiles-Allen's pupil Pamela Bowden sang Granados's 'The Lover and the Nightingale' on the same date and Evelyn Rothwell's pupil Bernard O'Keefe played arrangements for oboe of two movements from a Handel concerto grosso. Edna Hobson was now studying with Stiles-Allen, and sang Beethoven's 'Ah! perfido' on 11 July; Marjorie Thomas sang three of Elgar's *Sea Pictures on* 12 July. Nina Papadopoulos was now studying with Iso Elinson and played four Rachmaninov preludes on 12 July. On 29 November Holst's pupil Martin Milner played Bach's Chaconne; three of Walton's songs—'Daphne', 'Thro' Gilded Trellises' and 'Old Sir Faulk' were sung by Patricia Richards on 14 December. The first movement of Beethoven's B flat piano concerto was played by Marjorie Clementi, pupil of Lucy Pierce, on 6 March, 1945, when John Hopkins, cello pupil of Haydn Rogerson, played a sonata by Henry Eccles and Milner played the first movement of Beethoven's concerto. Ronald Stevenson, a piano pupil of Iso Elinson, made his students' concert debut on 4 December in a Haydn sonata. Elinson's pupils, who at this date also included Joseph Clough, Arni Björnsson, Maimie Woods, Dorothy Platt and Felice Pliskin, gave a concert on 13

December of music by Mozart, Haydn, Beethoven, Schumann, Brahms and Chopin.

Frank Mullings's pupil Joyce Gartside sang 'Ah! perfido' at the students' orchestral concert on 11 March, 1946, and joined John Chew in the Scene III duet from Act I of *Die Walküre* on 19 March, when Martin Milner played the first movement of Elgar's concerto and Eric Chadwick played three organ preludes from Stanford's op. 101. Milner produced a rarity on 4 June in Ernest Walker's *Variations on a Theme of Joachim*. Ronald Stevenson, also a member of Richard Hall's composition class, played his own piano sonata at an examination concert on 16 July; on 12 November Marjorie Clementi played Beethoven's *Thirty-two Variations in C minor* and Chadwick played some Reubke. Milner was now with Thomas Matthews and played the first movement of a Prokofiev concerto (number unspecified) on 25th February, 1947, and joined Stevenson in the latter's violin and piano sonata on 11 March. Other names soon to be known in wider spheres occur in this year as post-war expansion began to take effect. Elizabeth Godlee was in Clifford Knowles's quartet class and played in string quartets by Beethoven and Schubert, Geoffrey Buckley, an Elinson pupil, played mainly the classics and Elinson introduced his other pupils to the music of Shostakovich. Noel Rawsthorne played Bach's Dorian Toccata on 10 June, and Kathleen Moorhouse's pupil Manuel Alvarado played Fauré's *Elegy* and *Après un Rêve* on the same date, and Elgar's concerto on 1 July. Richard Hall had formed a madrigal class which sang examples by Dowland, Farmer and Morley on 8 July—it should be added that the music of Monteverdi and Caccini was also not infrequently performed at the College, and Elinson persuaded several of his pupils, including Stevenson, to play Bax's fourth sonata in G. Forbes conducted an ambitious vocal and orchestral concert on 15 December—Mozart's *Prague* symphony, Debussy's *L'Après-Midi d'un Faune*, the quartet from *Rigoletto* and the quintet from *Die Meistersinger*. Milhaud's *Scaramouche* suite was played by Donald and Geoffrey Greed on 9 March, 1948, and two extracts from Gerald Finzi's *Dies Natalis* were sung by Mullings's pupil Barbara Siddelley on 16 March. On 1 June Hindemith's Sonata for Two Pianos was played by Keith Swallow and Ernest Hall, three Blake settings by Stevenson were sung by Marie Reidy on 17 June, Pamela Bowden sang

Duparc on 30 June, and the cellist John Dow played the Symphonic Variations by Boëllmann at an examination concert on 6 July.

Keith Bond, yet another brilliant organ pupil of Dawber, played Parry's Fantasia and Fugue in G major on 9 November, 1948, and a new pupil of Elinson, David Wilde, played the first movement of Beethoven's B flat concerto on 23 November and the remaining two on 15 March, 1949. Lawrence Glover, a pupil of Claud Biggs, played the first movement of Beethoven's C minor concerto on 28 February and the slow movement of Brahms's B flat concerto on 31 May. Elsie Thurston's pupil Doreen Wedgwood sang Schubert songs on 29 June, and on 12 July Gordon Green's pupil Susan Tunnell made her first appearance in the first movement of Beethoven's C major concerto.

The examination concert on 8 July was by Richard Hall's composition students who at this date included John Graves, May Cusick and the trumpeter Arthur Butterworth. At a students' concert on 25 October, the quartet in Schubert's A minor string quartet comprised Elizabeth Godlee, her sister Rachel (viola), John Dow and Fred Crawshaw as second violin, Keith Swallow played works by Pitfield, Ravel and Chopin, Susan Tunnell played Chopin's G minor Ballade, Philip Challis (an Elinson pupil) played Beethoven and Bach, and Marie Reidy sang Delius and Debussy. In the Whitworth Hall on 2 December Forbes conducted an orchestral concert in which movements from organ concertos by Handel and Guilmant were played by Eric Chadwick and Keith Bond and the symphony was Vaughan Williams's *London*, an odd choice for Forbes, who once expressed to me some highly derogatory remarks about the music of this composer. One of Arthur Butterworth's compositions, a pianoforte suite *Lakeland Summer Nights*, was played by Jean Barker, a pupil of Hedwig Stein, on 14 February, 1950, and John Ireland's piano concerto was played by Geoffrey Buckley and the College Orchestra under Forbes on 24 March. The first pupil of Frederic Cox to sing at a students' concert was Jack Scott, who sang 'If with all your hearts' from *Elijah* on 28 March, but moved into more familiar Cox territory on 3 May with an arioso from *Fedora* and the ballata from *Rigoletto*.

Musically the next interesting concert was the examination concert on 14 July, when Sibelius's string quartet and Brahms's

F minor piano quintet were performed by the Godlee sisters, John Dow (who played Elgar's cello concerto with the orchestra on 24 July) and others. With David Wilde, Susan Tunnell and Keith Swallow as pianists at this date the concerts had considerable distinction. It will have been noticed that since the war there had been no opera performances, but Forbes increased the number and scope of orchestral concerts, conducting Shostakovich's first symphony on 18 December, 1950, and Sir George Dyson's symphony (which Barbirolli had once conducted at a wartime Hallé Concert) on 30 April, 1951, at a concert at which Lawrence Glover played Liszt's second concerto. Catherine Wilson, now well-known as a Sadler's Wells principal, sang for the first time at a students' concert on 1 May, choosing three songs by Delius. Jean Reddy, a pupil of Mrs Langford, sang an aria from *Figaro* on 5 June. Richard Hall's pupils gave another concert on 2 July, Roy Heaton Smith having a suite for piano duet performed, David Freedman a Fantasia for String Trio and David Wilde a Rhapsody for Violin and Piano. It is extraordinary how rarely the Chopin sonatas occur in these programmes, but the B flat minor was played by Keith Swallow on 18 July and the B minor on 21 July, when it was played by Geoffrey Greed after Geoffrey Buckley had played the *Hammerklavier* and before Gerald Keenan played the Liszt in B minor. The violist in Beethoven's string quartet, op. 18, no. 1 on 15 November was Ludmila Navratil, a pupil of Paul Cropper. A violin pupil of Clifford Knowles, Davina Hart, was also prominent in College recitals at this date and many will remember these two exceedingly attractive and talented girls playing together in performances of Mozart's Sinfonia Concertante for violin and viola, performances which penetrated to the heart of this glorious work. The first result of Michael Brierley's taking over the Opera Class was a performance of the sextet from Mozart's *Cosi fan tutte* on 25 March, 1952, by Marian Callear, Florence Smith, Beryl Hyland, Kenneth Ormston, James Shuker and Gwilym Jones. Two of Cox's pupils, John Mitchinson and Joseph Ward, sang a duet from *The Barber of Seville* on 17 June. Kenneth Ormston was the soloist on 2 July in Roy Heaton Smith's cantata for tenor, women's chorus and strings, *Phantasy*, which had won a Royal Philharmonic Society prize. This was again performed at an orchestral concert on 21 July (conducted by Gerald Wragg) at which Forbes conducted the first movement of Brahms's B flat concerto, with David Wilde as soloist and Saint-Saëns's G minor concerto with Susan Tunnell, and Brierley conducted the finale of Act II of *Figaro*, with Marian Callear, Joyce Craig, Florence Smith, Gwilym Jones, James Shuker and Joseph Ward. Three nights previously vocal pupils of Elsie Thurston, Mrs Langford and Miss Donaldson had sung arias from *Don Giovanni* and *Werther*, Schumann's *Frauen-liebe und Leben* and 'Asie' from Ravel's *Shéhérazade*. Jean Hindmarsh, a pupil of Mrs Langford and later to become a leading exponent of the Sullivan operettas, sang Handel's 'Subtle Love' on 14 November, and Elsie Thurston's pupil Jean Cooney sang three of Elgar's *Sea Pictures* on 15 December at a concert which marked Cecil N. Cohen's debut as conductor of the College Orchestra. Davina Hart was the latest in a long line of R.M.C.M. students to play part of the Elgar violin concerto (24 March, 1953). Brierley conducted the finale of Act IV of *Figaro* at an orchestral concert on 30 March when Cohen conducted the Adagietto from Mahler's fifth symphony and Brahms's second symphony. New names occur at the students' concert on 23 June: Honor Sheppard, a pupil of Elsie Thurston, sang Purcell's 'Music for a While' and Handel's 'Light is my heart', and the pianist in the first two movements of Brahms's horn trio was Brenda Lucas, with Barry Castle as the horn player. Miss Lucas was a pupil of Iso Elinson, and she played the first movement of Beethoven's B flat concerto on 30 June.

The last two concerts of the summer term of 1953 marked the end of Forbes's Principalship. On 16 July, in the Whitworth Hall, Cohen conducted Hart and Navratil in Mozart's Sinfonia Concertante, Jean Reddy and John Mitchinson sang the love duet from Verdi's *Otello*, and David Wilde played Beethoven's B flat concerto. On the 17th Keith Sellors played a piano sonatina by Robert Elliott, a fellow-student; Honor Sheppard sang two of David Wilde's songs; and the term and an era in the College's existence ended with Brahms's *Liebeslieder* Waltzes.

An 'extra-mural' College activity which should briefly be recorded was the work of the Manchester Contemporary Music Centre. At its monthly concerts many important new chamber works—such as sonatas by Scriabin and Prokofiev and the Bartók quartets—were introduced to the city. Its 'founding fathers' had been Frank Merrick, John Wills, Edward Isaacs, Lucy Pierce and Dora Gilson. Others such as Thomas Pitfield followed them.

14
Cox at the helm

'Freddie' Cox's appointment to the Principalship was a surprise. He applied for the post only when he heard the names of some of the other applicants and decided that 'if they were looking in the bargain basement' he had a chance. The College certainly got a bargain. He was, to a large extent, unknown except to connoisseurs of vocal training. Until he went to the College in 1949 he had had no experience in an academic establishment. He brought to his task, therefore, a fresh mind untrammeled by conventional attitudes, an infectious enthusiasm, a kindly and courteous approach to staff and students, and a winning personality capable of rock-like firmness on matters close to his heart. Opera was his chief interest, as perhaps it had been Forbes's, and his advent coincided with the growing international reputations being made by British singers. Yet he was also determined to maintain and improve the College's instrumental reputation, notably the piano-playing department, 'its special pride' as the 1953 annual report said.

He took over when the Treasury had increased its grant to the College for 1953–4 to £7,500, a sum that included the Treasury's contribution to Forbes's pension. The College's case for an extra grant had been presented by Jack Thom, in the absence of Forbes through illness, in January, 1953. Costs of running the College were increasing sharply, although no increase in professional salaries was sanctioned. The post-war financial results on each year's working since the war had been:

1946, surplus of £258 19s. 5d.
1947, surplus of £212 16s. 3d.
1948, surplus of £506 17s. 11d.
1949, surplus of £496 16s. 11d.
1950, surplus of £204 6s. 6d.
1951, deficit of £215 0s. 11d.
1952, surplus of £200 15s. 4d.
1953, deficit of £309 14s. 0d.

When Cox took over, students' fees were bringing in £12,800

in a year, grants amounted to £7,875, subscriptions to £51 and interest on investments to £1,011. The cost of salaries, fees, superannuation contributions and travelling expenses of staff in 1952–3 was £15,778, and the canteen was running at a loss of £387. Seven years earlier, salaries etc. ran at £8,493, students' fees at £6,567, and investments brought in £780 and grants £4,765.

At a meeting during the summer vacation in 1953, Cox put forward his first requirements, all being approved. Nancy Hislop (Mrs Joseph Hislop) was appointed to the singing staff to take over 12 students who had been with Cox himself. The chief consideration here was that the students would suffer the smallest possible break in the continuity of their training if they were taught by Mrs Hislop whose methods were similar to Cox's. Grahame Clifford, who took over some of Cox's duties during the time of his Joint Principalship, was retained on a temporary basis until Cox had presented his report to the Treasury and sounded their reaction to his proposal that College teaching expenditure should cover a new department of operatic, choral and vocal training—a department, he pointed out, which was already mentioned in the College prospectus although it did not exist. Three or four senior students were appointed to undertake various teaching duties under their professors' supervision, at a grant of £24 a term with free tuition. This was to give them extra teaching experience and to provide more supervised tuition for first-year students. On a lighter note, the Council decided to mark the diamond jubilee by an orchestral concert on 7 December. Sir John Barbirolli was invited to conduct but was unable to fix a suitable date. The concert was conducted by George Weldon, associate Hallé conductor since 1952, who had taken charge of the College Orchestra class earlier in 1953, and by Cecil Cohen, his assistant. On the day of the concert, at the annual meeting, jubilee year Fellowships were conferred on Dr Norman Andrew, Harry Blech, Louis Cohen, Gordon Green, Clifford Knowles and Richard Lewis.[1] Afterwards Forbes was presented with a Bechstein grand pianoforte and his photograph was accepted for hanging in the Lees Hall.

---

[1] There is a legend in the College that, when he left, Richard Lewis was advised to take up a career other than singing or music. If this is true, he has had a very loud and long last laugh, and his Fellowship must give him all the more pleasure.

It will, incidentally, come as no surprise to those who knew that great gentleman and under-rated conductor, the late George Weldon, to learn that he was adamant in his refusal of any kind of remuneration, even in the form of a gift, for his work at the College. The Council could only record their gratitude and appreciation in the minutes.

A new spirit was abroad. Not only did Barbirolli and Weldon conduct the College Orchestra but the University offered accommodation for College staff and students in the University Refectory. Lady Barbirolli returned to take a master class of oboe students and helped to coach the senior ensemble class. When Henry Holst resigned the violin professorship to take a similar post in Copenhagen, it was Sir John Barbirolli who recommended that an attempt should be made to persuade Endre Wolf to leave Sweden and settle in Manchester. Heddle Nash joined the singing teaching staff in 1954, and among other staff appointments in that year were those of Terence Usher, Information Officer of Manchester Corporation, to be professor of the guitar, and Eric Chadwick, a former student, as an organ teacher. Barbirolli, who acted as an external examiner for viola, cello and wind instruments in the diploma examination that year, was elected an Honorary Member at a Council meeting on 20 July, 1954.

But another kind of spirit was abroad, too. Financial stringency was still the national order of the day, and Manchester Corporation, which had grudgingly given the Hallé Concerts Society a grant which bore no comparison with those given to orchestras by other cities, was in no mood to be generous to cultural activities of any kind. At a Council meeting in February, 1954, Leonard Behrens reported that in an informal talk he had had with Norman Fisher, then director of education in Manchester, he had learned that the Education Committee of the City Council was considering further reducing its grant to the College—it had been dropped from £250 to £225 in 1952–3. The Council wrote to Fisher deploring that the first intimation of any dissatisfaction should have come 'in such a brusque guise'. (At the same meeting Cox read a letter from Lady Macdonald, a Council member who represented Lancashire Education Committee, in which she said that the County Council was prepared to consider an application for an increased grant. But she added that in her opinion it would be best if the College 'let sleeping dogs lie' because she believed that the L.C.C. 'had not yet realised that the College was in receipt of Treasury assistance'. Not surprisingly, the Council followed her advice!) In fact Manchester restored its grant to its former level of £250 after Cox had had talks with the Education Committee, and he told the Council in March of his concern over the Burnham Committee's decision to review the grounds on which graduate status was conferred on all holders of the College teachers' diploma who also fulfilled certain other conditions of age and experience. He was not altogether happy with the existing 'set-up' in the College, he said; there were several ways in which tuition and examination fell short of the Burnham requirements and he thought they should be brought more into line with the practice at the Royal Academy of Music.

Parallel with this was the decision to reorganise the school music department and to appoint a woman tutor as its head. The Council also approved admission of instrumental students who were not taking the full course but were of satisfactory standard. The annual report of 1954 summarised the College's policy on school music and training of teachers: 'They feel that the training of teachers and of performers should be carried out by one and the same institution. . . . It is most desirable that teachers should be, in a modest way perhaps, performers . . . and that performers should have the variety of interest and the broadness of outlook that are the mark of the teacher.' Miss Louisa Lamigeon was appointed as 'adviser' on school music, but Dr Andrew became professor in charge of the department, with Miss Lamigeon in charge of a new junior exhibitioners department. All students working for the teachers' diploma now had to take full part in the activities of the school music department, part of which was a series of lectures by university staff. The idea of a junior department, providing special tuition on Saturday mornings, originated from a talk between Cox and Dr Eric James (now Lord James of Rusholme), the then High Master of Manchester Grammar School. The scheme received no encouragement from Norman Fisher nor from the Ministry of Education, but Cox went ahead and as soon as it was announced there were 60 applicants, of whom 20 were accepted. A by-product of Cox's concern for early training was the decision to strengthen the College Council by the election of people deeply interested in education. The advent of Maurice Pariser to chairmanship of Manchester Education Committee won the College a wise new friend and he, Alderman Abraham Moss, Gordon Thorne, then Head of Music, B.B.C. North Region, and Professor R. A. C. Oliver, Manchester University Professor of Education and dean of the faculty of music, were all elected to the Council during 1955.

Early in 1955 Cox and Thom visited the Treasury where they were promised additional aid on the basis of several new principles:

(1) the grant should enable the College to balance its annual account without adding to or drawing on reserves;

(2) the College was to use for current purposes all investment income and donations legally available;

(3) the College, while providing out of revenue for depreciation, would finance any capital improvements either out of past reserves or out of future donations.

The College decided to raise its fees by 25 per cent from the 1956–7 session to bring them into line with the two London Royal colleges, and the Treasury at the end of the year increased its grant by £3,000 a year to £11,500. Cox had drawn the Government's particular attention to the deteriorating state of the College building and its general inadequacy. As he said in the 1955 report:

The facilities and space available . . . are inferior to those of any other comparable institution in the British Isles. . . . The allocation of teaching rooms remains a vexatious problem requiring, for its solution, considerable ingenuity and improvisation; it causes members of the professorial staff, as they are moved from studio to studio, much discomfort and exasperation; it affords students little opportunity to practise on the premises during the inevitable waits between their various lectures and classes. It is ironic, in a city which prides itself rightly on its fine musical tradition, that an institution devoted to the study of music should work under such difficulties.

Yet work it did; and as far as gifted students were concerned this was an exceptional period, as a brief recital of some names will prove. This was the time when the composition students included Alexander Goehr, Peter Maxwell Davies[1] and Harrison Birtwistle; John Ogdon, Brenda Lucas, Lawrence Glover,

[1] Maxwell Davies was on a University music course but received tuition at the College.

David Wilde and Susan Tunnell were among the pianists; the singers included Honor Sheppard, John Mitchinson, Jean Reddy, Joseph Ward, Barbara Robotham, Mary Baines, John Lawrenson and Jolyon Dodgson; Ludmila Navratil and Elizabeth Holbrook were the star viola players; Jennifer Nuttall and Rodney Friend were among violin students; David Ellis, organ and composition; Elgar Howarth was learning the trumpet; Elizabeth Walker and Philip Hill the oboe. Whatever the staff changes, too, replacements were always of high qualification, willing to work in these unsatisfactory conditions. Grahame Clifford left the singing staff because of other commitments, and two Hallé professorial stalwarts retired, Joseph Lingard (flute) and Charles Collier (harp). Both had served for many years and were succeeded respectively by the English Bernard Herrmann (who soon gave way to Peter Lloyd) and Jean Bell. Cox encouraged students, individually and as groups, to perform professionally. Two College string quartets gave school concerts in the Lancashire County Council area, David Ellis won a Royal Philharmonic Society prize for composition, the soprano Jean Reddy won the *Daily Mail's* Kathleen Ferrier Prize and Richard Hall took his New Manchester Group—Goehr, Birtwistle, Ogdon and Peter Maxwell Davies— to perform new music in London. Richard Hall was a remarkable and complex man, a disillusioned composer with more talent than was recognised at the time, but lacking the rebelliousness which might have lifted him out of the rut. As a teacher he was neither forceful nor demanding but somehow he helped men like Goehr and Birtwistle a great deal. Like them he had a speculating mind and an interest in the experimental, also a magnificent irony which kept them, as one of them puts it, 'from going overboard'. Young composers often felt that the College had no interest in them, they were 'extras' who were not bothered as long as they didn't bother anyone else. Yet Goehr, for instance, looked back on his days there with some affection, perhaps because he was left alone to do what he wanted! He was often to be seen poring over scores in the Henry Watson Music Library.

Two other changes merit special record. Harold Dawber died 'in harness' on 14 March, 1956, sadly missed not only for his musicianship but for his 'realism, integrity and lovableness': it was said of him that he neither preached nor practised austerity. Sir John Stopford retired from the Vice-Chancellorship of the University, and consequently from the chairmanship of the College Council, during 1956. This beloved figure, who was elected an Honorary Member, presided at his last annual meeting in November, 1955, when he urged that the College and the University should 'draw still more closely together spiritually and physically' and should 'combine together to obtain and share new premises worthy of their work'. The opportunity which now presented itself might not recur for some very considerable time, he said. Events were to prove this wise counsellor very right indeed. Stopford's successor as Vice-Chancellor, Professor William Mansfield Cooper, became chairman of the Council and presided at his first meeting on 3 October, 1956.

The 1955 annual meeting was also notable as the first occasion on which all students receiving the diploma wore gowns and, in the case of graduates, a specially designed hood. Members of the Council and staff wore academic robes.

During 1956 Dr Eric Wilson's term as Registrar came to an end. No successor was immediately appointed, Miss Dorothy Redhead acting in this capacity. Richard Hall left the staff to become Director of Music at Dartington Hall, Mrs Hislop resigned from the singing staff, and Cecil Cohen from his duties as conductor of the College Orchestra. In his place came Arthur Percival, strongly recommended by Barbirolli. In addition to Hall, the theoretical side suffered by the death of Dr George Armstrong: their places were filled by Leslie Clifton and Robert Elliott, both former students. In December of this year, the Council received a delegation from the teaching staff (Dr Andrew, Gordon Green and Albert Hardie) who presented the case for an increase in salaries, which had not altered since 1948 and were well below those paid in training colleges and at the colleges of art. It was accepted that the case was unanswerable and Cox agreed to approach the Treasury. In April of the following year, the Treasury agreed to a 30 per cent increase for the teaching staff, retaining a small differential between the London rates and Manchester's but agreeing to consider a pension scheme.

In 1956, too, the practice of having representatives of the Board of Professors on the Council was revived after it had been allowed to lapse in Forbes's time because the Royal Charter made no provision for it. (Dawber had been on the Council as an individual and not as a representative of the

9

staff.) One objection had been that their presence might be embarrassing when salaries were discussed, but this proved groundless; and on 19 December, 1956, Lucy Pierce and Clifford Knowles attended the Council meeting.

The College was still without a Registrar throughout 1957. It was decided to advertise the post but the Council recognised that a good salary would have to be offered if a suitable candidate was to be attracted. They therefore first raised Cox's salary to £1,900 a year, with £100 expenses, and offered the Registrarship to Noel E. Kay at £1,200 a year. He assumed his duties in May, 1958.

Cox continuously urged the need for more accommodation. He told the Council in September, 1957, that he had to vacate his own room on one day each week to make room for a professor. Professors were growing tired of teaching 'in holes and corners, cellars and attics' which possessed no amenities, and he had had to hire rooms elsewhere to accommodate the larger intake of students. The Council agreed to a plan for extra studies in the basement of the original building. The Treasury was informed of the urgency of the position, and while it expressed concern it promised nothing and suggested that an appeal be made to local authorities. This eventually yielded £300 towards new pianofortes. It was also decided to raise the fees to £30 a term from September 1958. After the basement had been cleared of rats and some dry rot eradicated, the alterations began and were completed in the autumn of 1958, providing three new studios and an extra administrative room. At the same time came news of an increase in the Treasury grant to £15,000 a year, to be stabilised at that figure for a number of years. During this year a Capella pipe organ was installed, in place of the electronic organ, which had never been really successful. A plan to install a Jardine four-manual organ a few years earlier had been scrapped because of financial considerations.

Academically the most important change at this time was in the College diplomas. Having precipitated the College into setting up its new teacher-training and school music courses, the Ministry of Education now, only a year or so later, decided that music colleges should no longer be responsible for teacher training, only for musical instruction. Teacher training would be covered by an additional year's course in a university education department or training college. So after more long discussions with the Ministry and the Burnham Committee, it was decided to have four College diplomas:

(1) Graduate of the Royal School of Music (Manchester), holders having graduate-equivalent status;
(2) A.R.M.C.M. (School Music);
(3) A.R.M.C.M. (Teacher);
(4) A.R.M.C.M. (Performer).

Holders of any of these were granted qualified teacher status, but after 1959 holders of A.R.M.C.M. (Teacher) were not eligible for consideration for graduate-equivalent status. Students with G.R.S.M. (Manchester) or A.R.M.C.M. (School Music) proceeded for a year either to a university education department or to a training college. These changes brought the College closer to the two Royal colleges in London. But they can still hardly have satisfied Cox, whose concern for a new approach to the whole of musical education was reflected in several sentences of the 1958 annual report when he wrote of the 'hand-to-mouth' basis of work in the College, citing not only the outworn equipment and inadequate premises but the 'lack of provision for the early and systematic training—combining general and musical education—of the talented children who abound in this part of the world' and 'the happy-go-lucky acceptance of three years as a reasonable period for a course in performance, when the most talented musicians find that a lifetime is barely sufficient'. In his tribute to what had been achieved by the junior department in the short time available —'three hours a week for some 33 weeks a year'—he remarked that it showed what might be achieved 'if the training of young musicians in this country were to receive the same serious attention as is given to the training of ballet dancers'.

Marjorie Clementi, a greatly gifted pianoforte teacher, joined the staff of the junior department in 1958. Other changes included the retirement after many years of the Hallé trombone stalwart Sam Holt. One of his former pupils and successor as principal of his section in the Hallé, David Want, succeeded him as trombone professor. Gwilym Jones joined the singing staff and Rudolph Botta, a Hungarian exile, joined the violin staff in place of Martin Milner, who was appointed Leader of the Hallé Orchestra.

And in May, 1958, R. J. Forbes died, aged 79. It can be assumed that in his five years of retirement in Bowdon he looked with pride on the achievements of his successor and took pleasure from the successes increasingly being registered by College students. He had lived to see the College's musical activities on a bigger scale than in the establishment's history; and, as a relief from the tortuous world of finance, let us turn now to review them.

15
The music, 1953–8

Henceforward the College's programmes become more numerous, more ambitious and more public. Cox's accession to the Principalship coincided with the post-war flowering of musical activity in Britain. The austerities of the immediate post-war period were abating, the long fight to win more generous State and civic aid for the arts was being won, music in every shape and form was in demand, and training establishments were playing their full part in this burgeoning of activity. Long past were the days when the Council had to debate whether to admit critics to open practices; long gone was the custom in the newspapers of referring to a student performer as 'a pupil of Mr So-and-So' and never by his or her own name. In the 1950s and 1960s it was possible for a gifted student to make a national reputation while still at College, and several did. The College's opera productions became a bright feature of Manchester's musical life; Barbirolli's conducting of the College Orchestra provided several memorable occasions; yet glamorous as these were, the fundamental background from which they grew was still the open practices, the examination concerts and the Review Weeks. An immediately noticeable feature of the new régime, however, was the shortening of the programmes of the open practices to three or four works instead of—as had occasionally been the case—fourteen or more.

Brenda Lucas played Bach's *Italian Concerto* on 28 October, Laura Birchall, a pupil of Clifford Knowles, played Beethoven's Romance in F on 11 November, and Jean Hindmarsh sang songs by Warlock and Catherine Wilson sang Purcell's 'The Blessed Virgin's Expostulation' on 25 November. On 7 December the College's diamond jubilee was marked by an orchestral concert at which George Emmott played Schumann's piano concerto and George Weldon conducted Dvořák's G major symphony. Staged opera returned at last on 16 and 18 December in the University's Arthur Worthington Hall in Dover Street, a small theatre (now demolished) with several imperfections but a real theatrical atmosphere which counted for a great deal. The first two acts of Donizetti's *L'Elisir d'Amore* were performed under Michael Brierley with Grahame Clifford as producer. Adrianne Sherlock sang Adina, John Mitchinson was Nemorino, Joseph Ward Belcore and Gwilym Jones Dulcamara. The orchestra was led by Davina Hart and the répétiteur was Hazel Vivienne, later to be chorus-master at Sadler's Wells. On the intervening evening the opera class gave a recital in the College, with extracts from Verdi, Mozart, Gounod, Saint-Saëns, Massenet, Rossini and Offenbach. *L'Elisir d'Amore* was performed in full in the following March, for three performances, with the same cast. Grieg's violin and piano sonata, absent from students' concerts for many years, was revived twice by Brenda Lucas and Jean Carr in March, 1954. Davina Hart played Tchaikovsky's violin concerto at an orchestral concert on 1 April, conducted by Cecil Cohen, with George Weldon taking over for Brahms's third symphony. Poulenc's Sonata for Trumpet, Horn and Trombone was played by Elgar Howarth, Barry Castle and Paul Lawrence on 26 May. On 16 June Honor Sheppard sang two songs by Pitfield's composition student Robert Elliott (whom she was eventually to marry) and the name of John Ogdon, a 17-year-old pupil of Claud Biggs, occurred for the first time at this same practice. He played Balakirev's *Tyrolean Dance, Reverie* and *Islamey*. Ogdon had been for several years at Manchester Grammar School whence he won a scholarship to the College. Biggs said of him later: 'From the start I knew he was exceptional. . . . In one week he learned what would take months for other pupils.' On 22 June Catherine Wilson sang three Wolf songs and Ludmila Navratil played five movements from Bach's Suite no. 5 in C minor. On 6 July Sir John Barbirolli conducted the College Orchestra in the Whitworth Hall. The programme was the *Oberon* overture (Weber), *Elgar's* Serenade for Strings, Richard Strauss's first horn concerto (soloist Barry Castle) and Brahms's fourth symphony, a testing evening from which everyone emerged with credit. At a chamber concert conducted by Cecil Cohen on 20 July in the Houldsworth Hall, two of Villa-Lobos's *Bachianas Brasileiras* were performed: no. 1 for two violas and six cellos and no. 5 for soprano and eight cellos (members of Oliver Vella's cello class). Jean Cooney sang three of Mahler's Rückert settings on 21 July (including 'Ich bin der Welt abhanden gekommen') and the following evening, at another examination concert, Joseph Ward, then studying with Heddle Nash, sang Massenet's

'Vision fugitive', Jean Hindmarsh also sang some Massenet and Debussy, and Ludmila Navratil and Geoffrey Arnold played Bliss's viola sonata in D minor.

Ogdon played a sonatina by his fellow student David Ellis on 27 October and another of Robert Elliott's compositions, his Divertimento for Piano Duct, was played on 3 November by the composer and George Emmott. This was preceded by Elsie Thurston's pupil Felicity Harrison's singing of two Handel arias. On 1 December Ogdon played a sonata in one movement by his fellow student Alexander Goehr at an open practice which also contained Webern's Variations, op. 21, played by Keith Sellors, a pupil of Gordon Green, and Hindemith's sonata for clarinet and piano played by Harrison Birtwistle and David Jordan. Jean Reddy sang three of Schubert's most popular songs on 13 December, and 1954 ended with performances of Bach's *Italian Concerto* by Bettie Ackerman and of a suite for oboe and piano by Alan Richardson, with Pat Liversidge as the oboist. Avril Roebuck, another of the galaxy of singers who have been taught by Elsie Thurston, sang the 'Willow Song' and 'Ave Maria' from Verdi's *Otello* on 16 February, 1955. Miss Roebuck may be cited here as a symbol of the hundreds of gifted people lost to music because they put marriage before a career. During her time at the College she sang the title-rôle in *Madam Butterfly* with a touching passion that seemed to herald a distinguished career. Certain details in her performance, particularly her scene with Suzuki as they prepare for Pinkerton's return, linger in my mind while other more famous and probably more accomplished performances fade. She was young, she was fresh-voiced, for those two hours she *was* Butterfly.

John Ogdon played Liszt's *Dante Sonata* at a students' concert on 22 March and at an open practice the next day you could have heard Book I of Brahms's *Paganini Variations* played by Robert Marsh and his *Handel Variations* played by Brenda Lucas. The spring opera performances were of Cilèa's *Adriana Lecouvreur*, the first of a series of lesser-known Italian operas which Cox was to choose as vehicles for developing young voices. It is noteworthy that, in contrast to Forbes, he never selected a Mozart opera, regarding them as too difficult stylistically for students. In *Adriana*, which in a shortened version the students later broadcast, the title-rôle was sung at two performances by Mary Baines and two by Marian Callear.

Similarly Jean Reddy and Elizabeth Davidson divided the Princess. John Mitchinson sang Maurizio, Joseph Ward the Prince and Jolyon Dodgson Quinault (at two performances only). Mary Baines and John Mitchinson were partners, too, at the College orchestral concert on 13 July in the Whitworth Hall when they sang the love duet from Act I of Verdi's *Otello*, conducted by Barbirolli. The solo violinist in Mozart's A major concerto was Endre Wolf's pupil Jennifer Nuttall, and Dvořák's D minor symphony was played, Sir John, as the annual report happily put it, extracting rather more than a quart from a pint pot. The examination concerts in July included Ogdon playing *Islamey*, Birtwistle playing clarinet pieces by Satie, Ravel and Stravinsky and Honor Sheppard singing Dowland.

The new term in October brought two new women singers who were to achieve success, Barbara Robinson, pupil of Mrs Langford, and an eventual winner of the *Daily Mail* Kathleen Ferrier competition, and Barbara Robotham (Elsie Thurston). Some of the open practices at this date if given now by the same artists would have the queues forming. For example, on 8 November Felicity Harrison, with Elizabeth Walker as oboist, sang 'Qui sedes' from Bach's Mass in B minor, Joseph Ward sang Quilter songs, Ogdon played studies by Alkan (a composer it was inevitable he would unearth!), Brenda Lucas played Bach and Jean Hindmarsh sang Schubert. On 15 December Rodney Friend, a pupil of Endre Wolf, played Saint-Saëns's *Introduction and Rondo Capriccioso* and later the same day David Wilde conducted a performance of Mouret's suite *Les Festes de Thalie*, with Honor Sheppard as soloist. Ludmila Navratil's successor as 'star' viola pupil was Elizabeth Holbrook, another Paul Cropper pupil, who played a concerto by K. F. Zelter at an open practice on 1 March. The next weeks were dominated by Ogdon, who played the *Hammerklavier* on 6 March, gave a recital of Chopin, Liszt, Debussy, Bartók, Bach, Brahms and Franck on 15 March, joined Rodney Friend in the Busoni sonata on 20 March, gave another generous recital on 19 April and another on the 24th which ended with the B minor sonata of Liszt, preceded by shorter works by Alkan, Bach, Balakirev (*Islamey*), Chopin, Bartók and Debussy. The making of a virtuoso! Though to mention them is really outside the scope of this book, he was at this date also one of the group of College students who, guided by Richard Hall, performed advanced music at concerts in Manchester. Early works by Goehr, Maxwell Davies, Birtwistle and Ogdon himself were played. Goehr in 1955 had won a French Government scholarship to the Paris Conservatoire. On 20 March also, Brenda Lucas played Liszt, Debussy, Bartók and Chopin, and John Lawrenson sang Quilter's 'Go, lovely rose'. Lawrenson sang *Rigoletto* in part of Act I, Scene 2, during a miscellaneous operatic evening (staged) at the Arthur Worthington Theatre on 31 May and 1 June. Mitchinson was the Duke. Act I, Scene 2, of *Falstaff* was also performed, with Sylvia Jacobs, Barbara Robinson, Avril Roebuck and Barbara Robotham as the women, and *Il Tabarro*, with Mary Baines, Jolyon Dodgson and Mitchinson. A concert performance of Purcell's *Dido and Aeneas* was given on 13 June conducted by George Armstrong, with Avril Roebuck as Dido, Honor Sheppard as Belinda, and Leslie Jones as Aeneas. David Jordan, on 3 July, conducted David Ellis's *Diversions on a Theme of Purcell* for strings at a chamber concert which included Ireland's *Concertino Pastorale*, Delius's *Air and Dance*, Bach's A minor violin concerto (soloist Jean Brier) and Mozart's 'Exsultate Jubilate' (Honor Sheppard). An examination concert (6 July) which included Brenda Lucas playing Franck's Prelude, Chorale and Fugue, Ogdon playing Busoni's second sonata, Hindemith's trumpet sonata played by Elgar Howarth, Mary Baines singing 'Ernani, involami' and Barbara Robinson singing arias from Gluck's *Orfeo* makes exciting reading in the light of hindsight. This was the first year, too, of the junior department, and among those who took part in its first examination concert on 7 July was the pianist Anthony Goldstone, who played a Bach toccata. As was only to be expected, the choice of soloist with Sir John Barbirolli when he conducted on 11 July was Ogdon, who played Brahms's D minor concerto, no less. It was a memorable performance with, as I wrote at the time, 'assurance, power and sensibility . . . [he is] a young man of exceptional accomplishment with the seeds of great brilliance within him'. Well, at least that was one critical assessment of a student that time proved right, though it needed very little perspicacity to make it. Ogdon was already a virtuoso and his artistry and musicianship were astonishingly mature.

The pattern of College music-making under Cox was now becoming settled: two staged operas a year, several orchestral concerts with Barbirolli's (if he was available) as the climax, and an encouragement to the students to form chamber ensembles and a string quartet. College string quartets and a section of the orchestra gave concerts for schools in the Lancashire County Council area, and students were on several occasions 'borrowed' by the Hallé, Liverpool Philharmonic and B.B.C. Northern Symphony Orchestras. In 1957 the operas were Rossini's *William Tell*, on 6 and 7 June, with John Lawrenson as Tell, John Mitchinson as Arnold, Avril Roebuck as Jenny, Barbara Robotham as Hedwiga and Peter Leeming as Walter, and the *Madam Butterfly* production I have already mentioned, with Roebuck as Butterfly, Robotham as Suzuki, Leeming as Sharpless and Brian Casey as Pinkerton, on 25, 26 and 27 November. Michael Brierley conducted both works, which were sung in Italian, the College policy being, roughly, tragedy in the original language, comedy in English. Later the students broadcast Act II of *Butterfly* with Brierley conducting the B.B.C. Northern Orchestra. At an open practice on 27 February Rodney Friend and Ogdon played sonatas by Mozart (K.379), Fricker and Brahms (op. 108). These ensemble teams were taught, or coached, by Forbes, who returned to the College for this purpose and must have received satisfaction from working with students of their quality. They repeated these works at an evening concert in March, adding Busoni's second sonata to the programme. Ogdon played Beethoven op. 109 on 19 March, when Mary Clibran was joined by Rodney Friend in Holst's *Four Songs* for voice and violin. The comparative rarity of an organ concert was given in the Whitworth Hall on 3 April when pupils of Eric Chadwick and Shackleton Pollard—among them Neil Chaffey, Graham Williams and John Askey—played works by Bach, Rheinberger, Franck, Brahms and Bairstow. Malcolm Arnold's wind quintet was played by Lucy Pierce's ensemble class on 29 May and a sonata for solo violin by David Ellis was played by Rodney Friend on 26 June. An extra operatic event in the Arthur Worthington Hall on 25 and 26 June was performances of Mozart's *The Impresario* conducted by David Jordan (singers were Honor Sheppard, Maria Harvey, who later became a member of the Salzburg opera company, and John Lawrenson); a mime, *The Shawl*, with music by Ellis; and the revival of a fantasy *Polonaise*, written by Frank Sladen-Smith, of the famous Unnamed Society, for College students in 1930, when James Bernard had produced it. Interspersed among the stage events were readings of poetry and performances of Mozart's clarinet quintet and Tippett's first piano sonata (Ogdon). On 3 July Barbirolli conducted his own suite from Purcell's *Dramatick Music,* Mozart's 39th symphony, and Brahms's violin concerto, with Jennifer Nuttall as soloist. During the July examination concerts, Ogdon played his own Variations and Fugue, Rodney Friend played Bach's Partita in E, Brenda Lucas played three of the '48', Honor Sheppard sang Duparc, Debussy and Fauré and Elinson's pupil Maureen Challinor played Beethoven's op. 109.

An important new name, a pupil of Elsie Thurston, comes into the programmes on 3 December when the soprano Elizabeth Harwood sang three songs by Mozart, Armstrong Gibbs and Warlock. Sibelius's second symphony was conducted by George Weldon at the orchestra's last concert of the year on 12 December. Review Week from 24 to 28 February, 1958, contained several notable performances: Iso Elinson and Maureen Challinor in Brahms's *Haydn Variations,* Mozart's Serenade K. 361 by Fritz Spiegl's ensemble class, Ogdon playing *Gaspard de la Nuit,* Ogdon and Friend in the *Kreutzer* sonata, Honor Sheppard singing Delius and Purcell, Holst's Fugal Concerto and Stravinsky's *Pulcinella* conducted by David Jordan, and the second symphonies of Beethoven and Brahms conducted by Arthur Percival and George Weldon respectively. Much greater emphasis than in the past was now laid on the work of the drama class, and undoubtedly it had the intended effect of raising the standard of operatic acting. Early in 1958 the class staged the *Antigone* of Sophocles and Shaw's *Man of Destiny* and on 20 and 21 March Anouilh's *Ring round the Moon* was performed with Elizabeth Harwood in the cast. The producer was Sheila Barlow. The 1958 operas were Giordano's *Fedora,* on 22 and 23 May, with Avril Roebuck as Fedora, Brian Casey as Loris and Peter Leeming as De Siriex, and Massenet's *Werther,* on 27 to 29 November, with Casey as Werther, Roebuck as Charlotte, and Elizabeth Harwood singing Sophie on the first two evenings. The leader of the orchestra was Rodney Friend. Acts III and IV were later broadcast by the B.B.C. On 18 June works by composition pupils of Thomas Pitfield were performed, among them Roy Bennett's *Chiaroscuro* for two pianos, David Ellis's quartet for violin, viola, horn and bassoon, John Ogdon's *Studies* and Robert Black's topical *The Congo* for two pianos, speaker and

percussion. On 2 July Barbirolli, in the Houldsworth Hall, con-
ducted a concert in memory of Forbes, beginning with Elgar's
Elegy and including Tchaikovsky's violin concerto (soloist Rodney Friend) and Franck's symphony. The July examination concerts included Felicity Harrison singing *Frauenliebe und Leben,*
Peter Leeming singing King Philip's great aria from *Don Carlos*
and Beethoven's *Thirty-two Variations in C minor* played by
Rowena Ferguson. Bliss's viola sonata was played by Elizabeth
Holbrook and Margaret Brownbridge on 2 December. By then
Jean Reddy, Ogdon and Brenda Lucas had left College and it
remained to be seen if talent of similar exceptional quality
would emerge to fill the gap.

16
Increasing activities

At midsummer 1958 the College had 332 students, 117 men and 215 women. The altered pattern of financial assistance is shown by the fact that only 98 were fee-paying; 234 others were holders of scholarships, exhibitions or grants from the College, the Education Ministry or local authorities. The piano-forte students among them, numbering 158, were fortunate in 1959 when, by spreading payments over three years, the College bought six new Bechstein grand pianos and two new Danemann 'uprights'. In addition Mrs Forbes sold back to the College the Bechstein grand piano with which R. J. Forbes had been presented on retirement. Male piano students were among those who benefited from a bequest to the College of over £12,000 from the estate of Oscar Rothschild for the foundation of scholarships for male students of the piano, violin, composition and allied subjects.

New members of the staff in the 1958–9 session included a distinguished former student, Geoffrey Gilbert, the great flaut-ist, who took over from Peter Lloyd when Lloyd went to the Scottish National Orchestra. Pat Ryan, who had retired from the Hallé Orchestra, returned to the College staff to train woodwind and brass in ensemble work, succeeding Fritz Spiegl. Keith Bond and Ronald Frost joined the harmony department and Otto Freudenthal the pianoforte. Freudenthal, who was 25, was Swedish and had lived in London since 1951. Albert Hardie, for many years a popular member of the staff, died in August of this year. John Wills temporarily agreed to take accompaniment class, and John Ogdon joined the pianoforte staff. 'It is particularly gratifying', Cox said, 'when distinguished old students return to the College to teach and pass on the traditions they themselves received from the past.' It had not been possible to utilise Arthur Percival's services with the College Orchestra as easily as had been hoped, and Michael Brierley, the director of opera, was asked to take the G.R.S.M. conducting class. Brierley also stepped into the breach in April, 1959, when the Registrar, Noel Kay, left the College before the end of his probationary year. He became

Acting Registrar. Dr Andrew was appointed Warden, Laura Birchall became Librarian, and David Jordan, like Miss Birchall a former student, helped with the concert and orchestral schedule. There were changes, too, at this time on the Council. Following a suggestion that some younger members should be co-opted, George Furniss and Rex Hillson were elected; both were already members of the Hallé Committee. Gordon Thorne left the Council on appointment as Principal of the Guildhall School of Music; his successor as Head of B.B.C. Music in the North, Paul Huband, joined in his stead.

College students continued to win prizes. John Ogdon came second in the Liverpool Philharmonic international piano competition and, in 1960, achieved world fame at a stroke by becoming joint winner (with Vladimir Ashkenazy) of the Moscow Tchaikovsky piano competition.[1] Barbara Robinson won the Kathleen Ferrier prize, Barbara Robotham won the Liverpool international singing competition. In 1959 the Sustentation Fund paid for a fourth year's singing tuition for the soprano, Elizabeth Harwood. Despite Cox's urgent recommendation, her local authority had refused to renew her grant. A few months later she too won the Kathleen Ferrier prize, and her subsequent career has justified all the faith shown in her youthful ability.

The year 1960 was the first in which, under the new diploma regulations, graduate students completed a year's professional training in teaching in the University Department of Education. It was felt that keyboard requirements of the new diploma ought to be eased in the case of string players—existing standards made it virtually impossible for a string player of performance standard to obtain a graduate diploma. School teaching practice no longer formed part of the curriculum of the College's teaching diploma, but associate diplomas in teaching would be issued for all instruments including woodwind and brass.

Because of the vitally important and long-drawn-out events which will occupy Chapter 18, the story of the 1960s in the College is largely a record of staff changes, of musical achievements (detailed in the next chapter) and of more individual

[1] To mark this achievement, the College presented Ogdon with an autograph letter in which Tchaikovsky congratulated Brodsky on his 'recent success in Moscow'.

successes: for example David Wilde was placed equal first in the international competition for pianists at Budapest and second in a similar contest in Rio de Janeiro; Barbara Robotham came second in the singing section of the Geneva international competition; Rodney Friend, the violinist, won a television company's competition; John McCabe, pianist and composer, won a Royal Philharmonic Society prize for composition (and has since amply fulfilled this promise); Katrina George won an I.S.M. young artist's award; and Pearl Fawcett, who was a piano student at the College, became world champion piano accordionist.

During 1960 Marjorie Thomas, the contralto, joined the singing staff, Michael Winfield became an oboe teacher, Eva Warren and Brenda Lucas joined the piano department, and John Wills resigned from the accompaniment class, being succeeded by Clifton Helliwell. William Johnson, the bassoon professor, died after a long illness, his pupils being taken over by Charles Cracknell. In 1961 Claud Biggs retired after 20 years' service as piano professor, a very great teacher indeed, and was elected professor emeritus. Oliver Vella was compelled by illness to resign from the cello professorship, being succeeded by Christopher Gough. In 1962 Annie Lord, a piano teacher for over 30 years died, Otto Freudenthal left to join Covent Garden, John Ogdon and his wife Brenda Lucas resigned because of increasing pressure of outside engagements. Their places on the piano staff were taken by Clifton Helliwell and Antoinette Wolf, wife of the violin professor, and by the advent of George Hadjinikos, a Greek pianist whose friendliness, personality and brilliant musicianship soon won him many friends and admirers. The singing staff was strengthened by Ena Mitchell.

Changes in 1963 were the resignation of Shackleton Pollard and his succession on the theoretical staff by Derrick Cantrell, Manchester Cathedral organist. Alfred Livesley, oboe professor, whose department had increased in size, was succeeded by John Williams and Sheila Bickerdike. The Hallé trombonist Terence Nagle took over from David Want.

A new generation of students—the post-Ogdon generation, it may be called—was maintaining the College's new high standards and reputation. It included John McCabe, Janet Hilton the clarinettist, Lynn Brierley oboist, Owen Wynne, Rhiannon Davies, Paul Smith, Anne Howells, Ryland Davies,

Patrick McGuigan, Caroline Crawshaw, Dianne Matthews, Carol Roscoe, Kathleen Smales—all singers—John Davies and John Brown, violinists, Anthony Goldstone and Darina Gibson, pianists and Anthony Halstead, horn. In the junior department was Nichola Gebolys, who in 1964 won first place in the National Youth Piano Competition.

The students, with their grants and scholarships, their opportunities for personal publicity while still under tuition, their subsidised studies abroad and, at the end of it all, their chances of a rapid rise to fame, might be considered much better off than the dedicated people who taught them and who, in 1960, could still not contemplate a decent retirement pension. The Council had long been unhappy about this. Something had been done but not nearly enough; and no one was more deeply concerned about this subject than Jack Thom. Throughout 1960 and 1961 he negotiated with the Treasury for a comprehensive retirement benefits scheme for the staff and in 1962 it came into operation, applying to all teachers who were paid by the hour and who did not receive a pensionable salary. Under this non-contributory scheme a sum of money representing 15 per cent of all earnings was paid into a special fund to be distributed at the Council's discretion to teachers, who had been in the employ of the College for at least 10 years, on attaining the age of 65 or earlier retirement from the College staff. Thom was enabled to bring this scheme into swift effect by the decision of Mr R. A. Moorhouse, trustee of the £8,500 estate of Arthur Jowett which was bequeathed to the College, to allow its use for the pension scheme. The College fees, which had been raised by £4 a term to £34 in September, 1960, were again raised in September, 1961, to £45 a term for all courses. This was on a level with the London Royal schools.

The Jowett bequest was not the only sign that the College was still the object, even in the age of the Welfare State, of generous private patronage. Margaret Furness, an old student, left the College £4,000 for scholarships; Mrs Risegari left £1,000 to found a violin scholarship in memory of her sister Edith Robinson; and Dora Gilson gave £1,000, wishing the interest on it to be used to further the careers of talented and deserving pianoforte students.

Accommodation, or the lack of it, was still the College's biggest problem. Extra rooms had been rented and on four

nights a week the College annexe stayed open from 6 to
8.30 p.m. so that students could practise. At the end of 1961
Cox reported that there might be the chance of buying the
whole or part of premises occupied by a synagogue. It was
also possible that No. 31 Ducie Grove, adjoining the College,
might be on the market. The purchase of the house was completed in 1962; the synagogue too was rented and converted
into seven new studios, which came into use in September,
1962. The College bought six new pianos for the new rooms for
over £7,000, an expenditure that was eased by an increase in
1963 of the Treasury grant by £2,000 to £17,000. Grants by
local authorities hardly equalled this munificence—Manchester, in fact, gave more in 1904 than it did in 1963. This
caught the eye of the Mayor of Hyde at the annual meeting in
1963, when he called Cheshire's £50 'a miserable grant' and
turned to the Lord Mayor of Manchester and told him that
Manchester's £250 was miserable, too. 'I will promise you',
he said, 'that when I go back to Cheshire I shall say, "Well,
you give more than this for a potato-pie supper for the Boy
Scouts."'

In the summer of 1963 the College was saddened by the
sudden death of George Weldon, who had worked unstintingly
for the College Orchestra. In May, 1964, Iso Elinson died
during the interval of a London recital he was giving. He had
been on the professorial staff for 20 years, and his pupils were
taken over by Colin Horsley.

Elinson was a delightful man and a fine musician, as his
pupil David Wilde eloquently described in a memorial
tribute:[1]

One cannot think of Iso without laughing, not at but with him
... he was one of the happiest people I knew.... He was the
living embodiment of the popular image of a musician, with his
big gestures, broken English, long hair and recently a beard. But
all this was the real Iso. He had no affectation, he was just naturally
the sort of man everyone noticed. At College he taught at the
farthest end of the top floor. He never walked there. He always ran,
two or three stairs at a time, and I well remember breathlessly
chasing after him.

Though small, he was immensely strong, and his hands were like
bundles of muscles. Like Horowitz he had studied with Blumenfeld
and believed in developing sufficient finger strength to uphold the

---

[1] *Worthing Gazette*, 15 May, 1964.

10

weight of the whole arm. Accordingly he played with a consistently big, rich sound which I have rarely heard equalled and
never bettered. When he wanted a fortissimo, he dropped those
thick arms on to those powerful fingers and the piano shouted in
exultation. But he could be gentle too. I remember one day, at the
end of a lesson, he played Chopin's 'Study in Thirds' to me—a
spider's web of silvery sound. Two other students came in, and in the
breathless silence that followed he turned to them and said 'You
wanted something?' 'No', was the reply. 'We heard the "Study in
Thirds" and came to listen.'

Mr Wilde's tribute was perceptive. I remember Elinson
playing the posthumous A major Schubert sonata at a Mid-day
Concert in 1952, and I have yet to hear a better performance
technically or one that so perfectly caught the spirit of the
music.

The piano staff was further depleted by the retirement, after
50 years, of Lucy Pierce. She was elected professor emeritus.
Another resignation was that of Endre Wolf. The violin staff
had already been strengthened by Clifford Knowles; and Sir
John Barbirolli, deeply concerned about the quality of string-
player recruits to the orchestras, recommended György Pauk
and Alexander Moskowsky, then principal professor at the
Israeli State Conservatoire and a former member of the
Hungarian Quartet, to the College. Both were engaged and,
in addition, Vilmos Schummy, a former pupil of the Liszt
Academy, Budapest, was engaged as full-time violin tutor.
The importance of maintaining the violin reputation of the
College was reinforced because at this date four of Britain's
major orchestras were led by former R.M.C.M. students: the
Royal Philharmonic (Raymond Cohen), Covent Garden
(Charles Taylor), the L.P.O. (Rodney Friend) and the Hallé
(Martin Milner). Frederick Riddle replaced Paul Cropper
as chief viola professor, Peter Lloyd returned to flute
teaching and Marjorie Thomas resigned. Sir John had conducted a concert in the Free Trade Hall on 24 April, 1964,
when the orchestra contained 50 students and about 60 past
students, of whom 14 had also played under Forbes at the
memorial concert for Brodsky in 1929.[1] This concert launched

[1] They were: Sydney Partington, Norah Winstanley, Margaret Ward,
Philip Hecht, Clifford Knowles and Don Hyden (first and second violins);
Norman Cunliffe (viola); Sydney Wright and Charles Meert (cellos);
Geoffrey Gilbert (flute); Pat Ryan (clarinet); Archie Camden (bassoon);
Sydney Coulston (horn) and Michael Brierley (percussion).

the Forbes Memorial Fund and also marked Sir John's 21st season in Manchester.

The Council had been depleted by the resignation of W. R. Douglas, the surgeon (he died shortly afterwards leaving the College £1,000), and the death of Abraham Moss. New members in 1964 were Edgar Stowell and Richard Godlee, son of Philip and a former cello student under Kathleen Moorhouse.

The College had recently created two Honorary Members— in 1961 Ruth Railton, founder of the National Youth Orchestra, was given this honour, and in 1962 it was bestowed on Richard Wignall, the College solicitor who had drawn up the Royal Charter in 1923. In 1964 it was conferred on Wilhelm Backhaus, then 81, and Jack Thom. The latter had been seriously ill, but his good recovery enabled him to continue as treasurer. The honorary memberships were conferred at a joint ceremony on 20 May, 1965. It had been hoped that Barbirolli would be present to receive his own honorary membership in person and then confer it on his colleagues, but illness prevented his attendance. Lucy Pierce acted in his stead—she had been a pupil of Backhaus 60 years earlier and had taught Jack Thom —and reminded the audience that it was Thom who had won the staff their pension scheme.

Another sadness had befallen the College on the eve of the 1964 annual meeting when Dr Andrew had died a few hours after signing diplomas with the Principal. He was succeeded as Warden by Dr John Wray, organ scholar of Keble, who had been director of music of the City of London School. Verdi's *Requiem* was performed on 31 March, 1965, in memory of Dr Andrew. Cox paid tribute to him in the programme:

There surely lived no more lovable a man. Generally, with 'lovableness' there goes a certain disorderliness or absentmindedness. Not so with Dr Andrew; he never forgot—he always forgave —and nothing was ever misplaced or left undone. When he died his in-tray was empty, his reports were all filed and his schedule of examinations was prepared: a model to any aspiring and efficient business executive, though music and education were his life.

Andrew had for some years been a member of the Council; another resignation from that body in March, 1965, was that of Gerald Sanville. In January, 1965, the author of this book was elected to the Council (thereby, at that date, giving it two members under the age of 40, the other being Richard Godlee) and later in the year Dora Gilson was elected to represent the

College staff; Sir Robert Platt resigned on his retirement to Cambridge (and, a little later, the House of Lords). In May, 1965, the College also honoured one of its most famous sons, Alan Rawsthorne, on his 60th birthday, with a concert of his works and a party. These social occasions, so pleasant and combining dignity with informality in a remarkably effective way, bore in every respect the imprint of Freddie Cox's personality. In him a natural sense of fun and a perennially youthful delight in the lighter side of life are the obverse of his dedication to his job and his kindliness and loyalty towards his staff and students. With no Mancunian associations before he came to the city in 1949, he soon developed an over-riding pride in the College's traditions and achievements. In his quiet firm manner, combining tolerance with high principles, he perhaps resembled Charles Hallé more closely than any other of his predecessors; and to his skill as a singing teacher the successes of College students since 1953 bear ample witness. In John Wray and Michael Brierley he had two lieutenants who acknowledged their Principal's determination to maintain and improve all that the College stood for; and it was indeed fortunate for the institution that at this time of expansion in face of heavily increasing financial responsibilities the treasurer should have been Jack Thom, whose diffident, apologetic manner concealed a superb fiscal brain and a shrewdness which classed his services to the College with those of Charles Lees and Gustav Behrens.

The staff in 1965 was larger than ever before in the College's history: 12 on the singing staff; 17 pianoforte—strengthened by the addition of the composer and executant Franz Reizenstein, when Gordon Green asked to reduce some of his teaching duties—five violin; four clarinet; three oboe; 17 harmony and general musicianship; one composition and a variety of smaller classes. In the next few years there were, of course, several changes, often necessitated as in the case of John McCabe by the encroaching demands of a wider career. Additions to the piano staff included Marjorie Clementi (from the Junior department), Maureen Challinor, Patricia Griffin, Daphne Spottiswoode, Robin Harrison and David Wilde. William Waterhouse took over the bassoon professorship from Charles Cracknell, and Ludmila Navratil and Elizabeth Holbrook joined the viola staff. Sydney Coulston returned to the horn staff. In 1967 Raphael Sommer became principal cello professor and Yossi Zivoni in 1968 succeeded György Pauk when Pauk left to become senior violin professor at the Royal Academy of Music. The number of students was now over 450 and another house in Ducie Grove was bought and turned into studios as a contribution towards relieving the ever-increasing strain on accommodation.

Deaths and retirements of long-serving members both of staff and Council are the milestones of the College's history. Lady Macdonald resigned from the Council because she had gone to live in Anglesey, thereby ending a long association. Pat Ryan and Maria Valgimigli retired from the staff (the latter being succeeded by Ernesta Partilora), as did Clifford Knowles on his appointment as leader of the Royal Liverpool Philharmonic Orchestra. Miss Dorothy Porter, having served on the Council for many years as representative of Manchester Education Committee, was elected a member in her own right, but resigned in 1969. Dora Gilson, who had completed 52 years on the staff both as a singing teacher for many years and as pianoforte teacher, retired but remained an active member of the Council. Sam Holt, the trombonist, and Richard Wignall, Honorary Member and solicitor, died in 1967; Lucy Pierce died aged 82 in February, 1968: the College had been her life and her devotion to it had perhaps obscured her own fine talent as a pianist, though this was recognised in Manchester at any rate.

A former violin student whose name had been more widely known, Olive Zorian, died in 1965 aged only 49. A fund was established in her name to buy her valuable 1721 Gagliano violin (which had once belonged to her teacher Arthur Catterall) and to present it to the College for the use of its most talented students. In London on 26 November, 1966, Benjamin Britten and Peter Pears, who had performed so often with the Zorian Quartet and with Olive in the English Opera Group Orchestra, took part in a concert for the fund; and in the Free Trade Hall, Manchester, on the following evening those taking part in a similar concert included John Ogdon and Brenda Lucas, Elizabeth Harwood, Rodney Friend and Isobel Flinn. During the evening the violin was handed to its first holder, Jonathan Sparey.[1] After the purchase of the violin, over £1,000 remained which was handed to the College. Of this £200 was

[1] On 16 July, 1969, the violin was stolen from the College and has not been recovered.

sent to the Aldeburgh Festival as a donation towards the building of The Maltings concert-hall at Snape where a commemorative tablet was placed, and placed also in the new Maltings, rebuilt after the 1969 fire.

In April, 1966, tuition fees were raised to £180 p.a. The College continued to be the recipient of private generosity on a princely scale both in money and in musical instruments. Hallé's last surviving pupil Rosa d'A Blumberg, left her Bechstein concert grand pianoforte to the College; Joseph Lingard, flute professor for many years, gave it an historically valuable Böhm-Mendler flute; Geoffrey Galloway Payne left the College £8,000 in memory of his parents; Mrs Lucy Standen left £4,000 to found an organ scholarship; Mrs Herman Bantock gave by deed of covenant over £100 a year to help viola students; by the generosity of Jean Dalzell and Lucy McLaren Thompson who died in October, 1967, and September, 1966, respectively the College received a sum of about £12,000 to further the careers of talented pianists; talented singers and pianists from Accrington and district were helped by the income on a £650 trust fund in memory of Tom Bridge; a bequest of £20,000 to help piano students was made by George H. Lees; Lucy Pierce left the College £1,000 and her valuable library; another library to come to the College was that of the singer Derek Oldham, although he had not been a student there; and Dora Gilson made two further gifts, one of £2,000 and the other of £1,000, stipulating that the income should be available to past as well as to present students of talent and integrity. This was the first trust of that nature in the College's existence. Miss Gilson's name, too, had for many years headed subscribers to the Sustentation Fund. In all these ways people expressed their devotion to the ideal of music as exemplified by the College. Old and unsuitable the buildings may have been, exasperating the working conditions, but the spirit of the place triumphed over these disadvantages.

In September, 1967, a change was made in administration. Cox had told the Council that both he and Brierley, who had been confirmed in the post of Registrar since January, 1964, needed assistance with their duties. Cox still undertook a large amount of teaching and was also a member of various committees, while Brierley's operatic work was also increasing. Since, for reasons which will be explained in Chapter 18, the post of Registrar had ceased to exist in its old form, Clifton

Helliwell was appointed Assistant to the Principal and Brierley was released to devote himself wholly to operatic training. Helliwell's work in the accompanist and ensemble class was of the highest distinction. His rather diffident manner might leave a superficial acquaintance unprepared for the sterner seam in his personality which admirably equipped him to be a loyal, efficient and dependable aide-de-camp. The new system had been in operation for only just over a year when Brierley died suddenly, an irreparable loss, as the annual report rightly said, because he had an extraordinary gift for inspiring students to give of their best in opera productions. In his memory past and present students sang extracts from two of the operas he had conducted and Dr Wray conducted Brahms's *Requiem*. A few days after Brierley's death, news came that Reizenstein too had died. They were both men who would have insisted that 'the show must go on', and Brierley would have been pleased that the production of *Werther* on which he was working was given as planned, conducted at short notice by Roger Norrington. Some of the students who had sung recently under his guidance were well launched into their professional careers: Anne Howells and Ryland Davies, for example, Caroline Crawshaw, Vivien Townley and Norman Welsby (B.B.C. opera prize-winners and recipients of contracts with, respectively, Covent Garden and Sadler's Wells). Instrumental students, too, continued to shed reflected glory on the College, notably Anthony Goldstone the pianist, John Bimson, appointed first horn of the B.B.C. Northern Symphony Orchestra while only 18, and Janet Hilton, international prize-winner and much in demand as a clarinet soloist.

Staff changes in 1969 were necessitated in the piano department by the death of Antoinette Wolf, the resignation from full-time teaching of Elsie Dove and the departure of David Wilde on his appointment as resident pianist at Lancaster University. Sven Weber and Dennis Murdoch were of great help and the staff was further strengthened by the addition of Ryszard Bakst, former professor at Warsaw Conservatoire. Terence MacDonagh joined the oboe staff, although his orchestral commitments prevented his visiting the College as much as he would have liked. Ena Mitchell increased her College duties in anticipation of the retirement from full-time work during 1970 of Mrs Langford.

In June, 1968, the Council decided to confer Honorary Membership on Sir Percy Lord, chief education officer of Lancashire County Council, and on Sir Neville Cardus, the Manchester-born music critic whose 80th birthday was on 2 April, 1969. The ceremony was fixed for 6 May, 1969. Some weeks before that date Sir Percy died and the Council thereupon conferred Honorary Membership on its vice-chairman, Leonard Behrens, who at 78 was still as lively and provocative in his service to music in Manchester as his father had been. On the day itself Cardus was unable to travel to Manchester to be 'invested' because of gout—'possibly inherited from Sir Thomas Beecham', he wrote to Cox in a letter read out at the ceremony—but Sir John Barbirolli was admitted officially to the Honorary Membership he had held for 15 years and seemed delighted to be escorted to the platform by two of the prettiest girl students. Lord Harewood presided genially over a happy occasion. For Behrens it was an acknowledgment of a family tradition indelibly written into the history of Manchester's cultural life, and for Sir John it was a tangible demonstration of what his friend Freddie Cox had once written: 'It is a source of the greatest encouragement to students and staff alike that a musician of such pre-eminent international standing as Sir John should show a personal interest in the College and its activities as conductor, examiner, adviser and friend.'

Present at that ceremony were Jack Thom and his wife. Thom, after completing a large-scale reinvestment programme with certain College funds, had resigned from the treasurership in December, 1968, handing over to Simon Towneley, who had joined the Council in October, 1967. For once the unemotional words of the minutes are sufficiently eloquent of what was owed to Thom:

> The Council expressed their very great sorrow at the news. He had been so much part of the Council and the College for so many years that it would be difficult to think of either without him. The debt the College owed him was such that no expression of gratitude could adequately indicate the measure of their indebtedness . . . he must surely know what a secure and lasting place he held in the affection and esteem of all his colleagues.

The truth of those words can be judged from the chapter with which this book ends, an account of the long, intricate, and often frustrating events which led to the foundation of a new College of Music. Thom's last official words as treasurer were to point out that, since it opened, the College had received bequests of over £120,000. By the time the new college was open the R.M.C.M. would take with it trust funds of the order of £200,000. 'We bring to the new concern physical assets,' he said, 'but of far greater importance we come with a heritage and record of which we may well be proud.'

Part of that heritage was the freely given service of men like Thom. No one can tell what inroads on his precarious health were made by the hours he spent on College financial business and in the sub-committees dealing with the negotiations for the new college, but however despondent the latter sometimes made him, he never lost heart. Whatever imperfections successive Councils may have had, the fact that their members were giving their time, experience and energy because of enthusiasm for music and its practitioners has been a source of strength to the College and of support to the Principals. Meetings were frank and friendly and owed much to the link, through the chairman, with the University. This link and the intimacy of a 'volunteer' Council will be lacking in the new college. It is to be hoped that a governing body of aldermen, councillors and co-opted individuals, together with local government officers, will promote a similar splendid spirit.

17
The music, 1959–70

Before chronicling the long series of negotiations for the formation of a new College of Music, it is pertinent to examine the musical activities of a 10-year period, the busiest in the College's existence, because they give meaning to J. H. Thom's words about a heritage.

On 25 February, 1959, at an open practice, a pianoforte pupil of Gordon Green, John McCabe, played Brahms's Scherzo in E flat minor, thus beginning a career in which brilliance as a pianist and as a composer have gone side by side. The Review Week in March contained several interesting performances: Felicity Harrison sang Brahms's 'Vier ernste Gesänge', Rowena Ferguson and Elizabeth Weir played Stravinsky's Sonata for Two Pianos, Jennifer Nuttall and Otto Freudenthal played violin and piano sonatas by Brahms (op. 100) and Beethoven (op. 30, no. 2), Pat Ryan conducted the wind ensemble in Gounod's *Petite Symphonie*, Barbara Robotham and Robert Jones sang Britten's *Abraham and Isaac* canticle, Iso Elinson, Endre Wolf and Sydney Coulston played Brahms's horn trio, George Weldon conducted Brahms's first symphony and Gordon Thorne conducted Bach's cantata, no. 51, with Sylvia Jacobs, Honor Sheppard and Avril Roebuck as the singers, violin obbligati played by Endre Wolf and Clifford Knowles, and Robert Elliott providing harpsichord continuo. John Davies, a pupil of Endre Wolf, played Mozart's B flat sonata on 18 March. On 25 April singing students gave a concert of sacred and secular extracts, the first half including the quartet from Rossini's *Stabat Mater*, the quartet 'Come, everyone' from *Elijah* and the 'Benedictus' from Mozart's *Requiem*. In the second half, the duet from the last act of *Butterfly*, King Philip's aria from *Don Carlos* and the *Rigoletto* quartet were sung. The performers were Elizabeth Harwood, Avril Roebuck, Sylvia Jacobs, Barbara Robotham, Felicity Harrison, Jolyon Dodgson, Peter Leeming, and Brian Casey.

The new Concert Grand Bechstein was inaugurated on 6 July by Iso Elinson playing Beethoven's op. 111 and Endre and Antoinette Wolf in Brahms's D minor sonata. At the examination concerts Elizabeth Harwood sang 'Ach, ich liebte' from *Die Entführung*, Rodney Friend played a sonata by a fellow student, Ian Gleaves. Felicity Harrison sang Mahler's *Lieder eines fahrenden Gesellen*, Lucy Pierce's ensemble class chose Walton's piano quartet and Endre Wolf's distinguished quartet class—Jennifer Nuttall, John Davies, Elizabeth Holbrook and John Catlow—played Debussy's quartet. Barbirolli conducted two symphonies on 10 July, Mozart's 41st and Vaughan Williams's *London*, the latter being recorded and broadcast later. At open practices in September Rodney Friend played Mozart's fifth concerto, Bach's D minor Partita and Paganini Caprices. Owen Wynne, a counter-tenor, sang songs by Wilson and Arne on 28 October and Jill Spence (Elsie Thurston's pupil, as was Wynne) sang Bach and Schubert songs on 18 November. There was only one opera during 1959, the proposed spring performance of *Tosca* having been cancelled because of a severe flu epidemic: on 23, 24 and 25 November Bellini's *La Sonnambula* was performed as a vehicle for the already brilliant Amina of Elizabeth Harwood. Brian Casey was Elvino, and the opera was produced by Sheila Barlow, the first of her many splendid contributions to the College's operatic laurels. The drama class's choices this year were Clemence Dane's *Granite*, Terence Rattigan's *Separate Tables* and André Obey's *Noah*. On 26 November the College Quartet—Friend, Davies, Holbrook and Catlow—played in the City Art Gallery, choosing Mendelssohn's op. 44, no. 1, Beethoven's op. 18, no. 2 and the Debussy. These four students were an especially good team and they gave several 'outside' concerts in the following 12 months. On 4 December George Weldon conducted Sibelius's fifth symphony and Mozart's C minor piano concerto (soloist Margaret Brownbridge) and at the last open practice of the year, on 9 December, the name Anne Howells appears, singing Italian songs by Bononcini, Caldara and Paisiello.

The year 1960 began with a concert in the Free Trade Hall, organised on the initiative of the students in aid of World Refugee Year. Hundreds were turned away and box office receipts were over £800. David Jordan conducted, Rodney Friend was leader and John Ogdon, who since leaving College had studied with Egon Petri, Denis Matthews and Gordon Green, and was now launched on his fine career, returned to play Beethoven's G major concerto. Elizabeth Harwood and

Brian Casey sang an extract from Act I of *Rigoletto* and the symphony was Dvořák's *New World*. At open practices in February and March, Nanette Degg played Beethoven's op. 90 sonata, and Erika Harrison Bach's *English Suite*. Review Week in March included the College Quartet in Hindemith's third string quartet (of which they made a speciality) and Beethoven's op. 59, no. 1, a chamber concert under Arthur Percival at which Felicity Harrison sang Berkeley's *Four Poems of St Teresa of Avila* and Ruth Waterman played Mozart's third violin concerto (K.216), and a full orchestral concert under Weldon, with Elgar's *In the South*, Dvořák's G major symphony and Brahms's violin concerto, soloist Rodney Friend. The soprano Dianne Matthews sang music by Bononcini, Cesti and Jommelli at the open practice on 18 May, Dora Gilson's pupil Meriel Dickinson sang Wolf's 'Verborgenheit' and 'In dem Schatten' on 15 June and John Catlow played Elgar's cello concerto (first two movements) on 22 June. The drama class performed two Yeats 'plays for dancers', *The Dreaming of the Bones* and *At the Hawk's Well* on 29 June and followed them the next evening with 'The Seven Ages of Costume in Shakespeare', which gave the attractive girls a chance to wear pretty clothes from various periods. At an examination concert on 5 July Owen Wynne sang Dowland and Rossiter, Jill Spence sang Schubert and John McCabe played a Nielsen Chaconne and his own Five Impromptus. Victoria Sumner appeared on 5 July as Elinson's piano pupil in Chopin's B minor Scherzo and the next evening as Mrs Langford's singing pupil in Tatiana's Letter Song from *Eugene Onegin*. The Michaelmas Term opened with David Jordan conducting Bartók's Concerto for Orchestra and Mozart's fourth violin concerto (soloist John Davies) at the College of Science and Technology. (Incidentally on 4 July Elizabeth Weir had become the first student to play Bartók's *Allegro Barbaro* in a concert programme.) Now that Rodney Friend had left to join the London Mozart Players the College Orchestra was led by Barry Griffiths. On 28 November Ruth Waterman played Bach's Partita no. 3 and a young tenor, Ryland Davies, sang 'Sebben crudele' by Caldara and 'Amarilli' by Caccini. Barbirolli's concert with the orchestra was on 8 December when Erika Harrison played Mozart's 21st piano concerto and the symphony was Brahms's second. The operas in 1960 were both by Puccini—*Tosca* on 18, 19 and 20 May, with Mary Baines as

Tosca, Edwin Fitzgibbon as Cavaradossi, Douglas Stark as Scarpia and Patrick McGuigan, Paul Smith and Rhiannon Davies in small parts. *La Bohème* was performed on 23 and 25 November, with Mary Baines as Mimi, Elaine Hewitt (Musetta), John Winfield (Rodolfo), Patrick McGuigan (Marcel) and Paul Smith (Colline).

Beethoven's *Archduke* trio was played by Erika Harrison, John Davies and John Catlow on 15 February and a week later five of Vaughan Williams's *Ten Blake Songs* were performed by Ruth Stewart and James Hunt (oboe). The orchestra, under David Jordan and augmented by 15 former students to a total of 80, played in the Free Trade Hall on 14 February in aid of the Leonard Cheshire Homes. Otto Freudenthal played Beethoven's fifth piano concerto and the main orchestral work was Rimsky-Korsakov's *Scheherazade*. Barry Griffiths and Rosemary Hayes played Debussy's violin sonata on 1 March, which they repeated on 20 March at the first Review Week concert. They were preceded by Ruth and Wendy Waterman in Mozart's B flat sonata. Beethoven's octet, op. 103, was a comparative rarity played on 21 March. On the 22nd John McCabe played Liszt, and Maureen Smith played the Scherzo Tarantelle by Wieniawski. The College Quartet—whose members were now John Davies, Angela Caldwell, Barry Griffiths and John Catlow—ended the week with three quartets, including the *Quartetto Lirico* of Matyás Seiber and Schubert's D minor quartet. On 18 May George Weldon conducted the orchestra (now led by John Davies) at a Free Trade Hall concert in aid of Camp Lorch refugees. Erika Harrison was again the soloist, in Liszt's E flat concerto. Mary Baines sang arias from *La Forza del Destino*, and the symphony was Brahms's C minor. Another string quartet of younger students was now playing together and 'challenging' the seniors: John Brown, John Bradbury, Andrew Thomas and Martin Robinson played Haydn's op. 76, no. 1, at an examination concert on 11 July (when John Catlow also played Hindemith's unaccompanied cello sonata), Beethoven's op. 18, no. 4, on 12 July and accompanied Owen Wynne in Elizabethan songs and songs by Purcell the following evening. The Waterman sisters played Franck's sonata on the 14th, preceded by John McCabe's performance of Beethoven's *Thirty-two Variations*. During the five examination concerts songs performed included Gurney's 'Desire in Spring' and 'Spring', Warlock's 'Sleep', Mussorgsky's

'Nursery Songs', Schubert's 'Die Junge Nonne', Strauss's 'Wie-genlied', Purcell's 'Hark the Echoing Air', Milhaud's 'La Tourterelle', Fauré's 'Nell' and Duparc's 'Au pays'—all the singers being pupils of Elsie Thurston, whose consistent variety and range of choice mark her out year after year.

Open practices in the autumn began on 25 October with a young soprano, Janet Hilton, singing Scarlatti and Caldara. Versatile Miss Hilton's voice was soon to be overshadowed by her gifts as a clarinettist, but her singing teachers were convinced that her success vocally could have equalled her instrumental prowess. On 20 November, the orchestra—which by now had quite a busy independent life, touring to Cumberland, Blackpool and Staffordshire—took part with the Hallé Choir at an Albert Hall concert conducted by Eric Chadwick at which was given the first Manchester performance of Britten's *Cantata Academica*. The four soloists were Sylvia Jacobs (now returned to the College as a teacher), Anne Howells, Ryland Davies and Patrick McGuigan. Miss Jacobs and McGuigan were the soloists also in Brahms's *Requiem*. On 6 December McCabe played three Messiaen preludes and on 13 December the 'senior' quartet played McCabe's *Partita* for string quartet, and Jill Spence sang six of Pitfield's songs. The College was the venue for many of the concerts given by the newly formed Manchester Institute of Contemporary Arts and although these are not strictly student activities, students often took part and one very famous ex-student, John Ogdon, on 25 October played Messiaen's complete *Vingt regards sur l'enfant Jésus*, 'a feat of endurance physically and of concentration intellectually' wrote J. H. Elliot in *The Guardian*, wondering at the same time whether Messiaen was not 'a Massenet in wolf's clothing'.

The 1961 opera productions were of Gluck's *Orfeo* on 11, 12 and 13 May, conducted by David Jordan, with Rhiannon Davies in the name-part, Betty Pratt as Eurydice, Elaine Hewitt as Amor and Jill Spence as the Blessed Spirit. The ballet, as in previous College productions, was provided by members of the Hammond School of Dancing, Chester, never more effectively than in this production, which was otherwise memorable for Miss Davies's fine singing. On 29 and 30 November and 1 December Brierley conducted *The Barber of Seville*, with Ryland Davies as Almaviva, McGuigan as Bartolo (very funny), Jean Langfield as Rosina, Paul Smith as Basilio and

a new young singer Kenneth Langabeer as Ambrogio. Sets
were designed and made by the Regional College of Art, and
for *Orfeo* the costumes had been designed and made by the
Domestic and Trades College. During 1960–1 nearly 50 complete programmes were arranged by the College for various
music societies (for example, the chamber choir sang with the
Manchester Wind Ensemble in Stravinsky's Mass) and, on an
average, no evening during term passed without one or more
students performing in public. Typical of the programmes
arranged for other societies was that given on 3 February,
1962, for the National Federation of Music Societies: string
quartets by Schubert and Hindemith, part of Franck's sonata
played by the Watermans, operatic arias sung by McGuigan,
Langabeer and Jill Spence, Lieder sung by Meriel Dickinson
and Falla's *Spanish Songs* sung by Anne Howells.

Now must be chronicled one of the most memorable artistic
events in the College's history, the three performances on 8, 9
and 10 March, 1962, of Debussy's *Pelléas et Mélisande*, sung
in English (alas) but given in full, with a 60-minute interval
between Acts II and III during which the audience could have
a meal at the University. This was Debussy's centenary year
and in recalling this production I can do no better than quote
the review which appeared in the magazine *Opera* in May,
1962:

Sheila Barlow's production . . . brought out to a remarkable degree
the opera's pre-Raphaelitism: the preoccupation with sickness and
death, the veiled but none the less acute sexuality personified
by Mélisande's sensuousness yet her remoteness, the touch of
sadism in Golaud's assault on his wife. It was astonishing to observe
how students had absorbed the work's atmosphere and were trans-
lating it into their actions and voices. Yet this was always a
thoroughly operatic production. Not too much emphasis was
placed upon symbolism, and the characters emerged not as shadows
but as warm-blooded people caught up in a timeless drama. . . .
The orchestral playing was quite astoundingly good, rarely tenta-
tive, often extremely beautiful and always with a professional
polish. Michael Brierley, the conductor, guided his young players
expertly and was particularly considerate towards the singers. No
one would have dared foretell so much success for a student venture. The only non-student in the cast was Joseph Ward (Pelléas)
who was at the R.M.C.M. before joining Covent Garden. He had
the advantage not only of a voice of the true Pelléas timbre but
also of looking the part almost to perfection. His whole performance
was virile and sensitive, lit by flashes of intuitive artistry which

promise well for the future. Dianne Matthews (Mélisande) sang with the richness which the part requires if there is to be no suggestion of insipidity. She looked like a Rossetti woman. . . . Here was a genuine tragic heroine, strange, bewildered and passionate. . . . Altogether this was an operatic achievement which will long be talked about in Mancunian musical circles.

The Golaud of Patrick McGuigan was also remarkably distinguished, and in the small part of Geneviève Anne Howells first caught eye and ear. She had been a pupil before she went to the College of Alfred Higson, the famous conductor of the prize-winning Sale and District Choir. It would not be too much to claim that this and other College opera productions precipitated a new hunger in Manchester for a permanent opera company and an opera house and played their part in encouraging the ambitious scheme for a civic arts centre propounded by Maurice Pariser. Alas, the enthusiasm abated.

More of an exceptionally rich crop of vocal talent was heard at a song recital for Manchester Organists' Association held at the College on 31 March, when Ryland Davies sang Caccini, Pergolesi and Gluck ('O del mio dolce ardor'), Sylvia Jacobs sang Brahms Lieder, Jeannette Godard (accompanied by John McCabe) sang Gurney and Warlock, Anne Howells sang Falla, Jill Spence Wolf and Schumann, Barbara Robotham Mahler and Hélène Pax Fauré, Franck and Messiaen. At an open practice three days earlier Janet Hilton was the clarinettist with Andrew Thomas (viola) and Isobel Flinn (piano) in Mozart's E flat trio (K.498). She played in Mozart's clarinet quintet at the final Review Week concert on 6 April, when Bartók's sixth quartet and Brahms's A minor quartet, op. 51, no. 2 were played. Earlier in the week McCabe played Debussy and Ravel, his Concerto for Chamber Orchestra was conducted by David Jordan, David Lloyd played Schubert's A minor sonata, op. 143, John Brown and McCabe played Debussy's sonata, and Anne Howells, Andrew Thomas and Penelope Smith performed Brahms's two songs, op. 91, for contralto, viola and pianoforte. The Saturday of Review Week was given to the junior exhibitioners, among them in this year the pianist Nichola Gebolys. At the July examination concerts McCabe played the Schubert A minor sonata, Owen Wynne sang Schütz and A. Scarlatti, Erika Harrison played Beethoven's op. 109 sonata, Anne Howells sang Brahms, including the 'Sapphische Ode' and 'Die Mainacht', Hindemith's viola sonata was performed by Andrew Thomas and Russell Lomas and his *The Four Temperaments* was played by the chamber orchestra under David Jordan.

More Hindemith, his clarinet sonata, was played at an open practice on 31 October by Janet Hilton and Penelope Smith, Miss Hilton appearing a fortnight later singing Schumann songs. At the same practice, Anthony Goldstone, now a pupil of Derrick Wyndham, played Schumann's *Carneval*. On 21 November Sonia Wrangham was the oboist in Mozart's oboe quartet (K.370). On 4 December Andrew Thomas and Russell Lomas played Rawsthorne's viola sonata, Gillian Sarple sang Britten's *Charm of Lullabies* and John Davies played Bach's unaccompanied sonata, no. 2, in A minor. A new soprano, pupil of Elsie Thurston, sang Bach's 'Break in Grief' and two of Kennedy-Fraser's *Songs of the Hebrides* on 5 December. This was Caroline Crawshaw. On the 12th the 1962 open practices ended with Erika Harrison playing Schubert's A major sonata and John McCabe playing Elliott Carter's Sonata (1945–6). The autumn opera production, as strong a contrast to *Pelléas* as could have been found, was Rossini's *The Italian Girl in Algiers*, conducted by Brierley, on 14, 15 and 16 November, with Anne Howells as Isabella, Dianne Matthews as Zulma, Jean Langfield as Elvira, Paul Smith (the Arkel of *Pelléas*) as the Bey, Ryland Davies as Lindoro and Patrick McGuigan as Taddeo. John McCabe was répétiteur and Caroline Crawshaw one of the assistant stage managers—an all-star cast all round, in fact, and a production that caught the fun and sparkle of the music more successfully than some professional productions. Drama Class productions since October, 1961, had been of Lorca's *House of Bernarda Alba*, with Anne Howells, Jill Spence and Dianne Matthews in the cast, Edward Percy's *Ladies in Retirement*, and Enid Bagnold's *The Chalk Garden*.

The year 1963 opened with Sir John Barbirolli conducting the College Orchestra in the Whitworth Hall in Dvořák's seventh symphony, Mendelssohn's violin concerto (soloist Maureen Smith), the 'Salce' and 'Ave Maria' from Verdi's *Otello* (soprano, Dianne Matthews) and Wolf-Ferrari's overture to *The Secret of Susanna*. 'Perhaps there was occasional loss of perspective', wrote J. H. Elliot of *The Guardian* about the symphony, 'but there was never any lack of enthusiasm or

11

understanding. The performers were clearly inside the music and were not merely converting notes into sound.' He was impressed, too, by Maureen Smith's interpretation—'a more serious and thoughtful reading than the work usually receives . . . it was agreeable to find a young soloist revealing so much originality of outlook without stretching the framework of the music'. At the first open practice on 23 January, for the first time in College history, works for piano-accordion were played, by Pearl Fawcett, followed rather prosaically by Schumann's *Études Symphoniques,* played by Russell Lomas. Another Thurston pupil destined to achieve much, Vivien Townley, sang at the open practice on 6 February—Purcell's 'Hark the Echoing Air' and Gluck's 'O del mio dolce ardor'. This was followed by Shostakovich's cello sonata, played by Margaret Greenlaw and Michael Grady. Pearl Fawcett played nine piano-accordion items on 20 February at a concert at which the senior quartet played Schubert's Quartettsatz and Schoenberg's *Ode to Napoleon* was recited by Patrick McGuigan with George Hadjinikos (piano), John Davies (violin), Angela Caldwell (violin), Barry Griffiths (viola) and, from the Northern School, Ian Rudge (cello). This last work was repeated by the same artists at a M.I.C.A. concert at the University Faculty five days later when it was introduced by Procter-Gregg's successor in the chair of music, Professor Hans Redlich. Hadjinikos's championship of the music of his fellow-countryman Skalkottas meant that Manchester heard several of this composer's works at a time when they were unknown elsewhere in Britain.

The opera in March, on the 13th, 14th and 16th, was as ambitious a choice as *Pelléas*—a shortened version of Wagner's *Parsifal,* with Rhiannon Davies as Kundry, Paul Smith as Gurnemanz, Alan Ward as Klingsor and Kenneth Langabeer as Parsifal. (Act II had been sung on 6 February at a Manchester Mid-day Concert.) The fame of the College's opera productions had spread, and the chief critic of *The Times,* William Mann, attended the first night. He found the production

remarkably successful in conveying the simple spiritual grandeur of Wagner's last work as well as the flooding, languishing richness of this still curiously elusive music. . . . The most impressive features . . . . are a Gurnemanz of outstanding vocal accomplishment, a Parsifal who sang out boldly and with ingratiating tone . . . and who really showed the evolution of the dumb boy into the *deus ex machina* ...; and the strong, not flawless, but impassioned and often gloriously rich orchestral playing obtained by Mr Michael Brierley, a conductor who plainly knows his Wagner. The flower maidens would not have disgraced any production anywhere.

Mr Mann thought that Kundry 'was inclined to hoot in the bad old manner' and the critic of *The Daily Telegraph* suggested that Act I lay uncomfortably low for her. The *Telegraph* said of Brierley: 'There remains one hero—the conductor.... The man who can conduct *Parsifal, Pelléas* and *The Italian Girl* so that the music's essential flavour is realised—and, moreover, can extract this flavour from student players and singers—is no mean musician. The College, and indeed Manchester, ought to be proud of him.'

With such heady successes in the field of opera, the instrumental virtuosity displayed at open practices and students' concerts continued—John McCabe playing Copland's Variations, for instance, on 20 March and Samuel Barber's *Dover Beach* sung by Loretta Morgan with the 'junior' quartet; Brahms's piano quartet in G minor, with Margaret Gowland as pianist on 21 March; and Erika Harrison and John Davies playing Brahms's D minor sonata, op. 108, on 6 April. Informal operatic evenings were given in the Arthur Worthington Hall on 29 and 31 May, including Act III of *La Traviata* with Jena Milling as Violetta, the Letter Scene from *Figaro*, with Ann Dunn as the Countess and Carol Roscoe as Susanna, extracts from *Carmen*, with Anne Howells and Ryland Davies as Carmen and Don José, Act I of Britten's *Midsummer Night's Dream* (arranged for two pianos by John McCabe) with Owen Wynne as Oberon, Caroline Crawshaw as Tytania, Patrick McGuigan as Bottom and Nichola Gebolys among the fairies), Act IV of Gounod's *Romeo and Juliet*, with Graham Allum as Romeo, a scene from Act II of Verdi's *Falstaff*, and part of Act IV of *Otello*, with Dianne Matthews as Desdemona and Lesley Cookson as Emilia. On 12 June three of Elinson's pupils played: Anthony Halstead three preludes and fugues from the '48', Michael Holloway two Brahms rhapsodies and David Bowman Schubert's A minor sonata. In the first of the July examination concerts Halstead appeared as the horn player in Mozart's C minor wind serenade (K.388) and Dianne Matthews and Erika Harrison performed Debussy's *Five Baudelaire Poems*. On 16 July Reicha's Four Sonatas for Three Horns were played by Halstead, Alun Francis and Muriel Petty. Penelope

Smith played Debussy's *Estampes* on 17 July and Janet Hilton and Erika Harrison played Brahms's clarinet sonata. The wise and experienced W. R. Sinclair of *The Daily Telegraph* wrote of this performance: 'We had a glimpse of a youthful artist, Janet Hilton, whose technique, already remarkable, may conceivably take her into the Kell, Brymer, de Peyer class. Her tone was wonderfully rich and varied and her sense of style astonishing for one so young.' The College had in 1962 instituted a diploma in the harpsichord and its first holder, Joanna Bowker, played the Suite in E minor by Rameau and Howells's *Hughes' Ballet* on 18 July. Erika Harrison, a holder of the new diploma in accompaniment, played Beethoven's op. 111 at this concert, most of the accompanying being done by John McCabe—of Kenneth Langabeer in two Verdi arias, of Elizabeth Mason in Debussy's 'Chansons de Bilitis' and of Rhiannon Davies in Ravel's 'Asie'. On 19 July Anne Howells sang Schubert and Fauré, Caroline Crawshaw sang Walton's three most popular songs ('Daphne', 'Thro' Gilded Trellises' and 'Old Sir Faulk'), Vanessa Gold sang Berg's 'Frühe Lieder', and Pearl Fawcett gave the first performance of Pitfield's sonata for piano accordion.

The operatic activities in the autumn formed the climax of the College's busiest year—a year which took the orchestra to play under David Jordan in Guernsey and under Jordan and George Weldon in the Isle of Man, and to Lancaster (with McCabe as soloist in Bartók's third concerto), Blackpool (where Malcolm Arnold conducted his own *English Dances*) and several other towns. The ambitious double bill of Bartók's marvellous one-act opera *Bluebeard's Castle* and his one-act pantomime *The Miraculous Mandarin* was given twice, at the Royal College of Advanced Technology, Salford (as it then was), on 23 October, and in the Whitworth Hall on 5 December. Jordan conducted, Sheila Barlow produced, and in the opera Bluebeard was sung by Patrick McGuigan and Judith by Rhiannon Davies. In the ballet, Jean Bailey was the girl and McGuigan the mandarin. On 27, 28 and 29 November, Brierley conducted the first performances to be given in England of Gluck's *Paris and Helen*, his third 'reform' opera, written in 1770. Ryland Davies sang Paris, Dianne Matthews Helen, Anne Howells Eros and Caroline Crawshaw a Trojan woman. This enterprise attracted the critics of *The Times, Sunday Times* and *Financial Times* to Manchester. Mann of *The Times* was complimentary about the individual singers but added:

> Above all the performance was memorable because it allowed an 18th-century composer to speak, for the first time in my 30 years of opera-going, in the language he intended. Mr Brierley must have taken endless pains to realise Gluck's vocal lines according to contemporary practice and to teach his singers the spirit as well as the letter of gracing. As a result the vocal music sounded more truthful and beautiful than in any performance of Handel or Mozart, however brilliantly cast, that I have ever heard.

The opera was sung in a new English version by Arthur Jacobs.

On 13 November Vivien Townley, Janet Hilton and Isobel Flinn performed Schubert's 'The Shepherd on the Rock' and Iris Foley sang soprano arias from Massenet's operas. The students' concert on 10 December included Anthony Halstead's Fantasy for Clarinet and Piano played by Geoffrey Haydock and himself, Ravel's *Don Quichotte à Dulcinée*, sung by Patrick McGuigan, with Darina Gibson accompanying, Anthony Goldstone playing Beethoven's *Appassionata* sonata, and Britten's song-cycle *On This Island* sung, as it has often brilliantly been since that evening, by Caroline Crawshaw, who took up another modern English song-cycle, Walton's *Songs for the Lord Mayor's Table*, on 12 February, 1964. Brahms's clarinet trio was played by Janet Hilton, Margaret Greenlaw (cello) and Isobel Flinn on 5 and 12 February. On 18 February music by Loeillet, J. S. Bach, Telemann, Handel, Purcell and others was performed by Honor Sheppard, with Robert Elliott (harpsichord), Geoffrey Gilbert (flute), Clifford Knowles (violin) and Paul Ward (cello). Hadjinikos's pupil Philip Spratley played Skalkottas's *Fifteen Little Variations*, Halstead's *Salford Soliloquies* and his own *Six Places by the Trent* on 11 March, when Susan Hampson and Anthony Goldstone played Martinu's third sonata. The first of the 1964 operas was Beethoven's *Fidelio*, staged on 11, 12 and 13 March in the new Renold Theatre of the College of Science and Technology. The English libretto by Thomas Oliphant, dating from 1833, was used because its rivals were considered to suffer 'in varying degrees from a self-conscious effort to be an up-to-date improvement on the original'. Another special feature of this production was that the spoken dialogue was set to music—'almost all of it Beethoven's, and the greater part from the opera itself'—because it had been found 'impossible to achieve a successful alternation between sung and spoken words. Only highly specialised and experienced artists can effect a transition from song to speech acceptable to a modern audience.' The *Fidelio* overture was used and *Leonora No. 3* was played between scenes 1 and 2 of Act II. Rhiannon Davies sang Leonora, Kenneth Langabeer was Florestan, Alan Ward Pizarro, Caroline Crawshaw and Ryland Davies were Marcellina and Jaquino, and Patrick McGuigan was Rocco. 'Everything was stylistically apt', said Elliot in the *Guardian*, 'even (one might almost say especially) the scene which drew upon a piano sonata [op. 31, no. 1, orchestrated by John McCabe] for its material. . . . Rhiannon Davies gave a resplendent and finely dramatic performance'. Anne Howells sang Leonora at one performance.

On 24 April Barbirolli conducted 50 present and 60 past students in a Free Trade Hall concert which commemorated Forbes, inaugurated the fund in his memory and honoured Sir John in his 21st Hallé season. 'They make a lovely sound, I wish I could take them on tour', was the conductor's comment on a memorable evening. 'The combination of expertise and youthful zest produced sound of impressive richness and quality', said *The Daily Telegraph's* critic. 'The number of strings available enabled Sir John to give a stunning account of Strauss's *Don Juan*, with the great climax soaring in memorable fashion, and eight horns to drive the point home.' Several other events contributed their proceeds to the Forbes fund, notably an Ogdon Beethoven recital in the College on 19 November.

Bartók's viola concerto and Hindemith's clarinet sonata were in the programme of an open practice on 13 May, and on the 28th John McCabe, John Brown, Alun Francis (horn) and Caroline Crawshaw performed British music by Hoddinott (first piano sonata), Rawsthorne (violin sonata), Arnold Cooke (Nocturnes for Soprano, Horn and Piano), Berkeley (horn trio), and Walton (*Songs for the Lord Mayor's Table*). On 2 June Mussorgsky's *Songs and Dances of Death* were sung by McGuigan, with Russell Lomas, and Beethoven's sextet for two horns and string quartet was played with Alun Francis and Anthony Halstead as the horn-players. Two nights later extracts from Poulenc's opera *Dialogues of the Carmelites* were sung by Caroline Crawshaw, Vivien Townley, Janet Jaques, Patrick McGuigan, and others. On 2 July a concert honoured Lucy Pierce on her retirement after over 50 years on the staff. Two of her ensemble class, Michael Grady and Russell Lomas, played Britten's Introduction and Rondo alla Burlesca, Clifford Knowles and Clifton Helliwell played Geminiani and Smetana, Barbara Robotham, accompanied by John Wills, sang three Brahms songs and Schubert's 'Abschied', Haydn's *Farewell* symphony was conducted by David Jordan and the evening ended with an 'Ode to Lucy Pierce written by a Disconsolate Principal' and performed by Caroline Crawshaw and Frederic Cox. At the first of the examination concerts on 13 July McCabe played Britten's *Notturno* and his own Piano Variations of 1963, and John Brown played part of Bach's unaccompanied G minor violin sonata. On the 14th Nichola Gebolys, who had recently won the National Youth Piano Competition, played Beethoven's op. 78 sonata, Anthony Goldstone played Schubert's A minor sonata, op. 42, and Vivien Townley sang 'Elisabeth's Prayer' from *Tannhäuser*. Milhaud's Suite for Violin, Clarinet and Piano was played by John Brown, Janet Hilton and Russell Lomas on 15 July and Maureen and Hazel Smith were the violinists in Bach's D minor concerto. On the 16th the 'College Consort' sang Elizabethan songs, Dianne Matthews sang Purcell's 'Blessed Virgin's Expostulation' and Caroline Crawshaw sang songs from *The Fairy Queen*. Two of the staff, Endre Wolf and Clifton Helliwell, played Bartók's first violin sonata on 17 July. In the juniors' concert the next day, the pianist Christian Blackshaw played the first movement of Mozart's C minor concerto, K.491, and it was judged even then that another remarkable star was rising.

The end-of-year opera (on 25, 26 and 27 November) was Verdi's *Otello*, a vehicle for the Irish civil servant Edwin Fitzgibbon who was a part-time student at the College, and for Dianne Matthews, whose Desdemona had long been awaited by those who had heard her sing some of the arias. Alan Ward was Iago, Graham Allum Cassio, and Janet Jaques Emilia. 'Remarkable by any standards', was the comment by *The Daily Telegraph*'s critic. 'The stupendous music had brought out the best from everyone.' And Elliot wrote:

One might have thought [*Otello*] about the last thing for students ... to tackle. Once again fainthearted prophets have been proved wrong. The performance ... like that of some previous apparent impossibilities, was telling, moving and altogether exhilarating. Perfection? No, but something infinitely encouraging—a corporate endeavour, made possible by sincere enthusiasm and graced by genuine love and feeling for artistic truth. . . . There were indeed no weaknesses in the cast.

For some, the evening was made memorable in a pleasantly amusing way by a typical example of Cox's sense of humour. He had the programme printed entirely in Italian except for a translation of the synopsis of the plot, which was a genuine reproduction of one he had encountered in Italy, containing such gems as: 'But Jago insinuates that the woman will be early tired of the rude love of her husband. . . . He will have Othello gone into ruin. He looks with attention at the mating between Cassio and Desdemona. . . . At the mercy of delirium he falls down fainted. Jago triumphally enjoys.'

The year ended with three exceptional concerts. On 10 December David Jordan conducted the orchestra in the Whitworth Hall in Shostakovich's fifth symphony and Prokofiev's first violin concerto, played by John Brown, who according to *The Daily Telegraph*, 'rightly stressed the music's essentially lyrical and typically Russian emotional basis'. On 15 December Hilary Thornton (viola) and Mary Dalton (piano) played Britten's *Lachrymae* (Reflections on a Song of Dowland), Maryrose Moorhouse, accompanied by Isobel Flinn, sang two of Berg's Lieder and two songs by Duparc, and David Evans (flute), Andrew Thomas (viola) and Darina Gibson (piano) performed Duruflé's Prélude, Récitatif et Variations. Then on 16 December Hugo Cole's Trio for Flute, Clarinet and Piano was played by Patricia Waddington, Peter Fielding and Julia Wallace. Kathleen Smales sang Mozart's 'Voi che sapete'.

The advent of 1965 brought no abatement in the flow of interesting concerts promoted by the College. On 9 February, baroque vocal and instrumental music was sung by Caroline Crawshaw, with Geoffrey Gilbert (flute), Clifford Knowles (violin), Robert Elliott (harpsichord) and Paul Ward (cello). On 10, 11 and 12 February Daudet's *L'Arlésienne* was performed, with Bizet's music, in its original scoring for 26 players, conducted by David Jordan. Acts II and IV of *Otello* were sung at the Tuesday Mid-day Concert on 23 February, and at an open practice on 10 March Dianne Matthews sang Debussy's *Ariettes Oubliées*, accompanied by Darina Gibson, and Kathleen Smales sang A. Scarlatti's delightful 'Le Violette'. On 17 March Ravel's *Shéhérazade* was divided between two singers, Elisabeth Harrison, singing 'Asie' and Maryrose Moorhouse 'La flûte enchantée' and 'L'Indifférent'. Katherine Train sang Poulenc's 'Banalités', and Julia Wallace, a pupil of Derrick Wyndham, played Bartók's Three Rondos on Folk-songs. On 18 March, Janet Hilton joined Jane Venables (cello) and Mary Dalton in Beethoven's B flat trio, op. 11, and played Debussy's clarinet rhapsody with Darina Gibson. Seven songs from Schumann's *Dichterliebe* were sung by Raphael Gonley on 24 March, when John Brown and John Shufflebotham (now known as John Arran) played Paganini's Four Sonatas for violin and guitar. On the evening of the 24th the College Consort sang madrigals by Weelkes, Ford, Morley and Dowland, Campian's *Masque for the Wedding of Lord Hayes (1601)*, and three movements from Monteverdi's *Lagrime d'Amante*.

On 31 March, Eric Chadwick conducted Verdi's *Requiem* in the Whitworth Hall in memory of Dr Norman Andrew, with Vivien Townley, Barbara Robotham, Edwin Fitzgibbon and John Lawrenson as the solo quartet. Two old friends, Clifford Knowles and Ben Horsfall, played in the orchestra. The chorus contained most of the College's operatic 'stars' of a decade, and the hall was crowded. It was a moving and splendid evening. As Elliot wrote: 'It was worthy of the high standards which by now are taken as a matter of course for anything publicly undertaken by the R.M.C.M.' Frederic Cox's words in the programme remain eloquent of what the critics left unsaid: 'Philosophers and theologians can dispute whether there is a life hereafter; one thing we know for certain: Norman Andrew still lives on earth—in the hearts and minds of his dear ones, his friends, his colleagues and his students.' On 28 April John Brown, Andrew Thomas, Martin Robinson (cello) and Anthony Goldstone played the piano quartets of Brahms (op. 26) and Mozart (G minor) and the string players performed Hindemith's 1933 string trio.

Alan Rawsthorne, perhaps the most accomplished composer to have attended the College, was honoured on his 60th birthday by a concert of his music in the Lees Hall on 4 May. He heard David Newland and Mary Dalton play the viola sonata of 1937; the Bagatelles and Sonatina were played by John McCabe; the wind quintet of 1963 was performed by Darina Gibson (piano), Lynn Brierley (oboe), Patricia Sharp (clarinet), Anthony Halstead (horn) and Janet Firth (bassoon); and Clifford Knowles and Clifton Helliwell played the 1959 violin sonata. 'Good as his earlier works are, the latest phase is the richest', I wrote at the time. 'The quintet is a remarkable piece, tragic and dramatic in character. . . . In the violin sonata the hand of a master is everywhere apparent.' A week later Barbirolli conducted the College Orchestra in Dvořák's G major symphony and Beethoven's G major piano concerto. 'It was a young artist's view of the matter,' Elliot wrote of Anthony Goldstone's performance of the concerto, 'but clearly all the materials of a first-class performance have been assembled.' At the open practice on 12 May Charles Walker, a pupil of Hadjinikos, played Schubert's A major sonata and Kathryn Hardman (violin) and Penelope Turner (piano) played Handel's Sonata in F. On 2 June, David Jordan conducted the chamber orchestra in a Handel concerto grosso, Holst's *St Paul's Suite*, Vaughan Williams's violin concerto (soloist John Bradbury) and Mozart's 29th symphony. Caroline Crawshaw sang Mozart's 'Exsultate Jubilate', and a fortnight later she sang Ravel's *Cinq mélodies populaires grecques*, accompanied by Richard Holloway, who also accompanied Raphael Gonley in the complete *Dichterliebe*.

On 23 June members of Geoffrey Gilbert's wind class, with assistance from other instruments, were conducted by Mr Gilbert in Kurt Weill's *Kleine Dreigroschenmusik* and also played Gounod's *Petite Symphonie* and Dvořák's Serenade, op. 44. French songs formed the basis of the open practice on 30 June, with Katherine Train singing Poulenc's 'Le travail du peintre', Milhaud's 'Catalogue des fleurs' sung by Mary Waters, Fauré's 'Chanson d'amour' by Anthea Robb, Debussy's 'Air de Lia' by Elisabeth Harrison and Massenet's 'Air de Salomé' by Vivien Townley. On 7 July works for violin and guitar by Vivaldi, Azpiazu, Corelli and Max Paddison (a College student) were played by John Bradbury and John Shufflebotham. More woodwind and piano works—Mozart's E flat piano quintet, Poulenc's flute sonata, Quantz's flute trio and Hindemith's *Kleine Kammermusik*, op. 24, no. 2—were played by Darina Gibson, Janet Hilton, Anthony Halstead and others on 12 July. In the final concerts of the summer term Goldstone played Liszt's first *Mephisto Waltz*, Maryrose Moorhouse sang Duparc, Darina Gibson played Schumann's *Carneval* and was joined by Sonia Wrangham in Hindemith's oboe sonata, and Vivien Townley sang arias from *Aïda* and *Adriana Lecouvreur*. On 24 November Margaret Graf (violin) and Janet Adams played the first movement of Edward Isaacs's sonata in A major and the cellist Alan Turner, with Anthony Halstead, played Bruch's *Kol Nidrei*.

The autumn opera, Giordano's *Andrea Chenier*, on 1, 2 and 3 December, was the first to be given in the handsome and beautifully equipped new University Theatre, almost next door to the College and built for the University Drama Department. Though it had many advantages over the Arthur Worthington Hall, its acoustics (for music) left much to be desired and it had no proper orchestra pit. Nor could early rehearsals be held there. Elliot's successor on *The Guardian*, Gerald Larner, described the performance as

remarkable in many ways but particularly in its dramatic impact. Small things happen and fail to happen in Sheila Barlow's production but many scenes—the trial, the prison farewell—are irresistibly moving. . . . Not all the drama happens on the stage, of course, and Michael Brierley's conducting of the college orchestra was imaginative and richly emotional. Of the singers, Norman Welsby as Gérard (the revolutionary footman) was outstanding.

Chénier was sung by Edwin Fitzgibbon and Madeleine by Vivien Townley. Anthea Robb, who made an effective mark in the small part of Bersi, sang songs by Délibes at an open practice on 8 December. A major policy decision was that College Orchestra concerts should in future be given in the Free Trade Hall, and the first (with David Jordan conducting and John Bradbury now the leader) was on 18 December when Ruth Waterman played Max Bruch's G minor violin concerto and the other works were Liszt's *Les Préludes* and Vaughan Williams's *London Symphony*. The audience was small but the critics were enthusiastic, particularly about Miss Waterman.

The guitarist John Shufflebotham opened 1966 with music by Villa-Lobos, J. S. Bach and Max Paddison at the open practice on 12 January. More French songs were sung on 19 January, including two of Berlioz's *Nuits d'Eté*, 'Absence' and 'Villanelle', by Christine Paterson, two songs by Jean Françaix, by Mary Waters and Chaminade's 'L'Eté' by Elizabeth Kemp. Vitali's Chaconne was played by David Hadwen on 9 February, and on 16 February Raphael Gonley sang George Butterworth's *Shropshire Lad* song-cycle. At a Lieder recital by students on 26 February Gonley sang Beethoven's 'An die ferne Geliebte', a comparative College rarity over the years, Katharine Gerrard sang four Brahms songs including 'Von ewiger Liebe' and three of Elgar's *Sea Pictures*, Norman

Welsby sang five Ivor Gurney songs, and Maryrose Moorhouse took over Anne Howells's speciality, Falla's *Seven Popular Spanish Songs*. Three days earlier Anthony Goldstone played Brahms's D minor piano concerto with the orchestra under Jordan in the Free Trade Hall. 'The last College student to play this challenging work on a similar occasion was John Ogdon', *The Daily Telegraph*'s critic wrote. 'In many respects Mr Goldstone's was the finer performance, unless memory grossly deceives me, because added to a technique as secure as Ogdon's is an extraordinarily mature musical intelligence which time and again illuminated dark recesses of this craggy music.' The same critic remarked that the performance after the interval of Bartók's Concerto for Orchestra was 'professionally assured, brilliant and well rehearsed, at some cost, it seemed, to the accompaniment of the Brahms concerto'.

Operatic excerpts were sung in costume in the Lees Hall on 28 February, several of those destined shortly to take leading rôles appearing on this occasion: for example, Roydn Jones as Tamino, Kathleen Smales as Dido, Colin Jones as Rigoletto and David Lloyd Jones as Sparafucile. Direction was by Isobel Flinn. On 8 March Janet Hilton, Hilary Thornton (viola) and Darina Gibson performed Mozart's clarinet trio (K.498) and Maryrose Moorhouse sang Ravel's *Chansons Madécasses*. The College's foremost sonata team of the period, Margaret Graf and Janet Adams, played Beethoven's *Spring* sonata on 9 March and yet more French songs were sung on 23 March, ranging from Poulenc's 'Air champêtre' and 'Air grave', sung by Susanne Bradbury, to Grétry's 'Richard Cœur de Lion', sung by Elizabeth Kemp. On 23, 24 and 25 March, at the University Theatre, the spring opera production was a double bill of Ravel's *L'Heure espagnole*, conducted by Brierley, with Anthea Robb a delightful Concepcion, Norman Welsby as Ramiro, Roydn Jones as Torquemada, Graham Allum as Gonzalve and Patrick McGuigan (no longer a student) as Don Inigo. The second half, under Jordan, was Act III of *Die Walküre* (which had been performed at the Tuesday Mid-day Concert on 1 March), with Vivien Townley as Brünnhilde, McGuigan as Wotan and Barbara Walker as Sieglinde. Larner wrote: 'The Ravel . . . is particularly good, with scarcely a weak spot on the musical side, splendid playing by the college orchestra, and a most characteristic Concepcion.' His colleague on *The Daily Telegraph* concurred, and said of the Wagner:

Miss Townley's performance was an immense advance on her previous appearances, both in strength and quality of tone, and suggested that Wagner, rather than the Italians, is her composer. Her singing was radiant and moving both in its achievement and in its promise of richness to come, and much the same might be said of Miss Walker.

More Ravel, his Sonatine, was played on 30 March by Kathleen Uren, a pupil of Derrick Wyndham and before that a junior exhibitioner, and Roussel's *Joueurs de Flûte* was played by David Murray and Gerald Willis. The open practice on 18 May is notable for the inclusion, for the first time, of the 'Laughing Song' from *Die Fledermaus*, sung by Elsie Thurston's pupil Elizabeth Kemp. Also on 18 May the chamber orchestra, wind ensemble, string quartet, trombone quartet and soloists (Lynn Brierley, oboe; Elizabeth Hill, harp; John Bradbury, violin; and Neil McKinnon, tenor) gave a remarkable concert in which, after a first half consisting of Mozart's *Serenata Notturna* and Bach's D minor concerto in the version for violin and oboe soloists (conducted by David Jordan) four Stravinsky works were performed—the wind octet, the *Epitaphium, In Memoriam Dylan Thomas*, and the *Symphonies of Wind Instruments*—under the direction of Geoffrey Gilbert. More familiar ground was covered on 25 May in the Free Trade Hall when Barbirolli conducted Franck's symphony and Darina Gibson was the pianist in Rachmaninov's second concerto. 'It is a rare, probably uncomfortable, but obviously valuable opportunity for music's future to come under the influence of one of the great interpretative personalities', Larner wrote. 'Sir John was obviously moved by the magnitude of sound and directness of expression he was able to get out of his young instrumentalists, particularly in the highly colourful (at times over-colourful) performance of César Franck's D minor symphony.' Four of Wolf's *Mignon* Lieder were sung by Maryrose Moorhouse, with Isobel Flinn, at the first of the July examination concerts. On 18 July Geoffrey Hopkins played Liszt's *Dante* sonata, Trevor Bray three of Messiaen's *Vingt Regards*, and Jane Venables and Darina Gibson played Prokofiev's cello sonata. The following evening the consort, wind ensemble and chamber orchestra performed Mozart's wind serenade in C minor, Dvořák's D minor Serenade and Purcell's 'Welcome to all the pleasures'. Raphael Gonley sang Barber's 'Dover Beach' on the 21st, Darina Gibson played

Liszt's *Venezia e Napoli*, and John Bradbury and Danielle Sala-
mon played Franck's sonata. On 22 July Vivien Townley sang
four Strauss Lieder (including 'Allerseelen' and 'Cäcilie'),
Maureen and Hazel Smith played Bach's D minor concerto and
eight of Bartók's duos, Anthony Goldstone played Schumann's
Symphonic Variations and Katharine Gerrard and Raphael
Gonley, accompanied by Richard Holloway, sang ten of Wolf's
Italian Song Book.

The evening of the 20th was a sentimental occasion when
students and staff paid tribute to Dora C. Gilson on her retirement after 52 years as teacher of singing and the pianoforte.
In her honour Stephen Bettaney and David Hartigan played
Milhaud's *Scaramouche*, Meriel Dickinson, accompanied by
Isobel Flinn, sang Brahms and Strauss Lieder, and Anthony
Goldstone, holder of the Dora Gilson award 1966, played
piano solos by Liszt, Gottschalk and Schumann. Finally Geoffrey Gilbert, Sidney Fell, Clifton Helliwell and Anthony Halstead played a suite 'D.C.G.' for flute, clarinet, horn and piano
which had been specially composed by Frederic Cox. The
analytical note in the programme stated: 'She will be constantly in their thoughts as they play, for the three written
notes D C G, occasionally abbreviated to D G, appear from
bar to bar throughout the whole piece.' It was one of those
occasions which Cox devised with such thoroughness that the
whole evening appeared to be an inspired improvisation. And
no one enjoyed it more than Dora, her laugh gurgling away, her
comments as direct as they were shrewd. Happy the woman
who inspires such affection in all with whom she comes into
contact. No one has served the College longer or more de-
votedly.

During July College students gave morning concerts at the
Buxton Festival, among them Caroline Crawshaw, Isobel
Flinn, Anthony Halstead, Anthony Goldstone, Mary Dalton,
John Bradbury and the wind ensemble. In June 16 of the
College's singers had sung the solo parts in Vaughan Williams's
Serenade to Music at a Hallé Prom. Winter brought the opera
production, *Die Walküre* in full, with Vivien Townley and
Barbara Walker as Brünnhilde and Sieglinde, Norman Welsby
as Wotan, Neil McKinnon as Siegmund and Gwynne Howell as
Hunding (the last-named, a very fine bass, was a member of
the planning department of Manchester Corporation). David
Jordan conducted, having 'blooded' the orchestra on Bruckner's

fourth symphony in the Free Trade Hall on 26 October. The opera was on 29 November, 1 and 3 December. Barbara Walker's radiant performance particularly impressed the critics and Larner stressed the 'noble contribution' by Miss Townley. The notice in *The Daily Telegraph* stressed wider aspects of what the writer called 'the most ambitious venture yet undertaken' by the College: the extraordinarily high standard, he said, 'is certainly unmatched by similar bodies in this country and can probably hold its own in competition with most in Western Europe. Manchester has something special here'. A few days earlier Cox, applauding Pariser's plan for an opera house, had emphasised that the proposed new college would help to produce a first-rate opera company and another first-rate orchestra for Manchester. 'We have to start the job of preparing for that almost straightaway.'

On 30 November, Christian Blackshaw played a Chopin nocturne and scherzo, Patricia Taylor sang Schumann's 'Liederkreis', and an Australian student, Kerry Smith, played Beethoven's *Spring* sonata partnered by Goldstone. Another busy year ended with a Free Trade Hall concert by the orchestra, at which Janet Hilton played Mozart's clarinet concerto, and a concert on 8 December in honour of the modest, much-liked and multi-gifted Tom Pitfield. Seven of his works were played, including a new 'zoological sequence' called *Planibestiary*. As Gerald Larner said:

> The idealist in one might regret that the composer should so limit himself when he is capable of writing music as strong as that in the Preludio of the sonata for piano accordion (splendidly played by Pearl Fawcett) or as lyrical as the elegiac nocturne of the trio for flute, oboe and piano . . . but the friend is refreshed by contact with a composer who does not take himself too seriously and would rather make a joke about it.

To start its 1967 season the College Orchestra played Tchaikovsky's *Manfred Symphony* on 14 February and accompanied Darina Gibson in Mozart's D minor piano concerto (K.466). On 22 February Miss Gibson and Vivienne Blumfield played Mozart's G major violin sonata (K.301) and on the 27th Maryrose Moorhouse sang Debussy's *Fêtes Galantes*, Barbara Walker sang four Strauss Lieder, and Brahms's horn trio was played by the remarkable young horn-player John Bimson, Kerry Smith and Anthony Goldstone. For its spring opera, the College for the first time staged two full-length operas on alternate nights with different personnel in the chorus and orchestra for each opera. Verdi's *Falstaff* was given on 7, 9 and 11 March, conducted by Brierley, with Norman Welsby as Falstaff, Carol Roscoe as Mrs Ford, Jean Bailey as Mrs Page, Katharine Gerrard as Mistress Quickly and Barbara Walker as Nanetta. On the 8th and 10th David Jordan conducted Bellini's *I Capuleti e i Montecchi*, with Anthea Robb as Juliet, Kathleen Smales in the *travesti* rôle of Romeo and Roydn Jones as Tebaldo. This was the first British performance for many years of this fine opera, and the house was full, with lusty cheers at the end. College opera productions by now had a *cachet* which, while it brought dangers, was a reward for years of hard work and risk-taking. On 16 March Geoffrey Gilbert conducted the College training orchestra, which had been formed in September, 1966, in order that the younger students could familiarise themselves with orchestral playing before they earned a place in the First Orchestra. Haydn's 104th symphony, Copland's *Billy the Kid* and Tchaikovsky's *1812 Overture* alternated with performances by the wind ensemble of Handel's *Fireworks Music* and Holst's Suite in E flat. On 8 April Caroline Crawshaw, John Bimson and Kerry Smith, with Clifton Helliwell, performed Debussy's *Ariettes oubliées*, a Mozart concert rondo, and items by Brahms, Bloch and Prokofiev. On 20 April the orchestra, now led by Margaret Graf, played Beethoven's seventh symphony, Kodaly's *Peacock Variations* and Strauss's oboe concerto, with the brilliant Lynn Brierley as soloist. A month later, on 14 May, the programme included Debussy's *La Mer* and Brahms's second symphony. At open practices in May David Stevens, pupil of Hadjinikos, played Berg's sonata, op. 1, and Charles Knowles played eight Bartók bagatelles from op. 6. Throughout 1966 and 1967 students played a large part in M.I.C.A. concerts, which owed much to John McCabe's musicianship and enthusiasm. That on 7 June was given wholly by students, and included Hoddinott's second piano sonata, played by Geoffrey Hopkins, Britten's *Songs and Proverbs of William Blake*, sung by Raphael Gonley, Schoenberg's *Das Buch der Hängenden Garten*, sung by Dianne Matthews, and Roberto Gerhard's wind quintet of 1928. The last-named was also performed at the Buxton Festival in July, when students again gave five concerts, at one of which Goldstone gave a recital and at another Neil McKinnon sang Vaughan Williams's *On Wenlock Edge*. Kerry Smith was among the students at Buxton, having made her début as a Free Trade Hall soloist with the orchestra on 9 June in Beethoven's concerto, which was followed by Sibelius's second symphony. Hindemith's bassoon sonata was played by Janet Firth and Roger Clegg on 21 June. The 'musicals class', which in 1966 had sung extracts from German's *Tom Jones*, this year gave two concert performances on 27 and 28 June of Victor Herbert's *Sweethearts*.

Since the heyday two or three years earlier, it is noticeable that string quartets are fewer at open practices in the 1966–7 period. On 28 June Mozart's D minor quartet (K.173) was played by Maria Kyriakou, Susan Brown, Patricia Ward and Susan Thomas. On 5 July the unusual choices of music included four songs by Enesco, sung by Judith Quine, two by Koechlin, sung by Christopher Littlewood, a baritone, and two of Britten's *Les Illuminations*, sung by Carol Roscoe. The training orchestra took part in the 'students' opera workshop' performances on 6 and 7 July of Cimarosa's *Secret Marriage*. The end-of-term concerts between 17 and 21 July again threw up some interesting selections: Strauss's violin sonata, by Margaret Graf and Danielle Salamon, Arnold's wind quintet Sea Shanties, Poulenc's piano sextet, Prokofiev's seventh sonata played by Tony Brentnall, Brahms's *Liebeslieder* waltzes, sung by Anthea Robb, Judith Quine, Neil McKinnon and Norman Welsby, with Stephen Pilkington and Martin Holland the duettists. On the final evening, Kerry Smith and Dinah Levine played Debussy's sonata, Katharine Gerrard sang four songs by Mahler, and Christian Blackshaw played Beethoven's op. 10, no. 3. On 30 October, in the Free Trade Hall, Jordan conducted Haydn's G major symphony (*The Military*), Shostakovich's first symphony and Schumann's Konzertstück for Four Horns, in which John Bimson, Ralph Hall, Peter Lewis and Patrick Garvey were the soloists. Nielsen's wind quintet was played on 1 November.

The autumn opera was another double bill, an amazingly ambitious one which did in fact strain the resources of the College—Hugo Wolf's *Der Corregidor* and Wagner's *The Mastersingers*. The Wolf was sung in a new translation by Gerald Larner and had Joseph Ward as the Corregidor, McGuigan as the Miller, Jean Bailey as Frasquita and Roydn Jones as the Neighbour. Interesting as this work was, it was overshadowed in all respects by the Wagner, which Brierley conducted splendidly, though in neither opera was the orchestral

12

playing all that could be desired. Norman Welsby's Sachs was much the best thing he did in College operas, Barbara Walker was a radiant Eva, Raphael Gonley a notable Beckmesser, Neil McKinnon a stylish Walther and Gwynne Howell an act-stealing Pogner. The chorus, trained by Dr John Wray, was superb. Kathleen Smales was Magdalena, but was vocally more impressive a few nights later when, on 12 December, she sang Ravel's *Shéhérazade* with the College Orchestra. The symphonies on this occasion were the sixth of, respectively, Sibelius and Beethoven, admirably conducted by David Jordan. On 6 December, Peter Sage, a pupil of Franz Reizenstein, played a Chopin group and the now annual recital of French songs included on 13 December Gluck's 'Ah, si la liberté' from *Armide*, sung by Judith Quine, and Katharine Gerrard's performance of Poulenc's 'Le travail du peintre'.

Owen Wynne was in charge of the College Consort, who opened 1967 with Wilbye, Milton and Morley, and Jane Coulson, a pupil of Gordon Green, played Bach's Toccata in D. Hedwig Stein's pupil Caroline Marshall played Mozart's A major concerto (K.488) on 24 January and Beethoven's piano trio, op. 70. no. 1 was played by Margaret Graf (violin), Susan Thomas (cello) and Joan Greenburgh on 31 January. The first orchestral concert of the year was held in the Free Trade Hall on 30 January, when Jonathan Sparey, first holder of the Olive Zorian violin, played Kabalevsky's concerto and David Jordan conducted Mendelssohn's and Mahler's fourth symphonies, with Barbara Walker the soprano soloist in the last movement of the latter. Haydn's *Lark* quartet was played on 7 February by Jonathan and Carolyn Sparey (violins), Diana Hall (viola) and the cello professor Raphael Sommer as cellist. Ann Forbes, mezzo-soprano pupil of Mrs Langford, sang Gluck and Roger Quilter; and on 14 February Derrick Wyndham's pupil, David Gaukroger, played Schubert's A minor sonata, op. 143. Elgar songs ('Through the long days', 'The Shepherd's Song' and 'Song of Autumn') were sung by Gabrielle Lister on 21 February, preceded by Haydn's op. 33, no. 3, quartet, played by Alexander Moskowsky's quartet class. Geoffrey Gilbert conducted the wind ensemble, with Darina Gibson (piano), on 24 February in Gounod's *Petite Symphonie* (a College favourite, it seems) and Mozart's E flat Serenade (K.375) with smaller items by Ibert, Haydn and Dutilleux.

Studies by Scriabin emerged for the first time since Lucy

Pierce's day, when Wyndham's pupil David Hartigan played four on 28 February. Mendelssohn's octet—relatively a rarity at open practices—was performed on 6 March by Sommer's ensemble class (Maire ni Chuilleanain, Kathryn Hardman, Jonathan and Carolyn Sparey, Pauline Alston, Diana Hall, Mei Lee Ong and Ian Sharp). At the Free Trade Hall on 11 March, Granville Bantock's centenary was marked by a performance of his tone-poem *Fifine at the Fair* conducted by David Jordan, and Kerry Smith must have delighted the spirit of Brodsky by becoming the first College student for many years to play Elgar's concerto in public. A concert of works by student composers on 18 March included Christian Blackshaw's quintet for piano, flute, oboe, violin and cello, Max Paddison's sonatina for piano and *Orpheus* for voice and flute, and Stuart Pedlar's *Missa brevis*. On 20 March, an open practice of French songs included Kathleen Smales's performance of an aria from Berlioz's *Beatrice and Benedict* and his 'Sur les Lagunes' (*Nuits d'Eté*) sung by Patricia Hughes, and Weckerlin's 'Non, je n'irai plus au bois' sung by Anita Smith (soprano).

The two spring opera productions were again enterprising—Handel's *Xerxes*, with Roydn Jones as Xerxes, Robert Ferguson as Arsamenes, Barbara Walker as Romilda, Kathleen Smales as Amastris, and Anthea Robb as Atalanta, and conducted by Jordan. 'A courageous venture which deserved more success than it achieved', said *The Daily Telegraph*. 'There was much that was splendid, but many things that were just not quite right.' The critic confessed that he left the theatre feeling that he had had more than enough of *allegro moderato*. The other opera was Wagner's *Das Rheingold*, which it is melancholy to record was to be Brierley's last College opera. 'He was supreme', Cox wrote later, 'in that twilight world, the opera school, where the two elements of student and professional meet and mingle for the first time.' As a Wagner conductor he was exceptional and it was a tribute to his powers that, now that the 'experienced' Townley–Welsby era was over, he should have built a new team for this memorable *Rheingold*. I wrote at the time:

This was in some ways the most successful of the College's Wagner forays. . . . Two performances were outstanding: those by Gwynne Howell as Fasolt and Neil McKinnon as Loge. Both sang with assurance, and Mr McKinnon in particular has never before produced such consistently steady and pleasing tone to go with his natural sense of how to phrase. Raphael Gonley's Alberich was a good characterisation but too light vocally: we saw rather than heard the maliciousness. . . . Katharine Gerrard's Fricka was another mature performance, and Roger Heath (Wotan), Patricia Hughes (Erda) and Angela Bostock (Wellgunde) revealed voices with considerable virtues.

This performance of *Rheingold* and that of *Pelléas* will remain for those who saw them as prime examples (with Avril Roebuck's *Madam Butterfly*) of student opera at its best: professional performances of course have every advantage, but the enthusiasm, the sense of fresh dedication as yet untarnished by worldly considerations of vanity or greed give to student opera an appeal that lifts it out of the ordinary run of musical experiences. Of course critics have not been lacking of Cox's policy of performing Wagner on the grounds that the strain on young voices is too great.

On 30 March, at a concert for the National Federation of Music Societies, Hazel Smith (violin) and Martin Holland played the Pugnani-Kreisler Praeludium and Allegro, Janet Hilton and Penelope Smith played Debussy's clarinet rhapsody, Barbara Walker, accompanied by Stephen Pilkington, sang Strauss Lieder, Robert Ferguson sang tenor arias, Roger Heath sang three of the *Songs of Travel* and Christian Blackshaw played Chopin and Scriabin. Dittersdorf's double bass concerto was played by Paul Marrion and Christopher Cotton (piano) at an open practice on 8 May. On the 10th the Free Trade Hall season of concerts ended with Beethoven's eighth symphony and Liszt's *Faust* symphony, with Neil McKinnon singing the final tenor solo. On 25 May David Jordan took the orchestra, jointly led by Kathryn Hardman and Raymond Sidebottom, to Liverpool to play in the Philharmonic Hall where it was rapturously welcomed. Tchaikovsky's sixth symphony and Beethoven's fifth piano concerto (soloist Christian Blackshaw) were played. In the Whitworth Hall on 14 May Geoffrey Gilbert conducted the training orchestra, wind ensemble and chorus in Mozart's *Haffner* symphony, Holst's second military band suite, Handel's *Zadok the Priest* and Berlioz's *Symphonie Funèbre et Triomphale*, probably the first Manchester performance of the last-named since Harty's Hallé performance in the 1920s. On 16 May Maryrose Moorhouse, accompanied by Isobel Flinn, sang Mozart's concert aria 'Ch'io mi scordi di te', Schubert's 'Suleika', Poulenc's song-cycle *Fiançailles pour rire*, and three Rachmaninov songs, and Darina Gibson played Haydn, Chopin, Ravel and Field. On 29 May the College Consort sang Monteverdi's Mass for four voices (1651) and various English madrigals, and harpsichord works by Rameau and Purcell were played by, respectively, Alexander Brown and Kathleen Uren. On 10 June Kathryn Hardman, accompanied by Christine Bennett, played Bach's B minor sonata, Beethoven's Romance in F, Mozart's sonata in G (K.301) and the Bartók-Székely Rumanian Dances. A week later Margaret Graf and Danielle Salamon played Brahms's D minor sonata, op. 108, and Szymanowski's Notturno and Tarantella. Songs by Moeran were sung by Gabrielle Lister on 26 June, and Tony Brentnall played Samuel Barber's sonata. The following evening the opera department gave a mixed programme, arranged by the students, which included extracts from *Un Ballo in Maschera, Mefistofele, Faust* and *Lucia di Lammermoor*, and a complete performance of Puccini's *Suor Angelica*, with Carol Roscoe and Angela Bostock. Max Paddison's Concertino for Flute, Clarinet, Violin and Cello was played on 3 July by Patrick Taggart, Anthony Houghton, Clifford Bibby and Peter Brown. The end-of-term July concerts were notable for the College Consort's performance of Purcell's Te Deum in D, Rawsthorne's Theme and Variations for Two Violins, played by Jonathan and Carolyn Sparey, Schubert's A major sonata played by Darina Gibson, Bax's clarinet sonata played by Maxwell Benn and Max Ritchie (piano), Wolf songs by Katharine Gerrard, accompanied by Isobel Flinn, Christian Blackshaw playing Chopin's B minor sonata, Beethoven's op. 111 played by Elizabeth Altman, and Jonathan Sparey and Blackshaw in Mozart's B flat sonata (K.454).

David Jordan opened the 1968–9 R.M.C.M. Orchestra series in the Free Trade Hall on 13 October with Shostakovich's ninth symphony, Sibelius's fifth and Liszt's first piano concerto, played by Peter Sage. On 25 November Wendy Brown sang six Monteverdi *Scherzi Musicali*, accompanied at the harpsichord by Kathleen Uren, and five Rachmaninov songs, and Charles Knowles played Beethoven's op. 101. A throwback to another era was the performance at an open practice on 27 November of Liszt's arrangement of Isolde's Liebestod by Marjorie Clementi's pupil Martin Roscoe. The two autumn operas at the University Theatre were J. C. Bach's *Temistocle*, conducted by David Jordan on 6, 11 and 13 December and

Massenet's *Werther*, conducted by Roger Norrington (taking over from Brierley, whose death had occurred in the early stages of rehearsals). *Temistocle* was receiving its first performance in England and its first anywhere since 1773 except for a Stuttgart performance in 1965. It was performed in the edition by the American scholars Edward O. Downes and H. C. Robbins Landon, a version at which specialists in the period cavilled because a number of arias from other works by J. C. Bach were introduced into the score. Angela Bostock, Rosalind Plowright and Ian Caley were the outstanding singers. In *Werther* Anthony Holcroft, Judith Quine, Anthea Robb and Alun Jenkins sang the leading roles. This is perhaps the place to emphasise that the students in the College operas gained experience behind the scenes as well as on the stage, Neil McKinnon, for example, being stage manager of *Werther*. In the past John McCabe had been a répétiteur.

Open practices in January, 1969, included Brahms's clarinet sonata, op. 120, no. 1, played by Richard Griffiths and Christopher Cotton, and three songs by Grieg—surprisingly a real rarity—sung by Greeba Kieg, a soprano pupil of Gwilym Jones. On 27 January, in the Free Trade Hall, the College Orchestra and Chorus gave the Michael Brierley Memorial Concert. In the first half, conducted by David Jordan, the Jacquino-Marcellina duet from Act I of *Fidelio* was sung by Caroline Crawshaw and Ryland Davies, the originals from the 1964 production, the Act II trio by Anne Howells, Ryland Davies and Patrick McGuigan, and the Act I quartet was also sung. Then Dianne Matthews and Joseph Ward, the 1962 Mélisande and Pelléas, sang Act III, Scene 1 of Debussy's opera. In the second half Dr Wray conducted Brahms's *Requiem* with Miss Crawshaw and McGuigan[1] as soloists. 'There is, I fear, no question but that his zeal and talent for work and his devotion to duty were responsible for his relatively early death', Cox wrote of Brierley in the programme. His name ranks in College annals among the great servants of musical education who have worked in Manchester.

Three of Holst's *Hymns from the Rig Veda* were sung by

---

[1] Whether marriages are made in heaven is arguable; they are certainly made at the R.M.C.M. For example: Martin Milner and Elizabeth Walton, John Ogdon and Brenda Lucas, Terence Nagle and Ludmila Navratil, Patrick McGuigan and Caroline Crawshaw, Robert Ferguson and Barbara Walker, Ryland Davies and Anne Howells, Robert Elliott and Honor Sheppard.

Gabrielle Lister on 5 March, and Susan Cowden and Martin Holland played Prokofiev's flute sonata, op. 94. On 11 March and 7 May Stravinsky's *The Soldier's Tale* was performed, and Villa-Lobos's *Bachianas Brasileiras* no. 6, for flute and bassoon, was played on 19 March by Kathryn Lukas and Andrew Gordon. The opera, on 22, 25, 27 and 29 March, was Bellini's *Norma*, a vehicle for splendid singing in the title-rôle by Angela Bostock (first night) and Thea Morelle (the remaining three). Judith Quine was Adalgisa and Pollione was divided between Anthony Holcroft and Roydn Jones. David Jordan conducted. The open practice on 30 April was notable not only for Kathryn Hardman's playing of Prokofiev's *Five Melodies*, op. 35, but for the inclusion of *Opus in Pastels* by Stan Kenton, played by five saxophone students. On 8 May Geoffrey Gilbert's annual concert with the training orchestra, brass ensemble and wind ensemble (including performances of Mozart's 41st symphony, Ravel's *Bolero* and Milhaud's *Suite Française*) marked the culmination of Gilbert's fine work at the College, for he resigned shortly afterwards to take up a similar post at the Stetson University, Florida. The superb results he achieved among wind students during his time in Manchester will have echoes among the professional orchestras for several years to come. On 17 May five of these students played a movement from Hindemith's wind quintet, op. 24, no. 2, three Rachmaninov songs were sung by Patricia Taylor, accompanied by Stephen Pilkington, Peter Sage played Liszt's *La Campanella*, Anthony Holcroft sang an aria from *Werther* and Brodsky's 'I'll walk with God', and Jonathan Sparey and Danielle Salamon played Debussy's violin sonata. The orchestra, led by Clifford Bibby, again visited Liverpool on 24 May, playing Mahler's first symphony and Walton's viola concerto, in which the highly accomplished soloist was Carolyn Sparey. On 11 June Richard Wilkinson, Hedwig Stein's pupil, played Bach and Liszt, and Lesley Kemplay, a violin pupil of Vilmos Schummy, and Stephen Bettaney played Vitali's Chaconne from the Dresden MS.

On 14 June Kenneth Cleveland conducted Rossini's *Demetrio e Polibio*, his first opera, written at the age of 14 and not performed since about 1824. The four parts were sung by Anthea Robb, Patricia Taylor, Harry Coghill and Roydn Jones. Another enterprising venture was a dramatisation of the book *Beloved Friend*, in which some letters between Nadejda von

Meck and Tchaikovsky were printed for the first time. On 18 June Goltermann's third cello concerto was played by Allan Stephenson, John Ireland's Fantasie Sonata was played by Howard Rogerson (clarinet) and Simon Wright, and Arnold's brass quintet was performed by Sydney Coulston's pupils. *The Soldier's Tale* was transferred to the stage of the University Theatre for a 10 p.m. performance on 19 June, conducted by David Garforth, with Susan Howells as the Princess, Philip Griffiths as the Soldier, David Hitchen the Devil and Eric Roberts the Narrator. On 27 June students from George Hadjinikos's conducting class—Keith Bentley, Erica Seligman and Christopher Fifield—gave a concert which included Mozart's Sinfonia Concertante for violin and viola, with Jonathan and Carolyn Sparey as soloists, Chausson's *Poème* played by Antony Tarlton and Liszt's second concerto played by Charles Knowles. End of term concerts included Tatiana's 'Letter Song' sung by Judith Quine, Schubert's E flat string quartet, Brahms's A major sonata, op. 100, played by Viviane Ronchetti and Gillian Bell, Pitfield's oboe sonata (Hilary Clough and Martin Holland) and Schubert's D minor sonata played brilliantly by Christian Blackshaw in a manner that made some good judges present speak of 'another Ogdon', a comparison emphasised even more forcefully by his playing of Brahms's B flat concerto at a College symphony concert at the Free Trade Hall on 28 April, 1970.

The 1969 autumn opera production in the University Theatre on 29 November, 2, 4 and 6 December, was of Britten's *Peter Grimes*, with Ian Caley as Grimes, Angela Bostock as Ellen and Alun Jenkins as Balstrode. This was a moving performance of the great work and the College's first excursion into 20th-century opera since *Bluebeard's Castle* and its first on a large scale. The experiment was repeated in the spring of 1970 when, on 18, 20 and 21 March, Phyllis Tate's opera about Jack the Ripper, *The Lodger*, was also successfully produced although audiences proved unadventurously cautious. Alun Jenkins sang the part of the Lodger and Ann Murray made a strong impression as Emma Bunting, the humane landlady. Among the orchestral concerts in the 1969–70 season, David Jordan conducted performances of Nielsen's *Sinfonia Espansiva*, Berlioz's *Harold in Italy*, with Michael Beeston as soloist and Brahms's third symphony. Verdi's *Requiem*, conducted by Dr Wray, was sung on 23 January, 1970, in memory of Gwilym

Jones, a former student who for 12 years had been on the singing teaching staff and whose early death was a shock to his colleagues. The *Requiem* was also performed in Wrexham, where it was heard by Germans from Iserlohn, 'twin town' of Wrexham. This led to an invitation to the College to take chorus and orchestra to Germany in March, 1971, at Iserlohn's expense, to give concerts and to perform *Peter Grimes*. The first opera staged after Cox's retirement was *Così fan tutte*, at the University Theatre on 5, 8, 10 and 12 December, with alternative casts. The accomplished performance of the most difficult of Mozart's operas ranked with *Pelléas* among the College's achievements. Angela Bostock, Patricia Taylor, Eiddwen Harrhy, Arthur Davies, Anthony Smith and Harry Coghill were the singers in the first cast, and Rosalind Plowright and Ann Murray (winner of first prize at the 1970 Barcelona under-25 competition) sang the sisters in the second. Larner praised David Jordan's 'singularly sensitive interpretation' and summed up the performance as 'one of the best heard by an avid and, some would say, not uncritical collector of *Così fan tutte* performances.'

Further honours were won overseas. Patricia Taylor, mezzo-soprano, was awarded the 1970 Richard Tauber Memorial Scholarship, carrying a cash prize of £550 and a year's study in Vienna. Christian Blackshaw was awarded a pianoforte scholarship to Moscow Conservatoire. He had distinguished himself in the July, 1970, Review Week concerts with a fine performance of Liszt's B minor sonata, as had Elizabeth Altman with Schumann's *Kreisleriana*. At a Free Trade Hall concert in honour of Frederic Cox on 26 November, the College Orchestra and Chorus and Chetham's Hospital Boys' Choir were conducted by Dr Wray and David Jordan. In the finale to Act I of *Norma* Elizabeth Harwood, Barbara Robotham and Joseph Ward were the singers. Vivien Townley sang 'Abscheulicher' from *Fidelio*, and Patrick McGuigan sang 'Wotan's Farewell' from *Die Walküre*, Anthony Goldstone was the solo pianist in Rachmaninov's *Rhapsody on a Theme of Paganini*, and the evening began with the Prologue to Boito's *Mefistofele*, with Norman Welsby as soloist. In a speech as witty and gracious as any of its kind, Cox declared the evening to be the highlight of his life.

During the 1970–1 season the College contributed handsomely to celebrations of Beethoven's bicentenary, with David

Wilde playing the 32 pianoforte sonatas, Raphael Sommer and Clifton Helliwell playing all the cello sonatas and cello variations, and Yossi Zivoni or John Brown and Helliwell performing all the violin sonatas.

In addition to these concerts the College in recent years has acted as impresario, or joint impresario, in promoting recitals by John Shirley-Quirk, Janet Baker, David Wilde, Yonty Solomon, Richard Lewis, Benjamin Britten and Peter Pears, Richard Rodney Bennett, Ronald Stevenson and Malcolm Williamson. College students, as has been seen, have been the mainstay of M.I.C.A., and the students themselves promoted a recital by Roger Smalley at which music by Stockhausen was heard for the first time in Manchester, and invited Peter Maxwell Davies and Harrison Birtwistle to bring their Pierrot Players to perform works by the two Englishmen and to give their renowned account of Schoenberg's *Pierrot Lunaire*, with Mary Thomas. In October, 1970, Anne Howells returned to give a fine Lieder recital. These Students' Union concerts were organized by Judith Serota.

Each Principal has faced different problems and has had to work within the context of conditions prevailing at the time. Great names stud these pages from the very start—Catterall, Camden, Maaskoff, Wearing, Rawsthorne, Barker—and among the teachers, from Brodsky, Backhaus, Petri and Forbes to Wolf, Gilbert, Gilson, Thurston and Brierley, a common thread of devotion binds the 'space age' to the age of Queen Victoria. Yet the post-1945 years more than any others vindicate Hallé's belief in the musical potential of the North of England. Aided by better general education and by the benevolence of local authority grants, students poured into the College and emerged from it into a richer and more varied professional life than can ever have been imagined by the first Principal. Under Frederic Cox, the College prospered as never before—to have produced such artists as John Ogdon and Brenda Lucas, Rodney Friend and Elizabeth Harwood, Ludmila Navratil and Catherine Wilson, Joseph Ward and John Mitchinson, Honor Sheppard and Robert Elliott, Alexander Goehr and Harrison Birtwistle, Ryland Davies and Anne Howells, Caroline Crawshaw and Patrick McGuigan, Vivien Townley and Barbara Walker, John Bimson and Anthony Halstead, Janet Hilton and Lynn Brierley, David Wilde and John McCabe, Ruth Waterman and Anthony Goldstone, is a record that fully justified Jack Thom's proclamation of the 'heritage' that the College would take with it into the new Northern College of Music. Such a major step, involving the end of the R.M.C.M. as it had existed for nearly 80 years, could only have been contemplated in the widest interests of musical education; and the long and difficult years of negotiation detailed in the next chapter bear testimony to the emotions, loyalties and conflicts involved, for the Northern School of Music also had enlarged and improved its contributions to Manchester's musical scene within the period of this chapter and was no less proud of its achievements and independence.

18
The new College

The minutes of a Council Meeting held in the College on 15 November, 1954, state:

The question of amalgamation with the Northern School of Music was raised by the Principal, and after discussion it was resolved that authority be given the Principal to explore the possibilities and to discuss the matter with the chairman of the Manchester Education Committee.

In the years since the end of the war the Northern School had made considerable progress. It offered a three-year diploma course for entrants over 18, and its staff was enthusiastic and devoted. The large majority of its students were part-time, whereas all the College's were full-time. Undoubtedly a rivalry with the College existed, as is inevitable where two organisations in one city deal with the same subject, but in view of the growth of the numbers of people studying music and the restriction of entrants to the College, there was no commercial rivalry in any real sense. On the other hand, in view of Treasury grants and financial obligations, it was obvious to some that one combined institution might fare better than two separate identities. At any rate, early in 1955 Sir John Stopford and Frederic Cox met Hilda Collens, then Principal of the N.S.M., and discussed the subject of a merger in general terms. 'There was reason to hope for developments', the Council were told. On 29 July, 1955, Cox reported a further meeting with Miss Collens and her assistant, Miss Ida Carroll, daughter of Dr Walter Carroll, who, it will be recalled, had been one of the original members of the College staff and had resigned in 1920. He described the talks as 'quite friendly', and added that Bernard Shore, the Staff Inspector of Schools, favoured an amalgamation and thought it might lead to an increased Treasury grant.

No further moves were made, and on 20 February, 1956, Cox 'spoke at considerable length' to the Council, which now included Alderman Abraham Moss and Councillor Maurice Pariser, the then chairman of Manchester Education Committee, on the advantages of an alliance between the College and the Manchester College of Technology rather than with the University. The Council discussed his views at a later meeting, on 19 March, 1955, and resolved that the College's future policy should lie in a strengthening of the ties that already existed between the College and the University. Cox's advocacy of the alternative course was based on a possibility at that time that the College would be offered accommodation in the new Technology building and would have the use, for operas and recitals, of the new Renold Theatre which formed part of the amenities. A sub-committee of the Council met University delegates and began talks on various aspects of a closer association. These, the Council were told on 24 July, were 'marked by goodwill, understanding and a desire to achieve results'. No real progress was made, however, because of severe restrictions on University building programmes which precluded any College transfer to a site within the University precinct before at least 1962 and a restriction on student numbers to 250. But at the same meeting Cox said he had learned (by an accidental remark made in a telephone conversation by a civil servant) that the Northern School of Music were asking Manchester Education Committee for increased assistance. It was unjustifiable, he said, for taxpayers and ratepayers to be asked to pay for the provision of two music schools in Manchester. If funds were available they should be used for improving tuition rather than duplicating the overheads. It was decided that ways of re-opening talks on amalgamation should be examined. On 3 October, just before the Council met, Cox was told on the telephone by Alderman Moss that the Education Committee had decided to assist the Northern School 'on a substantial scale', and would shortly be inviting the College to a meeting at which there would be discussion of ways in which the College could co-operate in 'a wider scheme'. The Council therefore authorised Cox to act as he thought best when the invitation was received. 'It was felt', says the minute, 'that the occasion might well be a turning-point in the history of musical education in the North of England.'

On 19 December, Cox reported an 'inconclusive interview' with J. K. Elliott, Manchester's Chief Education Officer. Early in 1957 there was misgiving on the Council about a report that a municipal school of music might be established in Manchester with the aim of training professional musicians and 'graduate equivalent' teachers. This could not be justified, it was felt, on artistic, educational or economic grounds, and a delegation—Behrens, Thom, Professor Oliver and Cox—was appointed to meet the Education Committee to put forward these views. This meeting was held in March and the College delegates came away with the impression that the Education Committee would 'heartily welcome co-operation or amalgamation on the part of the Royal College and the Northern School' and Pariser asked the College to approach the School direct. Miss Collens had died since the first approaches were made and Cox now had an 'informal and inconclusive' talk with her successor, Miss Carroll, Acting Principal at this particular date. She appreciated the force of the arguments in favour of amalgamation; 'but, while not shutting the door, she could hardly be said to favour the proposal'. So the Council decided that their chairman, Professor Mansfield Cooper, should write to the chairman of the Council of the N.S.M., Mr Gerrard. A meeting between both bodies was held at the University on 16 April, at which the School's delegates stressed that in any merger the entity and the diploma of the N.S.M. would have to be preserved. The next move, it was agreed, should come from the School. Meanwhile Cox had mentioned the possible amalgamation to a Treasury official who had been strongly in favour and deplored spending public money on a duplication of costs of providing musical training in Manchester.

The representatives of College and School met again on 3 June. One suggestion fully discussed was that there should be a division of labour between the two schools whereby the N.S.M. undertook the teacher training of all graduates and associates (teachers). After the meeting Gerrard wrote to Behrens to say that this was no solution and there was no other course than 'to go back to where we were and attempt to find a solution with the Education Committee'. Mansfield Cooper then wrote to the N.S.M. hoping that the School would not hesitate to communicate further with the College if it ever wished to do so: there were other avenues of approach to the problem. He met Gerrard again later and stressed the College's sincerity and readiness to re-open negotiations. And there it was decided to leave the matter. Nothing more was heard, officially, of the scheme until December, 1958, when discussions were convened by Percy Lord, chief education officer for Lancashire, on musical education in general and the possibility that local authorities would assume some measure of financial responsibility for the operation of the College, possibly in some form of association with the Northern School of Music. At the meeting were representatives of the local education authorities of Lancashire, Cheshire, Manchester and Salford and of the College and School. Further meetings followed in the next six months between Cox and Miss Carroll and, more formally, between local authority officers, Mr Athol Page, a schools inspector, and the College and School. Cox told the Council on 10 June that discussions had mainly been on optimum numbers of students and the size and site of any new premises, and that he believed they had been friendly and fruitful and that there was the 'very real possibility' of a scheme being formulated. On Mansfield Cooper's instructions he had seen Councillor Pariser about the Royal Charter and kept the Treasury informed. Pariser's view was that the present charter might be retained with certain modifications. Because any new College would be controlled by a governing body drawn mainly from members of the present Councils of the two existing schools and from the local authorities concerned, this of itself did not mean that the charter would have to be abrogated: there was nothing in the charter to prevent the election to the Council of representatives of the local authorities and the Northern School. Indeed the existing College Council of 19 members included five representatives of local authorities and two of the Northern School governing body. The Treasury approved of the idea of local-authority financing but said it would support the College in refusing such an offer if the new scheme did not maintain existing standards of tuition or did not take into account the work the College had already done and its national status.

Another full meeting of the representatives concerned in the project was held on 21 July at which considerable headway was made in spite of certain reservations on the part of the Northern School. In the meantime reports were to be made on a more accurate assessment of the running cost of the new college, on details of the two schools' existing accommodation and (from the city architect) on music college buildings in Britain and abroad. The College Council were anxious that, while not allowing questions of traditions, independence, personalities or methods to stand in the way of a new college, these imponderables should be retained in any new establishment. In the autumn of 1959 the first reports of the new scheme reached the Press. Under the draft scheme the minimum cost of a new college, containing an opera theatre, based on the requirements of 500 full-time students, was estimated at £263,000, with running costs of £75,000 a year.

Progress for the next few months was slow, with sub-committee meetings held fairly regularly. Formation of a steering committee, or interim governing body, was the next vital step and on 21 September, 1960, Cox attended a meeting at which an agenda was prepared. Site, title and constitution of the new college were the principal considerations. The site, it was generally agreed, should be of two acres and as near as possible to the city centre. With the exception of Cox, who favoured 'The Royal School of Music, Manchester', the meeting proposed the title 'The Royal Northern College of Music, Manchester'. No one, apparently, suggested that there was no prescriptive right to the designation 'Royal'. In the matter of the constitution, the recommendation was that the new college's council should have 25 to 30 members. Of these 16 would represent the four local authorities concerned, four each would come from the two amalgamating colleges, and the rest be co-opted from other musical interests. A week later, on 28 September, Cox and Athol Page discussed the College's Royal Charter with Mr Todhunter, of the legal branch of the Ministry of Education. Todhunter thought the new college could retain the charter. However, opinion began to swing the other way and at the College annual meeting on 17 November Lord Harewood hinted at 'difficulties' and 'misgivings' over the new college. 'We are ready to compromise', he said, 'but we shall never compromise on essentials.' The College's tradition rested on the students' diploma requirements: 'The Council will not consider abandoning these, nor will we lower standards in any way'.

A full representative meeting of those interested in the new college was held in Manchester on 15 December. Here it emerged plainly that the abandonment of the Royal Charter was more than likely; and this was reinforced by the steering committee's decision, on 24 January, 1961, to recommend to the next full representative meeting that the new college should be fully maintained by local authority funds and that, in consequence, the Royal Charter would have to go. The College Council, meeting on 8 February, heard this with regret and called the decision 'retrograde', but believed that it would be wrong to withdraw from the scheme on this score alone. Recommendations had still to be made on such vital issues as diplomas, entrance standards, appointments of Principal, Deputy Principal and senior staff, and arrangements for co-ordinating the work of the two schools during the transition period until the new college was open, and the Council wanted to see what these would be. In addition, their final attitude would be determined by their responsibilities as trustees of the many large sums bequeathed to the R.M.C.M.

The full representative meeting on 10 March produced a 'final' draft scheme for the new college. This the College Council approved at its next meeting, but reserved final approval until receipt of a detailed agreement covering such points as periods of office of members of the governing body, types of diplomas, admittance of students, etc. Most important of all, the Council agreed that the College's funds and assets should be available to the new body, under a legal agreement whereby:

(a) instruments, equipment, music and so forth should be transferred unconditionally;

(b) scholarship and sustentation funds should be administered, according to the wishes of the benefactors, by a body of trustees (possibly the new college's council, or a section of it);

(c) Charter funds should be formed into a trust and administered by trustees first for pensions and gratuities to existing members of the College staff and secondly for other purposes consonant with the Charter.

Now a new snag arose. It had been proposed that the posts of treasurer and clerk of the interim governing body of the new college should be the responsibility of Lancashire County Council but Manchester won the treasurership. In July, 1961, Lancashire proposed two amendments: that the clerk of Lancashire C.C. should become clerk of the new body in place of the original choice, Percy Lord, chief education officer, and that Lord should have the new post of 'education officer to the governors'. Foreseeing the embarrassing nature of this post in relation to the future Principal, the College Council inquired which duties it was proposed should be performed by the education officer; they felt that the appointment could serve

13

no useful purpose. Their misgivings on other aspects were conveyed by Cox to the Treasury, particularly the fear that 'some of the parties concerned' might wish to stress the teaching-training aspect of the new college's work to the detriment of musical standards. Again the Treasury gave its backing to the view that any lowering of performing standards would be a retrograde step. The College wrote asking that the next meeting of officers connected with the scheme should consider a College memorandum on aims, standards, diplomas and conditions of admission. Cox and Thom attended the meeting at Preston on 31 January, 1962, but the memorandum was not discussed: the meeting was devoted almost entirely to the question of clerk to the governors, and the decision was taken that the Lancashire C.C. clerk should remain as clerk to the new governing body. The idea of an education officer was dropped, Percy Lord being recommended as a foundation member of the new body. In March Lord told the Press that although there was still likely to be 'much discussion on several contentious points', he was now sure the scheme would come to fruition. The Ministry of Education, to his delight, had provisionally included the new college in the further education programme for 1964–5, which meant that work could begin on the site selected in Oxford Road, Manchester, some time after April, 1964.

On 31 May Lord was chairman of a meeting at the Northern School, attended by Lord's deputy, Boyce, Miss Carroll and Cox, at which Cox's memorandum on academic, as opposed to constitutional, points was discussed. Lord argued for and won Miss Carroll's acceptance of the whole document. It was agreed that:

(1) the Interim Governing Body should become statutory as soon as was practicable;
(2) except for a few well-defined categories, entrance to the new college should be limited to full-time students;
(3) there should be three courses only—performer, graduate and teacher of specific instruments;
(4) the new college should *not* prepare students for school teaching below the level of graduate-equivalent;
(5) the college should *not* give instruction to junior students (other than to a small number of talented children on a Saturday morning).

Shortly afterwards the clerk-designate stated that the interim governing body would soon be constituted and invited the College to name its four representatives. These were Leonard Behrens, J. H. Thom, George Furniss and Sir Robert Platt, with Cox ex officio. It might be thought that all was now plain sailing, but such is not the way of committee-government. The officers preparing a memorandum for the interim body were at odds over the appointment of that body's chairman: some wished to restrict it to representative members, others felt that it should be open to any member (i.e. from among co-opted members). Also, the College's decision to deal as it thought fit with its Charter funds as they affected building and site values and general reserve caused dismay among the local authorities' treasurers. And the College officials in turn were dismayed to find that, despite the *entente* reached at the 31 May meeting, the academic aims of the new college were still being presented in their original, unsatisfactory form.

The first meeting of the interim governing body—henceforward to be referred to as the I.G.B.—was in Manchester Town Hall on 21 November, 1962. The chairmanship issue was left open and not restricted to representative members; the 'definition of aims' as drafted by Cox was accepted; the clerk undertook to report at the next meeting on appointment of a Principal-designate; sub-committees were formed to consider purchase of a site and selection of an architect; and an invitation was sent to the University to appoint a representative. The I.G.B. met again on 11 January, 1963, and selected five other bodies from whom representatives were invited: the Arts Council, the B.B.C. North Region, Granada Television, the Hallé Concerts Society and the Royal Liverpool Philharmonic Society. Appointment of a Principal-designate was postponed until the Joint Committee (the Council of the new College) was formally established with statutory powers. This, it was said, 'should not be long'. Five firms of architects were on a short list. The Ministry of Education gave its blessing to all that had been achieved so far. Again, it all seemed plain sailing; and again it was an illusion.

When the I.G.B. met on 15 March the main debate was on transfer of the College's charter funds. One proposal was that sums accruing from the sale of the R.M.C.M. site and buildings should be distributed equally between the cost of the new buildings and a discretionary fund. The College representatives proposed that there should be a discretionary fund, with a ceiling of £40,000, formed from the existing general fund and the proceeds of the sale of land and buildings. This fund would be used for a retirement pensions scheme and to educate executants. Any balance over the £40,000 would go towards cost of the new site and buildings, which was now estimated in the region of £600,000. The I.G.B. accepted the College proposal by a majority vote, but Manchester Corporation representatives said that no further steps would be taken towards acquisition of the new site until agreement had been reached on transfer of the College assets.

At a meeting on 26 March of Manchester finance committee, the chairman, Councillor Norman Morris, said that 'the understanding was that the assets of the College, with those of the Northern School of Music, should be used to offset the capital cost of building the new college'. The College, he said, was acting in an irresponsible manner and had shown bad faith. These statements were discussed by the College Council next day, when it was decided to write to the Town Clerk, Sir Philip Dingle, pointing out the mis-statements which had been made and also to send copies of the letter to all others concerned. As a result Morris withdrew his allegation of bad faith, as did some Salford councillors who had followed his lead. The deadlock continued until December, when at a meeting on the 20th, the I.G.B. was told that agreement had been reached on the Charter funds whereby the College's provisions as outlined above were accepted. These were eventually embodied in the Second Schedule of the final agreement for setting-up of the new college, which was to be known by the title Northern College of Music, Manchester.

Matters now moved more swiftly. The architect appointed, W. H. Allen, aimed at completion in 1966–7, and pointed out that the £600,000 estimate was unrealistic. The next delay was caused by an objection to compulsory purchase of the site. By July the College Council and College solicitor, Mr Shepherd, were discussing the terms of the final agreement, which was published in September, and accepted at an I.G.B. meeting on 17 July. Briefly it summarised the new college's functions as:

To train musicians, both performers and teachers, and to make a general contribution to musical life.
Without prejudice or detriment to the primary aims of the

College to promote as far as practicable courses in speech, drama and related subjects, and to issue diplomas in these subjects.

Diplomas in performance only to be awarded to those who have reached the level of efficiency required in a professional recitalist.

Students to be accepted only if they undertook full-time courses leading to one or other of the diplomas. Part-time students to be admitted only if they have the necessary promise and standard to benefit fully from advanced tuition.

Administration of both the College and the Northern School was now complicated by the need to refer all decisions on salaries and staff appointments to sub-committees of the proposed new college because whatever happened in either school had now to be considered in the light both of existing needs and of future repercussions on the new college. Although it was constantly urged that appointment of a Principal-designate would iron out many problems that might arise, the issue was continually postponed. 'We are preparing to hand over our independence in a wider interest of music and music education', Cox told the College annual meeting in November, 1964. 'The proposal that we should sink our identity and join in a scheme for a new college is a greater act of faith than when our doors were first opened in 1893 with £1,500 or less in the bank.' Sir William Mansfield Cooper (as he had become in June, 1963) stressed that the College was not impelled by any fears about its financial future. 'Generous gifts have again shown how firm our future prospects would be if we preferred our independence', he said. 'We are, however, convinced that the way of collaboration in the long run is the better way.'

Objections to the purchase of the site were overruled in April, 1965. The Department of Education and Science (as the Ministry of Education had now become) approved the compulsory purchase order and now assumed financial responsibility for the College and the new college. One immediate outcome was an increase in salaries for the Principal and staff. At extraordinary general meetings of members of the College on 16 February and 3 March, 1966, formal approval of the new college scheme was given. The document, signed by all the other parties, was received at the College on 7 March and the College Seal was affixed. The Privy Council had been consulted and had raised no objections but had asked that formal letters from the Patron (the Queen) and the President (Lord Harewood) should indicate their approval also. On 1 April, the Department of Education and Science conferred statutory powers on the Joint Committee of the new college and the College then appointed its four representative members, to hold office for life or until they resigned. They were Leonard Behrens, J. H. Thom, Richard Godlee and myself. (Simon Towneley replaced Thom when the latter retired.)

Cox and Miss Carroll now entered upon the difficult period of 'running down', a period made more trying for both by the lack of any decision on a future Principal and by the growing feeling that, because of the financial state of the country, the new college might still be a long way from becoming a reality. Nevertheless they co-operated on appointments and on procedures to reduce the number of admittances to their colleges so that the total student body should not be over 500 (in 1966 the combined total was over 700). The chairman of the interim governing body since its inception had been one of the Lancashire County Council representatives, Simon Towneley, of Burnley, himself a distinguished musical scholar. He had lost his seat in the 1966 municipal elections and was now ineligible to be a member of the Joint Committee. Already a member of the Council of the Northern School, he was now invited to be a member of the College Council.

On 27 October, 1966, the Joint Committee held its first meeting in the Town Hall, Manchester. Alderman Sir Maurice Pariser, whose diplomatic work behind the scenes had smoothed over many an impending crisis, was elected chairman, with County Councillor J. Hargreaves of Lancashire vice-chairman. Lancashire had six representatives, Cheshire four, Manchester four, Salford two, the College four, the Northern School four (A. J. Moon, A. Hague, W. P. Lockley and J. N. Padmore), the University one (Professor Oliver), and the remaining co-opted members were John Cruft (Arts Council), Gerald McDonald (B.B.C.), Clive Smart (Hallé), Stephen Gray (Royal Liverpool Philharmonic) and Douglas Terry (Granada), with Percy Lord, foundation member. In addition Simon Towneley was co-opted to the staffing and architectural sub-committees.

The proceedings of the Joint Committee do not belong within the scope of this book, but the Committee accepted financial responsibility for the College and the Northern School from 1 September, 1967 (the 'notional' rate for the College being fixed at £137,735 per annum). Architects' plans for the new college were now published. The college is part of the magnificent new education precinct which will eventually spread along Oxford Road and will house the University, the University Institute of Science and Technology and the Manchester Polytechnic. On a site 315 ft. by 190 ft. on the corner of Oxford Road and Booth Street West, the college will contain a 720-seat theatre, a 475-seat concert hall, an organ, 90 tutorial rooms, a concourse, a 125-seat recital room, lecture rooms, refectory, common rooms, library, kitchens and administrative offices. The latest techniques in sound insulation and acoustics will be used.

The R.M.C.M. Council continued to press for appointment of a Principal-designate as a means of easing many incipient problems. The post was to be advertised but this could not be done until the Department of Education and Science decided a salary and terms of service. It was hoped these would be known by the autumn of 1967, but the year came and went without any progress in this respect. But on 16 November, 1967, the Joint Committee approved new scales of pay for all teachers and clerical staff, an event described by Cox at the College's annual meeting as 'the day of the Bill of Rights'. It would set new standards for music teachers throughout the country, a 'down-trodden band' who in the past had been at a considerable disadvantage to their colleagues in other branches of teaching. The new administrative régime, with the College's finances governed by the City Treasurer, meant that the old post of Registrar was outmoded, and the Treasurer's task was eased, except that the Council was still responsible for the College's assets. An example of the kind of problem that arose was the Junior Exhibitioners' Department, the cost of which could not be met by the new college. To make it self-supporting could only be achieved by raising individual fees from 12 guineas to £25 a term. But the Council strongly opposed this increase, because the department did valuable work and such a steep rise could only mean that some worthwhile students would be forced to leave. Instead, all the teachers in the department agreed to continue teaching juniors at the old salary scale, thereby limiting the increase in fee to £15 a term.

At the end of 1967 the expectation was that the new college would be ready for occupation by September, 1970. But in January, 1968, the stringent financial squeeze and freeze applied to all public and private spending by the Wilson Government took full effect and in April the College project was excluded from the 1968–9 building programme for further education. Coming just after the death on 3 February of Sir Maurice Pariser, this was a severe blow to all concerned with this tantalising dream. Lancashire, Cheshire, Manchester and Salford had each recommended priority for the college even in the light of the Government's economies, but it was to no avail. Cox and Miss Carroll both expressed their disappointment. 'We have been waiting so long', Cox said. 'We were made to hurry over a matter like giving up our charter to get the project into the 1963 building programme.' On 29 August, 1968, the Department of Education and Science announced that a start on the new college would 'definitely be made early in 1969'. The postponement had increased the cost to £778,000, exclusive of furnishings, equipment and instruments, and another £110,000 in professorial fees. In July, 1969, a tender of £828,299 from H. Fairweather & Co. was approved and building began on 10 November. The total final estimate, with professional fees, site investigation and fixed equipment and fittings was to be £1,060,548 and completion was to be within 27 months, so that the college could open during 1972.

Even at this stage, however, there was still no appointment of a Principal of the new college. The post had been advertised and a short-list had been made for discussion by the special sub-committee appointed by the Joint Committee, whose chairman was now Kathleen Ollerenshaw. Cox applied for the post, as he informed the Council on 1 October, 1969, and so did Miss Carroll. Neither was considered, for reasons of age, and no other name was considered suitable for recommendation to the Joint Committee.[1] On 27 January, 1970, at a Council meeting from which Cox was absent through illness, a statement from him mentioned the 'invidious and anomalous position' in which he now was. The uncertainty had continued for many years and he was no longer willing to continue; it would be 'better all round if he resigned'. In the following weeks members of the Council tried to dissuade him but his mind was made up. He was 64, he had been ill, and in March, 1970, he suffered a personal bereavement which affected him deeply. On 6 March he tendered his resignation, to take effect in September, at a meeting of the Joint Committee. At a Council meeting ten days later it was unanimously decided

[1] Later, John Manduell, Director of Music, Lancaster University, was appointed Principal-designate as from September, 1971.

to give him the unprecedented title of Principal Emeritus and to appoint Dr Wray as Principal for the last months of the College's separate life. Cox was elected to the Council and to the Board of Professors. As Principal he had taken the College back into the mainstream of Manchester's musical life and made it count in musical circles outside Manchester as it had not counted since Brodsky's day. He achieved this without personal flamboyance, but simply by quiet and firm force of character, by picking the right men for the right jobs and letting them get on with them and by his uncanny ability for being on good terms with the students without patronising them in any way. He made the College, staff and students, into a team, but no team can succeed without a great captain and that is what Freddie Cox was. His team won trophies, too. Also he made it a family—the system of Members of the College was his idea—and whatever family quarrels there may have been, there was unity when it was most needed. With his departure, with the retirement of Sir William Mansfield Cooper from chairmanship of the Council, and with the death of Jack Thom at the age of 71, the end of a College era was sealed, not with a bang and certainly not with a whimper but with a muffled roll of drums.

A future historian will have access to the minutes of the Northern School's deliberations on the matter of the new college, and to those of Lancashire County Council and other bodies. My brief has been to write the history of the Royal Manchester College of Music, and my successor of 50 to 100 years hence will find this chapter an accurate record of the proceedings as they affected the College. To him I say: from your perspective of half a century or a century after the events I have described, do not underestimate the people involved in the birth of the Northern College of Music, Manchester, however tremendous the personalities with whom you yourself will have to deal and of whom I cannot know anything. Do not underestimate, in 2070, Frederic Cox and Ida Carroll, both remarkable individuals, each jealous of the traditions and achievements of his and her own college for which they had fought many single-handed battles long before amalgamation was suggested, but each ready, in spite, perhaps, of personal misgivings, to submerge pride for something they hoped would mean a better future for music students; do not overlook the perseverance of Jack Thom, the wisdom of Maurice Pariser and the vision of Percy Lord.

The new college had a long and difficult gestation. Its labour pains were painful and prolonged; the forecast of its date of birth was again and again miscalculated, although the date of conception was never in doubt. It issued from a marriage of convenience, a marriage for money, with municipal godparents ready to shower annual gifts on the offspring. But if the child takes after its parents, follows their example and improves upon their achievements, then all the frustrations, the heart-searching, the intrigues, the sacrifices recorded or only suggested in this chapter, will have been worth while.

Appendix

I. OFFICERS OF THE COLLEGE

Patron

Queen Alexandra (1901–25)
King George VI (1937–52)
Queen Elizabeth II (1952–)

President

Sir William H. Houldsworth, Bart, M.P., LL.D. (1893–1917)
Sir Thomas Beecham, Bart. (1917–22)
H.R.H. The Duke of York, K.G. (1923–36)
Lord Hewart of Bury (1937–42)
Viscount Lascelles, later Earl of Harewood (1945–)

Principal

Sir Charles Hallé (1893–5)
Dr Adolph Brodsky (1895–1929)
R. J. Forbes, C.B.E. (1929–53)
Frederic R. Cox, O.B.E. (1953–70)
Dr John Wray (1970–)

Principal Emeritus

Frederic R. Cox, O.B.E. (1970)

Chairman of the Council

Sir Adolphus W. Ward (1893–7)
George R. Murray (1897–9)
Sir Alfred Hopkinson, K.C. (1899–1913)
Professor Frederick E. Weiss (1914–16)
Sir Henry Miers (1916–26)
Sir Walter Moberly (1926–35)
Sir John S. B. Stopford (1935–56)
Sir William Mansfield Cooper (1956–70)
Arthur Armitage (1970–)

Treasurer

Charles E. Lees (1893–4)
Charles J. Heywood (1894–1905)
Gustav Behrens (1905–34)
Philip Godlee (1934–52)
J. H. Thom (1952–68)
Simon Towneley (1968–)

Registrar

Stanley Withers (1893–1928)
John Holme (1928–41)
Harold Dawber (1941–48, combined with Warden)
Dr Eric Wilson (1948–56)
Noel E. Kay (1958–59)
Michael Brierley (1959–67) (post abolished in 1967)
Clifton Helliwell (Assistant to the Principal, 1967–70)

Warden

Harold Dawber (1941–59)
Dr Norman Andrew (1959–64)
Dr John Wray (1964–70)
Ronald Frost (Director of Studies, 1970–   )

Honorary Members

Mrs Lawrence Haward (1928)
F. E. Weiss (1930)
Sir John Barbirolli, C.H. (1954)
Lord Stopford of Fallowfield (1956)
Dame Ruth King, O.B.E. (Ruth Railton) (1958)
Richard T. Wignall (1962)
J. H. Thom (1964)
Wilhelm Backhaus (1964)
Sir Neville Cardus, C.B.E. (1968)
Sir Percy Lord (1968)
Sir Leonard F. Behrens, C.B.E. (1969)
Earl of Harewood (1970)
Frederic R. Cox, O.B.E. (1970)
Sir William Mansfield Cooper (1970)
Sir William Walton, O.M. (1971)
Michael Kennedy (1971)

Professores Emeriti

Dr J. Kendrick Pyne (organ) (1914)
Max Mayer (pianoforte) (1924)
Olga Neruda (pianoforte) (1924)
Arthur Catterall (violin) (1929)
Jeanne Bretey (pianoforte) (1933)
Carl Fuchs (violoncello) (1945)
Claud Biggs (pianoforte) (1961)
Lucy Pierce (pianoforte) (1964)

II. Honorary Fellows (F.R.M.C.M.)
(in chronological order of election)

1923: Norman Allin, Sarah Andrew, Dr J. C. Bradshaw, Arthur Catterall, Richard Evans, R. J. Forbes, Edward Isaacs, Dr Thomas Keighley, Edna Thornton, Lillie Wormald

1924: Horace Alwyne, Anton Maaskoff, Charles Neville

1925: Archie Camden, Lucy Pierce, Leo Smith

1926: John Booth, George Whitaker, Dr A. W. Wilcock

1927: Harold Dawber, Harry Mortimer

1928: Charles Kelly, John Wills, John Armistead

1929: Elsie Thurston, Alfred Worsley

1930: Naum Blinder, Edward Dunn, Dr A. W. Pollitt

1931: Hamilton Harris, Jesse Stamp, Anderson Tyrer

1932: Sam Holt, Bertram Lewis

1933: Samuel Worthington

1934: Alfred Barker

1936: Elizabeth Muirhead

1941: Dora Gilson, Norman Walker

1943: Frank Park, Thomas B. Pitfield, Alan Rawsthorne, Haydn Rogerson, Pat Ryan, Stephen Wearing

1944: Kathleen Moorhouse, Otto Paersch

1947: Grahame Clifford, Geoffrey Gilbert, Dr C. Thornton Lofthouse

1948: Albert Hardie, Leonard Hirsch

1953: Dr Norman Andrew, Harry Blech, Louis Cohen, Gordon Green, Clifford Knowles, Richard Lewis

1954: Dr George Armstrong, Raymond Cohen

1955: Maurice Johnstone, Marjorie Thomas

1956: Sydney Coulston, Dr Eric Wilson

1957: John Hopkins, Philip Whiteway

1958: Clifton Helliwell, Charles Taylor

1959: Michael Brierley, Paul Cropper, William Johnson

1960: Pamela Bowden, Keith Cummings

1961: Dr Dennis Chapman, Martin Milner

1962: Eric Chadwick, John Ogdon

1963: John Mitchinson

1964: Ben Horsfall, Sydney Partington, Noel Rawsthorne

1965: Sidney Fell, Rodney Friend, Thomas Johnson

1966: Alexander Goehr, Elizabeth Harwood, Ronald Stevenson, David Wilde

1967: Robert Elliott, Lawrence Glover, John McCabe, Honor Sheppard, Ernest Tomlinson, Joseph Ward

1968: Irvin Cooper, Keith Swallow, Yvonne Tiénot, Catherine Wilson, James Kershaw (posth.)

1969: Manuel Alvarado, Elgar Howarth, Peter Maxwell Davies, Hazel Vivienne

1970: Harrison Birtwistle, John Brown, Barbara Robotham, Susan Tunnell, Gwilym Jones (posth.), Philip Lord (posth.)

III. Scholarship and Prize Winners

Hallé Memorial Scholarship (pianoforte)
1897–1900: Edith Webster
1900–03: Edward M. Isaacs
1903–06: Ellen Arthan
1906–09: Lucy E. Pierce
1909–12: Horace (Hy) Alwyne
1912–14: Will Pearce
1914–17: John Wills
1917–20: Edith Hothersall
1920–23: Donald Hargreaves
1923–26: Stephen Wearing
1926–30: Lilian Grindrod
1930–33: John Brennan
1933–34: Robert Keys
1935–38: Winifred Rooking
1938–41: Zoë Monteanu
1941–42: Marie Taylor
1945–48: Joseph Clough
1949–52: Brian Wright
1958–63: Joanna Bowker

Read Scholarship
1897–1900: Frances E. Baguley (singing)
1900–04: Bertha Orgill (singing)
1904–05: Mary G. Brookes (violin)
1905–09: Elizabeth A. Lees (singing)
1909–13: Maud Dunnington (violoncello)
1913–17: Annie Dalies (singing)
1917–20: Eva Critchley (piano)
1920–23: Lily Endlar (violin)
1923–26: Nanette Osborne (piano)
1926–30: Ruth Denman (violin)
1930–34: Dorothy Rice (piano)
1934–38: Brenda Old (violin)
1938–41: Joan Stirrup (singing)
1941–42: Jean Shorrock (singing)
1943–46: Joyce Lumb (piano)
1946–49: Irene Cookson (piano)
1953–54: Jean Brier (violin)
1955–57: Margaret Hallworth (singing)
1964–68: Patricia Hughes (singing)

Charles James Heywood Scholarship (pianoforte)
1907–08: Dorothy Cole
1908–12: Dora Gilson
1912–16: Edith Hothersall
1916–18: Ed. N. Constantine

1918–22: Elsie Broughton
1922–26: Phyllis Eley
1926–30: Arthur Berry
1930–34: Alan Soulsby
1934–38: Annie Waring
1938–41: Edith Halliwell
1941–44: Dorothy Smith
1944–45: Sylvia Hudson
1946–49: Barbara Platt
1954–59: Maureen Challinor

Percy Heywood Scholarship (pianoforte)
1943–44 and 1949–51: Geoffrey Greed
1952–55: George Emmott
1953–55: John Ogdon
1955–59: Joan Smethurst
1959–66: Mary Dalton

Arthur Walmsley Organ Scholarship
1944–47: Bernard J. Porter
1947–49: Audrey Kennedy
1949–50: Marjorie Ingham
1951–53: Robert Andrews
1954–57: David Ellis

Max Mayer Scholarship (pianoforte)
1935–38: Nancy Harris
1939–42: Joan Holt
1942–45: Sallie Hickling
1949–52: Gerald Keenan
1955–57: John Ogdon
1959–62: Patricia Griffin

Will Pearce Scholarship (pianoforte)
1914–18: Augusta Bertrand
1918–21: Edith Annie White
1921–25: Lilian Grindrod
1925–29: Jessie Hulse
1929–33: Hilary Davis
1933–34: George Mantle-Childe
1934–37: Madge Barlow
1937–40: Mary M. Hodgson
1940–42: Douglas Shaw
1945–48: John Ellis
1951–54: Catherine Day
1955–58: Keith Allen
1962–68: Darina Gibson
1969–70: Ian Sharpe

Julius Scholarship (pianoforte)
1930–33: Robert Keys
1933–37: Dorothy Best
1937–40: Clare L. Liversage
1940–43: Marjorie Thomas
1944–45: Doreen Davis
1946–50: Pamela Edge
1954–59: Patricia Shackleton
1963–66: Priscilla Jessop
1969–70: Raymond Hodkinson

Brodsky Memorial Scholarship (violin)
1929–30: Evelyn Thornton
1930–34: Charles Taylor
1934–36: Raymond Cohen
1936–38: Betty Robey
1938–41: Agnes Stephens
1941–44: Solly Scheck
1945–50: Chumleigh Hind
1954–59: Jennifer Nuttall

Sarah Andrew Scholarship (singing)
1925–26: Alice Smith
1929–32: Norman Walker
1932–34: John Caunce
1935–38: Jack Wood
1938–41: Minnie Bower
1941–42: Josephine Curtis
1943–44: Ann Allane
1944–49: Helene Mottram
1947–51: Mary Clough
1951–55: John Mitchinson
1956–60: Doris Harrison
1963–69: Josephine Foster
1969–70: Graeme Bruce
1967–70: Judith Quine

Meadowcroft Memorial Exhibition (church music)
1906–08: Samuel Wood
1909–13: John Wills
1915–16: J. J. Sidebotham
1916–20: Norman Andrew
1921–24: Harold Wolfenden
1924–27: Harold Robinson
1929–31: Ivor Jones
1931–32: Sydney Dell

1933–35: Douglas Steele
1936–37: Victor Hawkins
1937–40: John B. Hopwood
1940–41: Leslie Clifton
1942–44: John Peter Dootson

John Webster Memorial Exhibition
1902–05: William Warburton (violoncello)
1905–09: Seth Lancaster (violoncello)
1909–13: Carrodus Taylor (violoncello)
1913–17: Jo. Lamb (violin)
1917–18: Phyllis Russell (violin)
1918–21: Ellie Spivak (violin)
1918–22: Annie Shore (violoncello)
1922–26: Leonard Hirsch (violin)
1926–29: Michael Collins (violoncello)
1929–31: Doris Welch (violin)
1931–35: Alexander Young (violoncello)
1935–38: Peggy Robson (violoncello)
1938–39: Brenda Old (violin)
1939–42: Gerald Briscoe (violin)
1942–43: Yvonne Boenders (violoncello)
1943–46: John Hopkins (violoncello)
1946–49: John Mottershead (violin)
1950–54: Edith Hardman (violin)
1950–54: Brian Stait (violin)
1956–61: Barry Griffiths (violin)

Ruth Hewitt Scholarship (pianoforte)
1942–46: Rosamond Mott
1946–47: Frederick Wardle
1947–50: Roy Rimmer
1952–55: Eva Warren
1958–63: Rosemary Hayes

Candlin Wind Scholarship
1917–20: Jan Stedman (flute)
1920–23: Keith Whittaker (flute)
1923–27: Harry Mainey (clarinet)
1923–27: James Redfern (trombone)
1927–29: Leonard Nichols (oboe)
1927–30: Fred Walsh (flute)
1930–34: Alfred Livesley (oboe)
1934–38: Frank Reidy (clarinet)
1938–41: Edmund Atkinson (clarinet)
1941–44: Maisie Ringham (trombone)

Candlin Wind Scholarship—(*cont.*)
1944–47: Bernard O'Keefe (oboe)
1952–53: Anne Bennett (flute)
1954–55: James Murray (trumpet)
1957–61: Brenda Kay (clarinet)
1958–62: Joan Turner (flute)
1965–68: John Barrow (flute)
1968–69: John Butterworth (horn)
1966–69: David Robbins (trumpet)
1969–70: Alison C. Smith (flute)

Jeanne Bretey Scholarship
1946–49: Geoffrey Buckley (piano)
1949–51: Joan Mitchell (composition)
1952–55: Alexander Goehr (composition)
1953–54: John M. South (composition)
1954–56: Robert Elliott (composition)
1958–63: Pauline Smith (violin)
1960–62: Patricia Chippendale (oboe)
1960–63: John McCabe (composition)
1962–67: Anthony Goldstone (piano)
1964–69: Neil McKinnon (singing)
1968–69: Roydn Jones (singing)

Oscar Rothschild Scholarship
1958–62: David Wilson (piano)
1959–62: Kenneth Hogg (violin)
1959–63: John Oldfield (piano)
1960–63: Alan Pickard (violin)
1962–63: Rosalind Bieber (piano)
1960–65: Marjorie Baker (piano)
1958–65: Russell Lomas (piano)
1965–66: Hilary Thornton (viola)
1962–67: Maria Kyriakou (violin)
1967–68: Raymond Sidebottom (violin)
1964–69: Stephen Bettaney (piano)
1965–70: Christian Blackshaw (piano)
1967–70: Stephen Reynolds (piano)

Frederick Nixon Black Scholarship (oboe and cor anglais)
1957–58: Monica Leighton
1958–61: H. James Hunt
1965–66: Lynn Brierley
1964–68: Diana Wheatley
1965–69: Hilary Clough
1967–69: Sarah Kingsmill-Brown
1967–70: Paul Scott

Max Mayer Travelling Scholarship
1957–58: John Ogdon (piano)
1958–59: Rodney Friend (violin)
1959–60: Angela Caldwell (violin)
1960–61: Anne Howells (singing)
1962–63: Anne Howells (singing), John McCabe (piano), Pearl Fawcett (piano)
1964: John Brown (violin), Anthony Goldstone (piano)
1966: Viviane Ronchetti (violin), Patricia Ward (viola)
1967: Pauline Alston (piano), Christian Blackshaw (piano), Vivienne Blumfield (violin), Dinah Levine (piano), Danielle Salamon (piano), Kerry Smith (violin)
1968: Joan Greenburgh (piano), Jane Coulson (piano), Danielle Salamon (piano), Michael Beeston (viola), Christian Blackshaw (piano), Darina Gibson (piano), Max Paddison (piano), Stephen Reynolds (piano), Kathleen Uren (piano)
1969: Christian Blackshaw (piano), David Hartigan (piano), Dewi Watkins (cello)

Annie Cantelo Scholarship (pianoforte)
1956–60: Victoria Sumner

Elwell Scholarship (pianoforte)
1957–60: Elizabeth Weir
1957–61: Patricia Stevens
1964–67: Harold Forshaw
1965–68: Dinah Levine
1967–69: Stephen Reynolds
1968–69: Richard Wilkinson
1969–70: Yvonne Burdett
1965–70: Jon Earnshaw
1969–70: Charles Knowles
1964–70: Danielle Salamon

Musicians' Union Scholarship
1960–63: Janet Hilton (clarinet)
1964–65: Martin Robinson (violoncello), Sonia Wrangham (oboe)
1965–66: Jennifer Turner (bassoon)
1965–67: Michael Buckley (violin)
1967–68: Roy McGeoch (double bass)
1968–70: Clifford Bibby (violin)
1969–70: Antony Tarlton (violin)

William Furness Scholarship
1961–63: James Hodgson (organ)

Frederick Dawson Scholarship (pianoforte)
1961–66: Julia Wallace

Edith Robinson Scholarship (violin)
1961–66: Elizabeth Toner
1967–70: Clifford Bibby

Frances Furness Scholarship
1963–68: Kathleen Smales (singing)

John Henry and Elsie May Payne Award
1968–69: Beatrice Cheah (cello)
1968–70: Susan Mosco (singing)

Alfred Barnes Scholarship
1967–69: Simon Wright (organ)

Helen Porterhouse Scholarship (violin)
1965–69: Christiane McLean
1969–70: Antony Tarlton

George H. Lees Scholarship (pianoforte)
1968–70: John Rowland
1968–70: Peter Sage
1968–70: Thomas Wakefield

Jean Dalzell-McLaren Thomson Fund (pianoforte)
1968–70: Martin Roscoe

Curtis Gold Medal (singing)
1899: Lillie Wormald
1900: Fowler Burton
1902: Blanche Webb
1903: Ellen Sellars
1903: Frank Barker
1904: Webster Millar
1905: Annie Worsley
1906: Grace Shorrock
1907: Annie Knowles
1908: Hamilton Harris
1909: Richard Evans
1910: Edith McCullagh
1911: Juanita Aitken
1912: Ann Newton Hague
1913: Edith Thorp
1914: Alfred Grant
1915: Constance Mason
1916: Constance Felpts
1917: Elsie Thurston
1918: Norah M. Ward

1919: Sybil Maden
1920: J. H. Walsh
1921: J. Dale Smith
1922: Ernest Jones, Samuel Worthington
1923: Joseph Sutcliffe
1924: Edith Garside
1925: Leonard Platt
1926: Thomas H. Mosley
1927: Margaret Collier
1928: Wilfred Frith
1929: Edith Winston
1930: Dorothy Pearce
1931: Evelyn Duke
1932: Norman Walker
1933: Norah Sinclair
1936: Peggy Shorrock
1938: Gwendolyn Veevers
1941: Minnie Bower
1942: Mary Peters
1943: Marjorie Thomas
1944: Edna Hobson
1946: Alys Bridge
1947: Margaret Pollard, Leonard Mayoh
1948: Gladys Thompson
1949: Geoffrey Clifton
1950: Margaret Hyde
1951: Joy Pierce
1952: Peggy Castle
1953: Gwilym Jones
1954: John Mitchinson
1955: Jean Reddy
1956: Honor Sheppard
1957: Barbara Robinson
1958: Avril Roebuck
1959: Barbara Robotham
1960: Elizabeth Harwood
1961: Felicity Harrison
1962: Owen Wynne
1964: Anne Howells
1965: Caroline Crawshaw
1967: Vivien Townley, Norman Welsby
1968: Barbara Walker
1969: Katharine Gerrard

Dayas Gold Medal (Triennial) (pianoforte)
1906: Ellen Arthan
1909: Charles Kelly, Lucy E. Pierce
1912: H. Alwyne Browne

14*

Dayas Gold Medal (Triennial) (pianoforte)—(*cont.*)
1915: John Wills
1918: Annie G. Lord
1921: Arnold Perry
1924: Freda Johnson
1927: Hilda Singleton
1930: Dorothy Simpson
1933: John Brennan
1936: Charles Ellam
1939: Zoë Monteanu
1946: Joseph Clough
1949: Geoffrey Buckley
1952: David Wilde
1953: Susan Tunnell, Lawrence Glover
1956: John Ogdon
1961: Erika Harrison
1964: Anthony Goldstone
1967: Darina Gibson
1969: Christian Blackshaw

Chappell Gold Medal (pianoforte)
1921: Donald Hargreaves
1922: Stephen Wearing
1923: Albert Hardie
1924: Lilian Grindrod
1925: Phyllis Eley
1926: Gordon Green
1927: Clifton Helliwell
1928: Alan Rawsthorne
1929: Phyllis Sutcliffe
1930: Arthur Berry
1931: Ernest West

Mrs. Leo Grindon Prize (composition)
1925: Thomas B. Pitfield
1927: Alan Rawsthorne
1929: Annie Snowball
1930: Lewis Marlow
1931: John Lamb
1932: Douglas Steele
1933: Frederick Smith
1936: Alan Park
1938: Gordon Stubbs
1939: Joan Holt, Ruth Turton
1940: Evelyn Boyson
1941: Peter Shortland
1942: Ernest Tomlinson

1943: G. Herbert Whone
1944: Kathleen Hasty
1945: Elsie Broomhead
1946: Harry Wild
1947: Leonard Mayoh
1948: John Ellis
1949: Edward Holman
1952: David Wilde
1955: Robert C. Elliott
1957: David Freedman
1959: Ian Gleaves
1960: Roy Bennett
1962: John McCabe
1963: Alun Francis
1965: Anthony Halstead
1966: Max Paddison
1967: Christian Blackshaw
1969: Patrick Dailly

Hiles Medal

1930: Geoffrey W. Gilbert (flute)
1932: Charles Meert ('cello)
1933: Philip Hecht (violin)
1934: Charles Taylor (violin), Alfred Livesley (oboe)
1935: Alexander Young ('cello)
1936: Sidney Fell (clarinet)
1937: John Ayre (horn)
1938: Molly Blundell (violin), Peggy Robson ('cello)
1939: Eric Cotton (bassoon)
1940: Millicent Cossack ('cello)
1941: Patricia Stancliffe (oboe)
1942: Clifford Seville (flute)
1943: Oliver Bannister (flute)
1944: John B. Ward (tipmani)
1945: Bernard O'Keefe
1946: John R. Hopkins (violoncello)
1947: Martin Milner (violin)
1948: Ronald Gibson (viola)
1949: Michael Steane (violin)
1950: Patricia Ward (percussion)
1951: David Want (trombone)
1952: Sheila Bickerdike (oboe)
1953: Davina Hart (violin), Ludmila Navratil (viola)
1954: George Boardman (violoncello), Barry Castle (horn)
1955: Noel Broome (violin), Barry Gregson (clarinet)
1956: Joyce Sharples (violin), Elizabeth Walker (oboe)
1957: Jean Brier (violin), Christopher Ball (clarinet)

Hiles Medal—(*cont.*)

1958: Roger Best (viola), Monica Leighton (oboe)
1959: James Cropper (violin), Martin Wilson (horn)
1960: Barry Griffiths (violin), Frank Rycroft (horn)
1961: John Davies (violin), James Hunt (oboe)
1962: John Catlow (violoncello), Patricia Morris (flute)
1963: Michael Cookson (viola), Lois Jones (flute)
1964: Margaret Greenlaw (violoncello), Janet Hilton (clarinet)
1965: Anthony Halstead (horn), Annette Oakley (percussion)
1966: John Bradbury (violin), Lynn Brierley (oboe), Patricia Sharp (clarinet)
1967: John Barrow (flute), John Bimson (horn), Peter Gane (trombone), Maria Kyriakou (violin)
1968: Richard Park (violoncello), Paul Marrion (double bass), Stephen Wardle (percussion), Patrick Taggart (flute)
1969 Clifford Bibby (violin), Keith Hartley (double bass), Kathryn Lukas (flute)

Hilary Haworth Memorial Prize

1938: Gwendolyn Veevers (singing), Flora Kent (piano)
1939: Alfred Hallworth (singing), Beryl Dallen (piano)
1940: Patricia Richards (singing), Flora Kent (piano)
1941: Joan Stirrup (singing), Beryl Dallen (piano)
1942: Winifred Busfield (singing), Evelyn Boyson (piano)
1943: Marjorie Thomas (singing), Sallie Hickling (piano)
1944: Margaret Burton (singing), Marjorie Thomas (piano)
1945: C. Mary Ellson (singing), Albert Knowles (piano)
1946: Leonard Mayoh (singing), Dorothy Rowley (piano)
1947: Alys Bridge (singing), Elsie Broomhead (piano)
1948: Margaret Pollard (singing), Edith Rothwell (piano)
1949: Barbara Siddelley (singing), Nina Higginbottom (piano)
1950: Geoffrey Clifton (singing), Edith Rothwell (piano)
1951: Margaret Hyde (singing), Nina Higginbottom (piano)
1952: Joy Pierce (singing), Philip Challis (piano)
1953: Peggy Castle (singing), Keith Swallow (piano)
1954: Jean Reddy (singing), Geoffrey Arnold (piano)
1955: Cornelia Martin (singing), Jane Rowden (piano)
1956: Sylvia Jacobs (singing), Joan Ashton (piano)
1957: Felicity Harrison (singing), Brenda Lucas (piano), Mary Clibran (singing), Annabel Adams (piano)
1958: Margaret Hallworth (singing), David Lloyd (piano)
1959: Elizabeth Harwood (singing), Isobel Flinn (piano)
1960: Victoria Sumner (singing), Isobel Flinn (piano)
1961: Jill Spence (singing), John McCabe (piano)
1962: Anne Howells (singing), Penelope Smith (piano)
1963: Maurice Walsh (singing), Michael Grady (piano), Elizabeth R. Mason (singing), John McCabe (piano)
1965: Caroline Crawshaw (singing), Richard Holloway (piano)

Edward Hecht Prize (composition)
1945: Arni Björnsson
1946: Olga Townend
1947: Ernest Tomlinson
1948: Edward Holman
1949: Nina Higginbottom
1950: Joan Mitchell
1951: Joan Mitchell
1952: David Freedman
1954: Robert Elliott, David Freedman
1955: David Ellis
1957: Robert Black
1958: Ian Gleaves
1959: Roy Bennett
1960: Keith Cole
1961: John McCabe
1963: Philip Spratley
1964: Anthony Halstead
1965: Max Paddison, John Mallord
1966: Stephen Reynolds
1967: Stuart Pedlar
1969: Peter Gould

Royal Manchester Institution Medal
1949: Eric Chadwick (organ)
1950: Keith Bond (organ)
1951: Audrey Kennedy (organ)
1952: Harry Brown (organ)
1953: Robert Andrews (organ)
1954: Ronald Frost (organ)
1955: John Coates (organ)
1956: David Ellis (composition)
1957: Neil Wade (organ)
1958: David Jordan (conducting)
1959: Jennifer Nuttall (violin)
1960: Rodney Friend (violin)
1961: John McCabe (composition)
1963: Erika Harrison (piano)
1964: David Garforth (organ)

Royal Philharmonic Prize for Composition
1949: Edward Holman
1952: Roy Heaton Smith
1955: David Freedman
1956: David Ellis
1962: John McCabe
1967: Max Paddison

Royal College of Music Patrons' Fund Award for Composition
1951: Ernest Hall
1955: David Freedman
1957: David Ellis

Meadowcroft Prize (organ)
1953: Robert Andrews, Ronald Frost

Imperial League of Opera Prizes
1948: Rosalind Rowlands, Geoffrey Clifton
1949: Veronica Lawton, Fred Westcott
1950: Joy Pierce, William Joyce
1951: Joan Sellers, Jack Scott
1952: Marian Callear, James Shuker, Leslie Williamson
1953: Joan Hadland, John Mitchinson
1954: Adrianne Sherlock
1954 (divided): Gwilym Jones, Joseph Ward
1955: Mary Baines, Joseph Ward
1956: Elizabeth Davidson, Leslie Jones
1957 (divided): Avril Roebuck, Sylvia Jacobs
1957: John Lawrenson
1958 (divided): Avril Roebuck, Barbara Robotham
1958 (divided): Brian Casey, Peter Leeming
1959: Brian Casey, Peter Leeming
1960: Elizabeth Harwood, Douglas Stark
1961: John Winfield
1961 (divided): Rhiannon Davies, Elaine Hewitt
1962 (divided): Patrick McGuigan, Paul Smith
1962 (divided): Jean Langfield, Dianne Matthews
1963 (divided): Rhiannon Davies, Anne Howells
1963 (divided):   Paul Smith, Patrick McGuigan
1964: Ryland Davies
1964 (divided): Dianne Matthews, Caroline Crawshaw
1966 (divided): Vivien Townley, Norman Welsby
1967 (divided): Neil McKinnon, James Ward
1967 (divided): Barbara Walker, Kathleen Smales
1967 (divided): Anthea Robb, Carol Roscoe
1968 (divided): Barbara Walker, Kathleen Smales, Katharine Gerrard
1968 (divided): Roydn Jones, Robert Ferguson, Gwynne Howell, Roger Heath, Norman White
1969 (divided): Judith Quine, Angela Bostock
1969 (divided): Anthony Holcroft, Alun Jenkins

Ricordi Prizes
1957: Avril Roebuck (singing), David Ellis (conducting)
1958: Peter Leeming (singing), Oliver Broome (conducting)
1959: Brian Casey (singing)

1960: Douglas Stark (singing)
1961: John Winfield (singing)
1962: Patrick McGuigan (singing)
1963: Rhiannon Davies (singing)
1964: Ryland Davies (singing), David Garforth (organ)
1965: Russell Lomas (piano)
1966: Vivien Townley (singing), Roger Clegg (Piano)
1967: Keith Bentley (piano), Norman Welsby (singing)
1968: Barbara Walker (singing), Kenneth Cleveland (conducting)
1969: Anthony Holcroft (singing), Catherine Grainger (piano)

Pinson Book Prize
1959: Jennifer Nuttall (violin)
1960: John Davies (violin)
1961: Joanna Bowker (piano)
1962: John Catlow ('cello)
1963: Erika Harrison (piano)
1964: John Brown (violin)
1965: Caroline Crawshaw (singing)
1966: John Sheldon (harpsichord)
1967: Raymond Sidebottom (violin)
1968: Gabrielle Byam-Grounds (flute)
1969: Jane Coulson (piano)

Webster Memorial Prize
1959: Elizabeth Holbrook (viola)
1960: Rodney Friend (violin)
1961: Barry Griffiths (violin)
1962: John Davies (violin)
1963: John Brown (violin)
1965: John Bradbury (violin)
1966: Philip Sutton (violin)
1967: Margaret Graf (violin)
1968: Patricia Ward (viola)
1969: Carolyn Sparey (viola)

Dora Gilson Award
1966: Anthony Goldstone (piano)
1967: Tony Brentnall (piano)

Herman Bantock Award
1966: Patricia Ward (viola)
1967: Patricia Ward (viola)

Tom Bridge Award
1967: John Tomlinson (singing)
1968: Philip Kubilius (piano)
1969: Philip Kubilius (piano)

Index

15